RUGBY LEAGUE CHALLENGE CUP

John Huxley

GUINNESS PUBLISHING

To my wife Carol, who has sacrificed many hours to this book,
and our children Kerry and David.

First Published in 1992 by
Guinness Publishing
33 London Road, Enfield
Middlesex EN2 6DJ
The right of John Huxley to be identified as the
Author of this work has been asserted in accordance with
the Copyright, Design and Patents Act 1988.

A product of Forster Books

Designed & typeset by Peter Simmonett

Printed and bound in Great Britain by The Bath Press, Bath

A catalogue record for this book
is available from the British Library

ISBN 0-85112-511-5

ACKNOWLEDGEMENTS

In any book of this kind an author needs all the help he can get. This volume was no different to any other and I gratefully acknowledge the help, assistance and time of so many different people. Their generosity of spirit has reinforced my faith in the warmth of people who inhabit and follow the game of Rugby League. If I have accidentally missed anybody out of the following list please accept my apologies.

Brian Cartwright, Trevor Delaney, Ernest Day, John Edwards, Michael Flynn, Chris and Jo Forster, Robert Gate, Malcolm Hamer, Graham Hart, Leslie Hoole, David Howes with management and staff of Rugby Football League, Lancashire Publications Ltd., Michael Latham, Manchester Central Reference Library, Paddy McAteer, Graham Morris, Oldham Library, Oldham Evening Chronicle staff, Chris Park, Ian Proctor, Rochdale Library, Michael Rhodes, Irvin Saxton and the Rugby League Record Keepers Club, Alex Service, South Lancashire Newspapers Ltd., Andrew Varley, Dr Donald Walton, Gerald Webster.

We also thank and acknowledge the following individuals, libraries or newspapers for their help and co-operation in providing the illustrations for this book:

Bradford Telegraph and Argus; Robert Gate Collection; Mick Flynn Collection; Les Hoole Collection; Paddy McAteer, Barrow-in-Furness; Chris Park, Hull; Press Association; Mick Rhodes Collection; Rugby League Recordkeepers Club; Gerald Webster and the Rugby League Newspaper; Alex Service, St Helens; Russel Cox and the Sunday Mirror Picture Desk; Varley Picture Library; Warrington Guardian.

CONTENTS

Preface	*vii*
The beginnings	*1*
Going north	*4*
Lancashire at last!	*8*
The wages of sin	*10*
Little by Little	*14*
Farewell fifteen	*17*
The glittering Goldthorpes	*20*
Vale of tears	*23*
The Empire Strikes Back!	*25*
The four just men	*27*
Stuff of legends	*29*
All hail to the Prince!	*31*
Patience rewarded	*33*
Talent blossoms	*35*
Stranglehold on Rugby	*37*
Red rose revived	*39*
Hornets go west	*41*
The League of friends	*43*
Jim and Wigan's Ring of Confidence	*45*
The team that Billy built	*48*
Last of the four timers	*51*
The road to Wembley	*53*
A capital move	*55*
A solitary Springbok	*58*
Halifax Brown-ed off	*62*
The Lions and a ghost	*64*
The Royal Australian touch	*66*
Local boys make good	*68*
Wigan to Wembley - via Dublin	*71*
A fisherman of England	*74*
Chemics find right formula	*77*
The Red Devils	*79*
The Rochdale disaster	*82*
Wartime finals	*84*
Trinity's dry Wembley	*86*
Odsal to Wembley and back... three times	*89*
The prodigal returns	*94*
Gee force	*96*
The Old Master	*98*
A nose for success	*101*
The replay	*104*
Round the Horne	*106*
Saints at last	*109*
Wembley's mental blockage	*111*
More Wigan glory	*113*
Family fortune	*117*
The man from Bethlehem	*119*
Trinity Tales-continued	*122*
Drawing out the agony	*125*
The day David almost slew Goliath	*127*
Murphy's Law	*130*
The dream machine	*132*
A drop in time	*135*
By hook or by...	*138*
Murphy's Law - proved!	*142*
Kel the boot	*145*
Fox - Mark Three	*148*
It's that man again!	*150*
Bull in a china shop	*152*
Dad's Army	*154*
Cup birthright	*156*
Hello Luv!	*159*
Dodger's last stand	*161*
A recipe for success	*164*
To Hull and back	*166*
Wild Rovers	*169*
End of the beginning	*171*
Anniversary present	*174*
Flushed and confident`	*177*
The Fax of life	*180*
The Lowe down	*183*
Sweet revenge	*185*
The Central reason	*188*
Challenge Cup Roll of Honour	*196*
Index	*198*

PREFACE

However hard Rugby League Football struggles, it finds it hard to shake off the image, in Britain at least, of a northern game whose one major game a year is the Challenge Cup final at Wembley. To a certain extent this image reflects the truth.

Regrettably, for those of us who have been touched by the magic of Rugby League, the spread of the professional game remains stubbornly the province of the sporting population north of the River Trent with isolated outposts in London and the East Midlands. And, indeed, the Challenge Cup is by definition the pinnacle of the domestic game, the holy grail for every player, club official and supporter.

The growth of the sudden death competition has mirrored the fortunes of a game that was created out of the failure by the Victorian-era Rugby Union establishment to realise that life in the north was harder in terms of work and living standards; that, there, attitudes towards amateurism differed and, most importantly, the Corinthian ethic was completely alien.

Yorkshire Rugby Union, before the formation of the Northern Rugby Union in 1895, proved that a sudden-death tournament was popular with both players and spectators, the latter in large and growing numbers.

Once the break from Twickenham had been effected it was quite natural, and understandable, such a competition should be introduced and that its name should reflect the degree of difficulty required to win it.

Today, virtually a century later, the competition remains as problematical as it was in 1897, and the 1929 decision to switch the final to Wembley away from the sport's heartland has arguably made it even more popular with the people in the game and those who watch from without.

Challenge Cup final day has become a sporting festival in its own right; an unashamed propaganda exercise as good behaviour and sportsmanship both on and off the field are demonstrated in front of the soccer-cynical audience of Britain's capital city.

The Cup, however, is more than one day when the winner for each season is inevitably decided. From the instant that the Cup register closes (when the eligibility of player is committed to his club) the tournament attracts mystique, magic and moments of pure drama.

Once Wembley is attained most of those moments are eclipsed; I have tried to capture the way in which the whole competition has moved both the communities and the teams involved. The progress to the final can be torturous and filled with the kind of tension born of the realisation that defeat means elimination.

The men of the Northern Union and now the Rugby League are driven by ambition. Very few would place money before an appearance in the final; it is still that precious.

More than anything the Cup illustrates the northern approach to sport. From the moment you are released into the arena as a player you are confirmed in the belief that winning is the thing, that maximum effort is required at all times and that courage is something to be respected. As a spectator you demand full value, total commitment and a high grade of performance.

So many different communities have embraced Rugby League because the sport embodies those qualities needed to live and work in such communities. After emerging from the Victorian era the north remained a place where the labour was hard, the community spirit was strong and the sport was accessible.

My own introduction to Rugby League was unusual by northern standards. Brought up on a diet of Rugby Union at a south Manchester school, we were allowed to taste League by an enlightened mathematics master, Bill Hennig. Although he was a 'Union' player, 'Sir' was prepared to show us in two fixtures against a Rochdale school that another variety of rugby existed. It was a fleeting glimpse which had to be stored away in my mind.

My next encounter was the result of lunch time discussions with a colleague as we sought to numb the hours of boredom while working in a major industrial company's accounts department. I extolled the virtues of Union while Ken Hardy stoutly defended League's qualities.

The challenge was simple – each man would try the other's code. Ken hated Union but I fell for League. I was never good enough as a player to be a professional but each game of League was a moment to savour. To combine my interest in the game with a professional life came unexpectedly. It meant the end of my playing days but I have, however, enjoyed twenty plus years writing about and being involved in Rugby League.

I had the ultimate pleasure of first experiencing the Wembley Cup final with my late father, Richard, who as a keen soccer player had to endure the disappointment of knowing that his only son had little talent or interest in his chosen game. The impact of Leigh's unexpected 1971 win over Leeds gave us a memory which we shared with relish until my father's death in 1989.

We were able to acquire that memory because one of my colleagues on the Oldham Evening Chronicle, Roger Halstead, was ill and I was asked to cover the game in his place. Roger's misfortune was our gain, and experiencing the occasion for myself added fuel to my desire to cover Rugby League on my own account.

I have discovered for myself the importance and relevance of the Challenge Cup to the game and communities devoted to the sport. It is more than the single moment of triumph or despair: it is being part of one of Britain's greatest sporting traditions. For the players it is the desire to be recognised as worthy practitioners and to stand comparison with some of the most illustrious names the game has ever produced. For the spectators it is an identification with their club, their players and, more often than not, their community.

I have tried to capture the flavour of the competition rather than a record of each pass, tackle, try or goal. The importance of the modern Challenge Cup competition is based on what has gone before – and to understand that statement it is necessary to know what did go before.

Great men, great games and great moments. They are all part of the potion that creates the spell of the Rugby League Challenge Cup. I was caught within that cast many years ago and hope that you will enjoy sharing that particular northern brew with me.

JOHN HUXLEY

CHAPTER 1

THE BEGINNINGS

The date, 16 October 1880, does not figure prominently either among the notable milestones in the long, illustrious history of Rugby League Football or in the annals of one of the sport's most illustrious clubs, Oldham. The history books, however, can be deceiving, for this date brought on to the stage one of the most important characters in the early development of a game which had still to be conceived: a man who was to play a central role in Rugby League's formation and tradition.

Mr Joseph Platt, the man in question, was a pillar of professional society in Oldham, a cotton spinning and industrial town chipped into the side of the Pennine hill chain. He was an accountant and land surveyor and his membership to the Rugby Football Club was confirmed on that day. He was clearly a man who believed in participation because he was elected as the club's treasurer, a position he was to hold for 15 years, before, significantly, moving on to higher and more notable matters.

Platt's progress into sport followed a pattern. He was a businessman and it was the professional men who were the driving force of British sport at that period in history. They had to be, particulary in the north of England, because the working classes were generally too busy earning a living in the mills and factories. This contrasted,

markedly, with the situation in the south of the country where the professions and public schools provided sport with a plentiful supply of participants and administrators.

In general, the south enjoyed the luxury of healthier players with more leisure time available although, to utilise a modern phrase, 'the times they were a changin'.' In 1871 the laws which required people to work through until two o'clock on Saturday afternoon as part of their normal working week were amended and working hours ceased at one o'clock. This gave the workers a complete afternoon for sporting pursuits.

Oldham, at that time, had a reputation for being a forward-looking club. Just two years before Platt had joined them in 1878 they, along with other progressive clubs in the area, like Salford, had staged a partially successful experiment of playing under the Siemens electric light system. By 1889-90 they were able to launch a tour of South Wales facing such clubs as Swansea, Cardiff and Newport. Then the Maoris, the first ever overseas team to tour this country, played them at Clarksfield, one of Oldham's previous homes, and lost.

Given the speed of change it was almost inevitable that Platt was to be thrown into the middle of the storm that was breaking over Rugby Football. The spectre of professionalism

was rising over the northern outfits and Platt's Oldham club were involved in the controversy. They were one of the top Rugby Union clubs in the country, a fact that brought them to the attention of Huddersfield clergyman Reverend Frank Marshall, a self-appointed guardian of the amateur ethic. Marshall suspected Oldham, like many clubs in Yorkshire, of breaching the Rugby Football Union's strict amateur regulations.

The strength of the Oldham team was boosted by players from outside, such as Welshman Billy Mc-Cutcheon, who in 1891 he was joined by countryman Dai Gywnn. That was the final straw as far as the Reverend Marshall was concerned. He was convinced that Oldham were recruiting good players and offering them financial inducements, and so reported them to the Rugby Union.

A special meeting was called in Manchester to discuss the issue in April 1891 when Oldham had to face charges of professionalism. Mr Platt and his committee were clearly made of tougher stuff than Marshall thought because charges against the Lancashire club could not be proved.

Had the Lancashire County Rugby Union seen a certain incriminating document it could all have been so different for Oldham. A player lost a letter from the club in which they offered him financial terms. The finder confessed that the communication was in his possession but refused to return it. This individual also refused to reveal the contents to anybody else and must have been as good as his word because otherwise Oldham would certainly have been suspended from membership of the Rugby Union.

Indeed Reverend Marshall's luck was really out because a previous investigation by the Lancashire Rugby Union had not only cleared Oldham of the same offence but had also added a rider that no blame could be attached to the club!

Whether Oldham, on either occasion, were genuinely innocent, which seems unlikely, does not really matter. What was happening to them was symptomatic of the times.

Until the 1871 Factory Acts there was no time for football for the working classes. After that date they could, in theory, join the gentry and professional classes in sport. But the necessity of earning a living was still a major handicap. They needed the shift money from Saturday mornings to provide for their families. Enlightened businessmen such as Joseph Platt understood such realities and wanted to accommodate them.

Oldham's position with regard to this problem was far from unique. It was the Reverend Marshall and his crusade against the infidel professional that was out of step with both the times and the community. The acceptance of the need for some financial compensation for lost (broken) time was widespread in the north; the Reverend's principles made him more suited to the game in the south. However, although proving that clubs had transgressed the amateur rules had nearly always been difficult, the problem of compensation was bringing the question of professionalism to a head. By 1895 the Rugby Football Union, which had been formed in 1871, was

being forced into a corner by their northern members who did not want to pay their players for playing but wished to compensate them for their loss of earnings on Saturdays.

Marshall was a powerful figure in the world of Yorkshire Rugby Union. He pursued the Corinthian spirit within Rugby Football in the same way as he pursued his religion; vigorously. He was a high profile figure in the game; a member of the Huddersfield club committee, a referee of note and an author.

In 1892 he wrote 'Football, the Rugby Union game' which contained his thoughts on 'broken time'. This was the name given to the compensation that clubs wanted to give workers who sacrificed working time. Marshall left nobody in any doubt where he stood on the matter. He thought it was the thin end of the professionalism wedge and did not want it in the game. History was to prove him right but the arguments were as contentious then as they have been over the decades since.

The history of the game, as the 1880s became 1890s, is littered with references to Marshall, either campaigning on his own behalf or representing a club which had complained about a particular player being financially induced away by another. He was Rugby's 'Witch Finder General', seeking professionals at every turn. It must have been a source of considerable smugness in some folk when, in 1893, Marshall's own club, Huddersfield, were at the centre of a storm over alleged broken time payments.

Cumberland club Cummersdale Hornets complained to the English Rugby Union committee that they had grave suspicions about the transfer which took two of their best centre three-quarters, Boak and Forsyth, to Huddersfield. The players had quit Hornets at such speed that they were summoned to appear before Carlisle

magistrates for leaving their respective jobs without giving proper notice, but the case had to be put to one side because the two accused men were playing for Huddersfield against Hull.

The chief witness for the prosecution was none other than the Reverend gentleman. Prior to the hearing, which suspended Huddersfield, he had made a very damaging statement against his own club and resigned from their committee.

While the committee's decision must have been some source of satisfaction to him, because they suspended Huddersfield, Marshall himself almost became a victim.

The club were suspended from the date of hearing until the end of the year, that was eight matches – four away and four at home. The committee, who sat in Preston, also ruled that players who had played for Huddersfield during the tainted period were also suspended, which was tough luck on those who had transferred away.

Marshall, however, continued to referee during Huddersfield's period of suspension and he took charge of the Lancashire v Cumberland fixture. This seeming anomaly was brought up before the Yorkshire Rugby Union who, in turn, referred the problem to Twickenham. The English Union, however, did not allow one of their chief supporters in the north to be abandoned. They ruled that the suspension only applied to Huddersfield's players, although their decision was not greeted with universal acclaim in the West Yorkshire town. Similar situations occured in Lancashire, too, where both Salford and Wigan suffered periods of suspension for contravening amateur rulings. The fact that northern clubs were so strong and wanted to remain so, meant that they had to continually look outside their own catchment areas for better players. In doing this they were always suspected by the southern clubs of offering financial sweeteners. Whether they were guilty or not, the compensation issue just would not go away.

The northern clubs, to be fair to them, did not want open professionalism. They wanted to pay for broken time, the issue at the heart of the problem. The chief element of the broken time system was that players would receive six shillings (thirty pence) as compensation for lost wages. And this is where Joseph Platt starts to help shape Rugby League as a national sport. Oldham, like many of the top northern clubs, could not reconcile the amateur principle with the hardship being experienced by some of their working class members. They wanted to build, and keep, a successful team.

Confrontation had to happen. It was inevitable. The two sides of the problem were diametrically opposed. In 1894, at a secret meeting, twenty-one clubs from Lancashire and Yorkshire came together as a 'combination for their mutual protection in the future'. They assumed the name 'the Northern League'. Ironically, their meeting was staged at the George Hotel, Huddersfield, the venue of an even more momentous meeting almost a year later.

Into 1895, and the threat to form a breakaway Union was becoming a real possibility. Oldham were among the chief rebels and consequently Joseph Platt was one of three Lancashire delegates who met the Yorkshire Rugby Union to discuss future prospects for a Northern League. As a result of these discussions the senior

clubs from both counties agreed to virtual unilateral independence from Twickenham.

By 29 August 1895 a decision had been taken and, at an historic meeting again at the George Hotel, the Northern Rugby Union, the forerunner to the modern Rugby League, was formed. Joseph Platt was named as its first secretary. Clearly they knew a good man when they saw one, because he was to hold the post for 25 years during which time he was involved in many of the important events that helped shape the modern game.

Once the Northern Union had separated itself from the Rugby Union there came the business of supporting itself. It had not gone unnoticed that one of the most financially successful competitions prior to the big split was the Yorkshire Cup. This was a knockout tournament and, for the Northern Union, its major attraction was the numbers of spectators it attracted. Money for broken time had to be found from somewhere.

The Yorkshire Cup, known throughout the county as 'T'owd Tin Pot' had started life in 1877-78. Its attraction for spectators was undoubted; the 1892-93 third round meeting between Leeds and Halifax at Headingley attracted 27,654, a bigger crowd than the 1892 FA Cup Final between West Bromwich Albion and Aston Villa and 5000 more than the England v Scotland international the following season. It was big box office.

On 5 March 1896, during the first season of Northern Union operations, it was decided that a knockout competition open to all member clubs

should be introduced. Because there was so little time to complete arrangements for the new tournament its introduction was delayed until the following season. In the meantime the Northern Union's committee went about acquiring a trophy from Bradford-based silversmiths Fattorini and Sons. The 36 inch cup cost them £60 and weighed 189 ounces. They also bought in winners and losers medals at £3. 3s. (£3. 15) and £1. 10s. (£1. 50) respectively.

The entry for the first competition was:

Bradford v Oldham
Bramley v Morecambe
Broughton Rangers v Warrington
Castleford v Allerton
Eastmoor v Oldham Juniors
Halifax v Stockport Rangers
Holbeck v Latchford Rangers
Hull v Walkden,
Hunslet v Broughton Recreation
Leeds v Rochdale St Clements
Leeds Parish Church v Runcorn Recreation
Leigh v Wakefield Trinity
Manningham v Dukinfield
Rochdale Hornets v Waterhead Hornets
Runcorn v Warrington Loco
St Helens v Lees
Salford v Warrington St Mary's
Swinton v Huddersfield
Widnes v Atherton Hornets
Wigan v Radcliffe

There were byes for Batley, Bradford Church Hill, Brighouse Rangers, Crompton, Heckmondwike, Liversedge, St Helens Recs, Stockport, Swinton Church, Thornton Rangers, Tyldesley and Werneth.

CHAPTER 2

GOING NORTH

Welshmen and Rugby Football have been bound together since the game first reached the Principality. The connection between the game in South Wales and that in the North of England came shortly after, and records noting the arrival of Welsh players can be found in the 1880s. Clearly the attraction of 'liberal' expenses held good even in those far-off days.

Once the Northern Union became established in its own right and broken time became an accepted principle of its existence, then the attraction clearly became even greater. Given a straight choice between a career in mining or what amounted to professional Rugby there was very little choice other than a train journey north. As in the modern game when players cross from Union to League, it was a risky business; some players achieved greater success than others.

Wattie Davies of Batley was destined to be out of the ordinary. The contrast between his birth place near Milford Haven in Pembrokeshire and Batley was stark. The rural life of West Wales could hardly compare with the dark, satanic mill landscape presented by Batley, a town slotted in the hills of the heavy woollen district of the West Riding of Yorkshire.

Christened Wharton Peers Davies, he was plucked from Welsh Rugby be-

fore he had reached the dizzy heights of the national side. He was a natural Rugby footballer with a remarkable grip of the game's skills. His senior Rugby career started far away from West Wales, in the metropolis of Cardiff.

He was a full-back for Cardiff Northern but found fame first with Cardiff Harlequins and then the city's senior club Cardiff, as a winger. In their records he was labelled as 'Wat' Davies.

His career with Cardiff was short, just a matter of 17 games during which time he scored seven tries. In 1896 he decided to cast aside his Welsh Rugby heritage and join the embryonic Northern Union with Batley.

While Batley, who are known throughout Rugby League as the 'Gallant Youths', are one of the modern League's lesser lights, stuck away on their dramatically sloping pitch at the top of Mount Pleasant, in the late years of the last century they were a power in the Yorkshire game. Davies was not going to be tucked away in some dark corner.

Batley had not made the best of starts to their Northern Union life. They had won just 12 of their 42 games during the 1895-96 season and that was not good enough for the men from 'shoddydom'. They had been accustomed to better and it was decided

to freshen up the team by bringing in new players.

They looked to Welsh Rugby for the necessary injection of talent although, surprisingly, their first recruit from that part of the world was already involved in Northern Union. Welsh international centre three-quarter Dai Fitzgerald had left Wales to join Lancashire club Leigh but was clearly not happy with the Red Rose county club. He arrived at Mount Pleasant in February 1896, expressing a desire to join Batley.

The man who had scored all the Welsh points in their 7-0 beating of Scotland at Newport in 1894 soon proved himself to Batley by scoring a try in his debut, a win over Huddersfield. His presence helped his new team mates end a long run of defeats.

Fitzgerald was a more than useful player to Batley but it was his connections back in Wales that were to be of more long-lasting importance to a club which, prior to signing Davies, were looking for something more than just a player; they wanted somebody to replace a legend.

The main stay of the team since the early 1880s was a little half-back who rejoiced in the name of Herbert 'Dodger' Simms. He was an amazing man. His playing talent was established as early as 1882-83 when he scored 17 tries – virtually half the club's total for the season. He was, however, more than just a good player. He was a character who attracted people. He undertook the bizarre. In June 1889 he played a team of nine brewery draymen single handed and won. Shortly after, he took a bet to race against a greyhound and, with a 20-yard handicap in his favour, made it to the finish line at the same time as the dog.

By the time Northern Union Rugby was initiated, Dodger's career was on the wane, and Batley needed a character of his stature to provide both Rugby talent and charisma to keep attracting people through the turnstiles.

Fitzgerald must have known that his long-time friend Wat Davies fitted that bill. At least one source of Batley history believes that their club committee first heard about Davies from Fitzgerald and, considering the lack of general media communication at that time, that seems to be a very fair assumption.

Perhaps Fitzgerald was in contact with Davies during the Northern Union's first close season break, because no sooner had the 1896-97 season started than a Mr Wharton Peers Davies presented himself at Mount Pleasant. He made it plain that he would like to make his immediate future with Batley who, although they did not know it at that moment, had found the man to replace the irrepressible Dodger.

Wattie made his debut for the Gallant Youths on 10 October 1896 coincidentally, like his friend Fitzgerald, against the claret-and-gold of Huddersfield. The committee must have realised from that point they had found a wing three-quarter of real quality. The depth of Davies's talent was to reveal itself with each game he played for the Club, but it took until the end of the League season to pay off. Batley finished in sixth place in the Yorkshire Senior Competition table and then prepared themselves for the initial Northern Union Challenge Cup campaign.

The competition was open to all Northern Union clubs, unlike their league games which were zoned into counties to save travel costs. Rounds were played in successive weeks. The first round of the initial competition kicked off on 20 March 1897, and Batley were favoured with a bye. In the second round they were paired with Bramley, a club based in a southern Leeds suburb. In a match which Batley won 11-0 Wattie broke the no-score deadlock by kicking a penalty goal. Having beaten Bramley the Gallant Youths faced Widnes with a semi-final place at stake. Davies opened the scoring with a try after two minutes, and that set the mould with Batley winning 10-0.

A place in the inaugural final was the prize in their semi-final meeting with Warrington, a major power west of the Pennines at the time, at Huddersfield's Fartown ground. Torrential rain made the pitch into a virtual paddy field and at Warrington players' request the referee ended the game after 34 minutes of the second half – six minutes early.

Batley won the game 6-0 and Warrington's committee tried to rescue the situation by protesting that the result should not stand because the game had not run its full course. The Union's committee, however was having none of that and disallowed the challenge adding a £5 fine to Warrington's discomfort. The result stood and Batley went through to face

The first final. Batley (left) and St Helens (right) before the 1897 game at Headingley.

St Helens in the first ever final at Headingley, Leeds on Saturday, 24 April 1897.

Davies had established his own loyal following at Batley. He was the original Welsh superstar. His idiosynchratic style endeared him to the West Yorkshire spectators and he was one of the major factors in Batley's status as a Cup fighting force.

Travel, in the final years of Queen Victoria's reign, was nothing like as convenient as it is today and the selection of Headingley for the first Cup Final was not greeted with any real enthusiasm by Lancashire clubs and their followers. But Headingley was, and still is, one of the game's top venues, and with good enough facilities to cope with a large crowd, not even accusations of Yorkshire-bias would change the Union's mind.

For Batley it enabled them to play every round without having to take the trouble of leaving the county of the White Rose while St Helens had a lengthy train journey to endure before the game. In fact a large proportion of their fans missed a substantial chunk of the first half because their train was delayed. By the time they reached the ground, their team were already on the slide.

Neither side had excelled in their league tournaments. Batley had finished a respectable sixth in the Yorkshire Senior Competition while St Helens had trailed in ninth in the Lancastrian equivalent.

Batley made all the running and kept St Helens very much on the defensive from the first whistle. The Lancastrians had the advantage of the wind at their backs but it was not enough against Batley who kept applying the pressure through their forwards. It was no surprise when, eventually, Saints cracked. A surge through the line by the Batley forwards with the ball at their feet produced a split in the St Helens defence

and stand off half Joe Oakland landed a drop goal. And that drop goal remains unique in Challenge Cup history because it was the only one scored in the final before the value of that score was reduced from four to three points.

Reports at the time record that such a roar greeted the score that two youngsters who were watching the game from a nearby tree were taken by surprise and promptly fell to the ground!

Davies's football ability brought the next score. Batley had sustained their attack on the St Helens line and the Welshman lofted a kick towards the St Helens posts. The Batley captain and centre John Goodall gathered the ball to go over for a try. Although there was a substantial suspicion he was offside, referee Mr J. H. Smith of Widnes allowed the score to stand.

So St Helens, who had started the game in a faded blue and white kit which is believed to have served them in every round of the competition, went into the second half with the wind blowing into their faces. Batley continued to turn the screw and, in a perverse way, those tactics presented St Helens with a way back into the game. Goodall attempted a drop goal and, unfortunately for him, he sliced his kick. Winger Bob Doherty fielded the ball, shrugged off the attempted tackles of Davies and Fitzgerald before surging upfield.

Batley's defenders were further thrown into confusion when Doherty produced an impressive dummy and then released the ball to centre David Traynor. As both Batley defenders Shaw and Goodall bore down on the Widnes-born player he reached the line and grounded the ball for a try just as he was being tackled. Jacques missed the conversion so Batley now led 7-3, leaving the Saints with a mountain to climb. Batley regrouped

St Helens winger David Traynor, scorer of a try in the first final.

and returned to the offensive, finally ensuring their place in British sporting history as the first winners of the Challenge Cup when back row forward J.T. Munns struggled over the St Helens line for an unconverted try.

After the game, tea was taken at the Exchange Restaurant, Leeds, followed by train journeys back to the respective home towns. Batley went into the record books while St Helens were left pondering what might have been.

Wattie Davies and the Challenge Cup had grown to like each other and, just 12 months later, they met again. Batley, boosted by their 1897 victory, attained third place in the Yorkshire Senior Competition and demonstrated their confidence by beating St Helens 12-7 in a repeat of the previous year's final in the first round.

They persuaded junior club Walkden to concede home advantage in the second round and won 8-0 and, in the third round, they won 10-4 at Castleford. An impressive 3-0 win over Oldham gave Batley a semi-final placing against Salford at Oldham – their first Challenge Cup tie outside Yorkshire – which they won 5-0 in front of 15,000 spectators.

Their opponents in the final, which was again played at Headingley, were Bradford, the forerunner to the modern Bradford Northern club.

Batley's task was daunting as Bradford had reached the final by beating Swinton, Birkenhead Wanderers, Hull, Broughton Rangers and Widnes in the qualifying rounds. Their form was impressive. Since December 1897 they had been undefeated in 25 successive games including an 8-3 league win over Batley. They were confident of victory. Maybe a little too confident, because, before the game, a large victory rostrum was constructed in front of the town hall so that they would have somewhere suitable to display the Cup.

The power for Bradford's challenge started in the front row of the scrummage where their open side prop forward Tom Broadley held court. He had come up the hard way. At the tender age of fifteen he first made his impact on a rugby field playing as a wing threequarter in the Bingley junior team.

But his rate of growth ensured that by the time he was in line for his debut with the senior club he was 5 ft 8 ins and weighed in at 14 stone. Hardly slender enough for the wing, but perfect material for the powerhouse of the forwards.

Broadley, however, suffered like so many other working class footballers of his time. He was a maltster by trade and, as the eldest of eight children, had to supplement the income of his wheelwright father. His employer, one Benjamin Broadbent, was clearly unimpressed by Tom's Saturday afternoon sporting activities and journeys out of town. This restricted Tom's appearances to just two games with his new club Bradford. He returned to play for Bingley and, at the age of 20, he was good enough to play for Yorkshire against Durham.

In 1892, however, he returned to play for Bradford. He represented Yorkshire as well as the North against the South. That recognition paled into insignificance when he was selected to play for England against Scotland on 4 March 1893.

The following season he was recognised as one of the finest forwards in England and returned to Bingley to help them win the Yorkshire Shield. At the time of the schism between the Rugby and Northern Unions he was captaining Yorkshire who won the County Championship. He arrived back at Bradford in 1896 after a spell with an ill-fated Leeds-based club, West Riding, which fell out of existence.

A contemporary account records: 'It is not only as a sound scrummager and a fine dribbler that Broadley is known; in every position on the field he has shown himself a master. He is a man who can adapt himself to all conditions of the game with an ease which is unapproachable.'

Clearly the Yorkshire Rugby public anticipated a considerable game because 27,941 made their way to Headingley for that 1898 final. It broke the record attendance for the ground, reckoned to be the best in the country at the time, and there have been claims that it was probably then a world record for any game of Rugby at the time.

Bradford started with one small advantage. Batley's pack of eight forwards weighed at an average of 12 stone 11 lbs per man while Bradford tipped the scales at an average of 12 stone 13 lbs. Bradford started the game well but the effort of chasing the Yorkshire Senior Competition championship clearly hit their game because after the first quarter and a couple of goal misses by centre Fred Cooper, who was to become the AAA sprint champion for the year, the threat presented by their superior attacking game receded.

After a scoreless first half Wattie Davies drew first blood by stepping inside the Bradford defence to land a drop goal; then skipper John Goodall put the issue beyond any reasonable doubt with a try and a goal.

The Northern Union Challenge Cup remained at Mount Pleasant and ensured the Gallant Youths virtual immortality in the new code.

CHAPTER 3

LANCASHIRE AT LAST!

By the time the 1899 Northern Union Challenge Cup competition was being staged several vital changes had been made to the game. Most importantly professionalism had been finally embraced and, for the first time in the competition's history, the final was to be played in Lancashire. The lack of a suitable stadium for the anticipated crowd caused some concern and the chosen venue, Fallowfield Stadium, Manchester was not considered to be the perfect choice. There was even a suggestion that the game should have been taken to Crystal Palace, London which had held 73,833 for an Association Football game.

The two finalists represented opposite ends of the code's spectrum. Hunslet were very much the team of local boys who welded themselves together to become a powerful force while Oldham, continuing their pre-Northern Union traditions, recruited widely when building their team.

Batley, winners for the two previous years, fell at the third hurdle beaten in Lancashire by Leigh 16-6, while the beaten finalists Bradford were also victims in the same round losing 23-3 to Oldham in front of 18,000 people.

Hunslet had reached the final after a stormy semi-final with Salford. Six players were sent off: Rhapps, Brown, Woodhead, Gledhill and Jones from Salford and just one from Hunslet, Gillings.

The Goldthorpe brothers, Albert and Walter, played alongside each other in the centre for the Hunslet team. Albert was the captain of the team and by the time Hunslet reached the final he had been playing with the club for 11 years. He had a built up an impressive record as a goalkicker and was the first player in Northern Union to kick 100 goals in a season.

Oldham had a secret weapon up their sleeves because their Cumberland county centre Tom Fletcher had developed a tactic whereby he jumped over opponents although whether he actually used the device in the final was not recorded.

Hunslet spent most of the match under the cosh and the Cup was finally on its way to Lancashire for the first time when Walter Goldthorpe had to leave the field with a broken collar bone. Together with his brother he had done a great deal to keep the south Leeds team in the game.

Albert had kicked three goals and Walter went over for their only try. Oldham with 15 men still available were not to be denied. The Oldham tries came from former Northampton St James winger Sam Williams, who scored two, J. Lees, ex-Melrose forward J. Moffatt and Sammy Lees – who also kicked a goal, as did fullback R. L. Thomas.

The 1900 final, between Salford and Swinton, was a game to remember, not least because of the involve-

ment of one Jim Valentine. Superheroes have always been thrown up by sport and the infant Northern Union brand of Rugby Football was no different. Jim Valentine was a colossus who crossed the great divide of 1895, when the mantle of the Rugby Union was cast aside, with his status undimmed in the eyes of both the players and paying public.

The great man was a centre for the Swinton club. Based in a coal mining district just west of Manchester, the Lions helped introduce democracy to the grace and favour world of Rugby Football in the area. They were one of the clubs who forced an elected body on the socially exclusive clubs of Liverpool and Manchester, both of whom organised the game in Lancashire at that time.

Valentine was already an established player with Swinton when, in 1884, he made his debut for Lancashire. By 1891 he was captain of the Red Rose county side and took them to the County Championship. He led by example, scoring 16 tries in Lancashire's progress through to the title. The England selectors took a little more convincing because they delayed his debut with the national side until 1890, and after that first appearance against Wales made him wait six more years for his next cap.

He played in three internationals for England against Wales, Ireland and Scotland in 1896. But then his

Rugby Union career was ended when, in full bloom, Swinton decided to join the Northern Union for the 1896-97 season. Valentine chose to remain loyal to his club and made the transition without any problems.

He was to remain one of the five or six major Rugby personalities of the era, retaining his skill and charisma through those turbulent years. He was a consistent performer and, in the Northern Union seasons up to 1899-90, he figured in the top ten points scoring chart in three out of the four seasons.

By 1900 Valentine's career was in the veteran stage and he had moved from the three-quarter line into the second row of the forwards. Swinton's passage to the semi-final that year had been through a draw of contrasting fortunes. In the first series of games they had disposed of Wakefield junior club Eastmoor 53-0, while their second round meeting with Holbeck in Leeds was one of the most evenly matched games of the stage. Swinton's more fluid style proved decisive and they entered the third round by virtue of a 17-8 victory.

Their third round tie was a meeting of the giants because they faced the holders of the trophy, Oldham. Swinton won 14-2 in a tie that had attracted 15,000 hardy souls to Watersheddings. They beat neighbours Broughton Rangers 9-0 in the quarter final and gained a final place after beating Yorkshire's only remaining side in the competition, Leeds Parish Church, at Huddersfield.

The kick off was delayed because of a clash in colours. The Churchmen played in black and blue and Swinton in all blue. The impasse was broken when Leeds decided to change into all white.

For more than an hour Swinton pounded Leeds with 'some of the cleverest attacks seen in a rugby cup-tie' without success, but the Yorkshiremen were forced to capitulate and Swinton won 8-0 with tries from the right wing partnership of Messer and Lewis together with a goal by Jim Valentine.

Swinton had earned the right to face their close neighbours and rivals Salford in the final which was played on 28 April.

Originally the game was scheduled for the nearby Broughton Rangers' Wheater's Field but after the cup sub-committee's inspection had revealed deficiencies in facilities it was switched to the Fallowfield Stadium, Manchester for the second successive year.

While Swinton enjoyed a reputation for producing open, attacking football it was Salford who commanded the greater crowd support on the day. In spite of the fact that it was an all Manchester area final there was a disappointing attendance of 17,864. Although the Yorkshire teams had been virtually eclipsed in the period, they commanded greater spectator support for their games.

Salford scored first, in the seventh minute, when a Swinton attack broke down and Salford went the full length of the pitch for a try by Williams. Griffiths landed the conversion. Two minutes later, however, Swinton scored an attractive try through centre Messer and Jim Valentine – there were two Valentines in the Swinton team – kicked the goal.

The teams were still level when Swinton suffered what appeared to be a mortal blow. Valentine dislocated his collar bone. Players of yore were, however, made of stern stuff and he returned to the field of play. His injury made further life as a forward impossible, and so he was switched out of the pack as an extra three-quarter.

Salford, who were labouring under the handicap of playing with 14 men following the sending off of forward Brown in the first quarter, played attractive three-quarter rugby but they were facing a side who were clearly their masters in that department of the game.

Salford regained the lead when winger Pearson dribbled the ball over the line and dropped on it to register a try. The Lions, however, did not allow Salford much time to revel in the glory because they equalised for a second time with a long-range try by winger Lewis. Injured Valentine, an inspirational leader, missed the goal kick but Salford were a spent force. Late in the second half Swinton scored further tries through Bob Valentine and stand-off half Davies while Jim Valentine kicked one more goal. No wonder Jim Valentine became the first player to be awarded a benefit in the Northern Union; he was rewarded with a testimonial of 300.

Jim Valentine also had his reward for all the pain and suffering, a cup winners' medal. By 1900 he had been a recognised player for the best part of 20 years but there was not much time left for him, either as a player or a man. He suffered an untimely death when he was struck by lightning at Barmouth, North Wales in 1904.

CHAPTER 4

THE WAGES OF SIN

By 1901 the Northern Union game was starting to show noticeable differences from the accepted game of Rugby Union that it had left in 1895. In 1897, for example, the line-out was abolished to be replaced by a punt kick from touch. The biggest difference, however, related to the Northern Union's acceptance of professionalism. Not that their acceptance represented a full embrace because the Northern brand of the game was still not completely free from the philosophy of Corinthian spirit.

The Northern Union accepted the principle of payment for playing the game, but insisted that there should not be full-time professionalism. Players still had to maintain a full-time, recognised job. Billiard and snooker

Oldham's league and Cup winning side of 1898–99.

markers and bookmakers' runners were not acceptable.

The legislation enforcing this situation was known as the 'working clauses' and was rigorously enforced. Batley, winners of the Challenge Cup in 1897 and 1898, suffered from its enforcement. Dai Fitzgerald, their Welsh centre three-quarter was hauled before the Northern Union's investigatory committee as they were concerned he was 'Not following employment in a bona fide manner' while employed as a coal merchant. Batley defended their man stoutly but the specially convened meeting of the committee was far from happy.

Fitzgerald worked three hours a day for three shillings and ninepence a week, compared with the £2 a week he received for playing Rugby Football. The committee punished the player and the club heavily. Fitzgerald was suspended from playing for 16

months from November 1898 until 1 May 1900. The club were fined a massive £60 for not ensuring their player was properly employed.

The club survived, but Fitzgerald was missing from their two Cup campaigns of 1899 and 1900 and it can't be mere coincidence that Batley, who were at the height of their powers, failed to reach the final. With his suspension served the flying Welshman was returned to their team in time for the 1901 Challenge Cup competition. They were given a bye in the first round and accounted for near neighbours Huddersfield 6-2 in the second round, with Wattie Davies kicking three penalties to take credit for their entire points return.

St Helens, Batley's opponents in the inaugural Challenge Cup final and in the first round of the second tournament, were the next to suffer at Davies's hands. He scored five of Batley's points in their 7-5 win over the Lancastrians. It was not a popular victory in the glass-making town and Batley had to have a police escort back to the railway station.

Batley moved through to the semi-finals after beating Runcorn 5-2 in the quarter final with Davies among the scorers yet again. In the last four Batley came up against the club many people were tipping to win the Cup, Oldham. Batley, with Davies kicking three goals, however, reached their third final in five years with a 9-2 victory.

The last Batley team to win the Cup from 1901.

Warrington earned the right to meet them by beating exclusively Yorkshire clubs to reach the final. Leeds, Heckmondwike, Leeds Parish Church, Bradford and Castleford were all accounted for on Warrington's road to the final, played at Headingley on 29 April.

The popularity of the Northern Union brand of Rugby Football had reached such a state by 1901 that a record crowd of 29,569 was attracted to the final tie. Neither team was rated among the most popular clubs in the code, and the fact that such a massive attendance was registered indicated that the match itself was becoming an event and more than just another game for players and spectators.

The play itself was unremarkable and, apart from the fact that Batley won the Challenge Cup for the third time in five years, the major distinguishing feature was a sending off in the 50th minute when Batley forward George Maine was dismissed for foul play. He was later suspended until 1 December 1901. No wonder he decided to retire as a player at the end of the season!

Inevitably, it seems, Wattie Davies was to be the man to break the scoring deadlock. After 13 minutes Warrington lost possession, Joe Goodall picked up the loose ball and the move finished when the Welshman went in for the try. It was not converted. Nevertheless it was a notable touchdown for Wattie because it took him to the 100 point mark for the season, the third consecutive time that he had achieved that particular feat. It justified his position as the darling of the Mount Pleasant crowd.

The scoring was completed shortly after when Batley's opposite winger, Wilf Auty, went in for the second and decisive try. In the second half, with Maine dismissed, Batley were content to sit on their lead but both Davies and Warrington's outstanding winger Jack Fish kept the crowd interested with some penetrating runs. Davies finished on the winning side while Fish's glory was still to come.

Batley's victory signalled the break up of their Cup fighting team and a gradual slip from the top of the tree. They never regained the predominance of those infant years whereas Warrington, on the other hand, have remained one of the sport's elite.

The City of Salford lies in the cen-

tre of a region dominated by the mighty Association Football. However, the Royal Borough has fiercely kept its own identity by embracing Rugby League football.

At the turn of the century its contribution was even greater than today because it was able to support two teams, Broughton Rangers and Salford, a testimony to the demand for the game and the Northern brand in particular.

As if to mirror the demands for a 'super league' in today's Rugby League world, it was felt in 1902 that the bigger, and usually more successful, clubs should play each other on a more regular basis and so 14 of them split from the old County leagues to form the Northern Rugby League – an event marking the end of the opening era of Northern Union.

The power of the game within Salford was reflected in the fact that Rangers and Salford finished first and second respectively in the new league and, in King Edward VII's coronation year, they both reached the Challenge Cup final.

Broughton's captain Robert Wilson was a powerful influence on their success. He was a perfect example of how Northern Union clubs recruited players from outside their own hinterland to maintain the strength of their team. Born in the North Lancashire town of Carnforth and working in the local steel mills, he was spotted by Mr Fred Fearnley, the Broughton club secretary whilst a centre three-quarter with Morecambe.

His fine physique, speed off the mark, body swerve and ability to sell an almost perfect dummy brought him to the attention of other clubs; it was Broughton, however, who succeeded in attracting him to join them at the Wheater's Field ground.

He became a county and international player of note. Broughton had brought him in to replace another fine

Robert Wilson and Broughton Rangers, the 1902 Cup winners with the Challenge Cup, South East Lancashire League Cup and Northern Union League Cup.

centre Harry Jackson, and he formed a fine partnership with first Tom Jackson and later Andrew Hogg, a former Hawick Rugby Union club wing three-quarter. Wilson and Hogg became a feared combination throughout the whole league.

Beyond being a fine player in his own right Wilson was also a remarkable captain. He took over the role in October 1900, coincidentally against Salford, and helped blend Rangers into one of the outstanding teams of the era. It is he who was credited with helping blend Welsh imports Sam and Willie James into one of the best half-back partnerships of the age.

Both finalists had mixed opposition on the way to the final. Rangers escaped with a 5-0 second round win at Stockport and a fierce 9-5 semi-final win over Hunslet while Salford had to scramble for a 2-0 win at Dewsbury in the second round, hammered junior club Goole 67-0 in the third round with winger E.J. Bone scoring a record six tries, and removed holders Batley 8-0 in the semi-final.

A week before the final, staged for

the first time at Rochdale Hornets' home ground, the Athletic Grounds, disaster had struck when 25 people were killed and 500 injured at Ibrox Stadium, Glasgow at a Scotland v England International Association Football game. As a precaution the Rochdale ground was inspected for safety and one of the popular stands was closed on the recommendation of an expert.

Whether that limitation had anything to do with the fact that just 15,000 people made their way to the Rochdale venue is not recorded. Lancashire, however, had failed to match up to Yorkshire in terms of attendance.

The final itself was a one-sided affair. Salford were late in arriving and the kick-off was delayed until four o'clock, one hour later than scheduled. How they must have wished it could have been put back further because Wilson, and his Broughton side, were always in complete control.

The Broughton captain opened the scoring with a try which Willie James converted. He broke Salford down again shortly after and while he didn't score himself he ensured that his wingman Hogg went over for their second try; James converted. Before half-time Wilson struck again for his second and Broughton's third try which was improved by James.

Salford were behind 15-0 at half-time. Even though they trailed by such a large margin they took the game to Broughton in the second half. Winger E.J. Bone had several impressive runs but the Rangers defence remained watertight.

Wilson was in incomparable form and he completed his hat-trick of tries as the game drew to a close. Oram goaled and, to complete the Rangers' triumph Wilson's partner, scrum half Widdeson, gained their fifth try which was converted by Willie James.

It was Wilson's moment of triumph. When he returned to Manchester's Victoria station there was a huge demonstration. As he went to take his box seat in the charabanc the Rangers supporters swept round and carried him away shoulder high.

The moment of high drama marked Broughton's achievement of becoming the first club to win Northern Union's Cup and League double while the final itself was to be referred to as : 'one of the greatest games in the annals of Northern Unionism'.

Wilson died during the 1915-16 season, life expectancy being considerably less in those days, and his obituary recorded that after the 1902 final he: 'Did not play football many seasons after this, for he commenced to put on weight, and lost a lot of stamina.'

Players moving between one club and another had been quite usual from the conception of the game, but once the Northern Union moved towards professionalism the whole question became contentious. Players became precious assets of their clubs.

By 1902-03 the transfer system was subject to much controversy. Laws that were laid down to cover moves prior to the start of the new season were difficult to operate; charges of poaching were becoming more frequent.

Northern Union had, by this stage,

split into the Northern League, effectively a super league of the more powerful clubs, and the Yorkshire Senior Competition. The Lancashire Senior Competition was wound up and run as a second division to the new Northern League. The new code was emerging from infancy into early childhood and teething problems were still being worked through.

To help provide suitable arbitration between the clubs involved in transfer disputes a three-man committee was established to value players. Even in those days they had a transfer tribunal.

One of the bitterest wrangles was between second division Bramley and first division Salford. Centre three-quarter Jim Lomas had played for Bramley and been a star player with the south west Leeds club. In 1900 he moved to Salford, but Bramley were less than happy about the background to the transfer.

Bramley had been enjoying a run of success when Lomas's switch of clubs brought it to a sudden end. That started the feud which dragged on until the two parties were brought together at a tribunal meeting in Huddersfield on 18 April 1902 to sort out a settlement. The result was that the transfer was allowed to stand but Salford had to compensate Bramley for Lomas to the tune of £100. The settlement established a trend and was the basis of the transfer system that still exists today.

Once successfully settled into the Salford team, Lomas became part of a well oiled attacking machine. And, like many other losing finalists since, Salford returned to the final one year later. In the 1903 tournament they received a first round bye because Altrincham scratched, they accounted for Leigh in the second round, a crowd of 10,000 saw them win at Rochdale in the third round with Lomas scoring a hat-trick of tries, and they assured themselves of a semi-final place with a 25-2 win at York.

Halifax, too, had been making progress that year. The winners of the Northern League, they had the incentive of repeating Broughton's feat of a Cup and League double. They comfortably beat Halifax-area junior club Salterhebble in the first round, and moved through to the third round after a replay win over Castleford.

They needed a replay in the third round too after Brighouse, like Castleford, held them to a scoreless draw in the initial tie. Their fourth round match at Runcorn was almost as close but they accounted for the Cheshire side when full-back Billy Little landed a 50-yard penalty against the wind to prevent them facing a third successive replay.

Their semi-final kick off was delayed for 50 minutes by the 'unpardonable' late arrival of Halifax and Hull KR and, in spite of Hull's shock early lead with a Moxon try and Halifax having forward Langhorn sent off, Halifax took their final place by winning 8-5.

In the other last four encounter Salford faced their first division rivals Oldham at Broughton's Wheater's Field and were contained in a scoreless match. In the replay Lomas helped break the deadlock by scoring one of their two tries in an 8-0 win.

The final at Headingley on 25 April 1903 attracted a then record crowd for a Rugby match in England, 32,506, but the game failed to live up to the previous year's high standards.

At the start of the 1902-03 season the punt-in from the sideline, the method of restarting selected by the Northern Union to replace Rugby Union's line out, had been abolished and this brought an enormous increase in scrummages which reduced the game's attraction as a spectacle.

In ideal conditions Salford were dragged into a forward battle ignoring the fire-power their backs had at their disposal. In those days scrummaging

was not a refined art and Salford, for example, packed down in a line never more than two deep.

Halifax's pack must have relished the battle because of their eight only Billy Bulmer tipped the scales at less than 13 stone, while five of the Salford forwards were below that weight level. Salford came under pressure for virtually the entire first half but they succeeded in keeping Halifax at bay.

Halifax's stand-off half Johnny Morley engineered the break-through early in the second half when he slipped through the Salford line and hooker Ike Bartle scored a vital try. That, added to two penalties by winger Herbert Hadwen, saw Halifax take the Cup and complete the double.

The match, which failed to live up to its billing, had more important ramifications for the whole game. The Northern Union was so disappointed with the game as a spectacle that for the 1903 Annual General Meeting it was suggested that teams should be reduced from 15-a-side to 12-a-side. The proposal failed, but it shows the way they were thinking. A year later legislation was introduced so that the front row of the scrummage could contain no more than three forwards, and that change was linked directly to the authority's desire to keep the game as a product that people would pay to watch. They were aware of the growing popularity of Association Football and that growth made Northern Union legislators aware of the importance of open play.

One of the features of the modern Rugby League Cup final is the under-11 age group match as part of the build-up to the major game. They offered the same fare in 1903, the final being preceded by a schoolboy curtain raiser game between Hunslet Carr and Jack Lane School of Leeds. It is claimed their game was more attractive than the senior game.

CHAPTER 5

LITTLE BY LITTLE

In the northlands beyond the confines of both Lancashire and Yorkshire the game of Rugby Football has always appealed. The split with the parent Rugby Football Union also bisected the far north of England. While the Northumbrians and Durham men remained loyal to Twickenham and its brand, the men of Cumberland were attracted more to Northern Union.

The emigration of players from the rocky, lakeland county started as soon as it became clear that financial support for playing the game was available in the more populated, industrial Lancashire and Yorkshire areas.

Halifax, the 1903 winners, had been as active as many of the other clubs in their region in seeking reinforcements for their West Riding supply, and in 1901 they acquired William Beaty Little, a full-back from Cumbrian club Brookland Rovers. He was to play a major role in the development of Halifax as an important team of the era.

His background was typical of the age. He started playing when he was 17 years old. Initially he was with Brookland and by 1898-99, when Northern Union's influence was beginning to make itself felt in Cumbria, he switched to Siddick who had embraced the professional code.

At that point in his development he was playing at centre three-quarter. He was on the move again in 1900-01 switching to a still more senior club, Seaton, replacing Tom Fletcher who had joined Oldham. He kicked 26 goals for them during his first season in their colours, and the fact they won the North-Western League, bears further testimony to Little's contribution.

Halfway through that season they made an inspired switch, moving him to full-back which is where he was to spend the rest of his career. He must have made an incredible impact because, three weeks after the change, he was chosen for the Cumberland county side to play against Lancashire. He replaced Billy Eagers, who had joined Bradford; yet another emigrant.

He retained his place in the county team playing against Yorkshire at Hull. There was, however, a problem because he was a collier and after his second county appearance he was to play little more football that season. Travelling was proving a major headache and his particular difficulty provides an adequate illustration of the times.

Billy lived in a village called Flimby which was two miles from his club Seaton. A mere cockstride in modern terms but for him it represented a virtually insurmountable obstacle. Physically, reaching a game even such a short distance away, proved difficult on Saturdays.

In his own words: 'It was too much of a rush trying to get on the rugby field by half-past three when I only came out of the pit at half-past one. Besides, to play football in Cumberland costs money. We were supposed to be professionals but there was no such thing as getting paid. We used to have to pay for our own tea sometimes.'

In 1902 he was on the verge of quitting Rugby football completely when Halifax stepped in with an offer he could not refuse. He was transferred to the Yorkshire club, and made his debut for them in the third match of their season against Runcorn.

Little's arrival in the Halifax team maintained their strength. Although they failed to hold on to their League championship, they finished ninth, they did make their second successive Challenge Cup final.

The shape of the competition had been changed for the 1903-04 season. Instead of a massive free draw, the Northern Union adopted a new system of qualifying and intermediate rounds. This had the effect of reducing the numbers of junior clubs who took places in the 32-club first round proper.

Halifax passed through the first round with a comfortable win over St Helens, they had a tough second round 11-6 win at Barrow and in round three 17,000 people packed in to see them beat Leeds 11-3; two goals from Little as well as some astute tactical kicking saw them reach the final by beating a feared Hunslet 7-0.

They faced Warrington, who had reached the Challenge Cup final for a second time. A first round win over Swinton after a replay was followed by a 3-0 home victory over Wigan, a game which attracted a club record gate of 10,558. They travelled into Yorkshire to beat Pontefract in the third round to earn the right to play Bradford in the semi-final.

The first meeting at Broughton ended in a 3-3 draw but at Fartown, Huddersfield, in the replay, Warrington made sure with winger Jack Fish scoring a try and a goal as they won 8-0.

The final was brought back into Lancashire and again the game failed to bring anything like the kind of attendance that could have been anticipated had the match been played in Yorkshire. There were an estimated 17,500 at Salford's Willows Stadium on 30 April to watch the game.

Halifax's big pack outweighed their Warrington opposite numbers while Little's tactical kicking saved his forwards enormous amounts of work in seeking attacking position. Halifax captain Johnny Morley kept their approach tight and they emulated Batley's feat of winning the Challenge Cup in successive years by playing to their strengths and keeping the ball away from the dangerous Fish.

Halifax led 5-0 at half-time with a try from centre Joe Riley and a penalty by Hadwen. Early in the second half they had to withstand a barrage from Warrington, a team who had finished two places above them at seventh in the League table. Fish lofted a high kick and stand-off half Dai Davies beat Little to score a try against the run of play in the corner. That, however, proved to be the high-point of Warrington's performance and Halifax made sure of retaining the trophy when Morley, the archi-

tect of their game plan, shot from behind a scrummage to score the clinching try.

Two men from the opposite sides of the Northern Union were to play decisive roles in the 1905 Challenge Cup competition. Both were wingers: George Henry 'Tich' West of Hull Kingston Rovers and Warrington's legendary Jack Fish, and they were to come face-to-face in the final.

Tich stood five feet, four inches tall and he earned a special place in

the record books when Rovers, the club he joined from junior club Beverley Victoria, faced Cumbrian junior side Brookland Rovers in the first round on 4 March 1905.

He was not one of the game's great all time players but an example of a local boy made good in a reasonable grade of competition. The record from his date with destiny, however, re-

Warrington's Jack Fish and the Challenge Cup.

mains with us as these words are penned.

Hull KR won 73-5 with Brookland having conceded ground advantage believing that the greater financial advantage came from playing in Yorkshire.

West scored 11 tries and landed ten goals creating the record for the greatest number of points scored by one man in a professional game, 53! His tries also remain as the greatest number scored in one game too!

Like Bob Beamon, who established the world long jump record in the 1968 Olympic Games, Tich was never to reach those dizzy heights again. His tally for that game equalled more than half his total for the 1904-05 season; that remarkable performance can be placed in perspective by considering his entire career return for Hull KR: 98 tries and 44 goals, equalling 328 points.

West retired four years later and, unfortunately, died at the early age of 45. Nevertheless his legacy has stood the test of time even after the advent of the four-point try.

Rovers went on to become the first Humberside-based team to reach the final, by defeating Leeds, Hunslet and Broughton Rangers. On 29 April 1905 they faced Warrington, who had reached their third succesive final, at Headingley.

The Wire, as Warrington were and are still known, had disposed of Morecambe, Keighley following a replay, Wigan and the imposing Bradford in the semi final. The Wire, had been one of the outstanding sides of the early Northern Union epoch, and one of the major reasons for that prominence was Jack Fish.

The Warrington supporters idolised the try-scoring machine. The previous season he had finished third in the League's try-scoring list with 28 and third in the goal-scoring list with 37, which made him the second top points scorer on 158, behind Salford's Jimmy Lomas, who had amassed 222.

They demonstrated their affection for him by cutting out shapes of fish in either metal or cardboard, and during Cup runs they would nail the shapes to the top of poles or stick them to their coats when going to the match in the same way as modern supporters carry inflatable emblems.

Jack was not a tall man and he was blessed with natural speed; he became a sprinter of note who would undertake challenge match races against noted athletes of the time for sidestakes of £100.

He was christened John Fish in the Cheshire town of Runcorn on the opposite bank of the River Mersey from Widnes. In Rugby circles he became known as Jackie and he moved to live in Lostock Gralam near the Cheshire salt town of Northwich. He joined the village Rugby team and made such an impact that he soon came to the notice of the Warrington club committee. They arranged a special game against Lostock so that they could see young Jack's speed and skill for themselves; they must have been impressed with what they saw.

Negotiations for his contract took the form of heaping a committee table with £50-worth of silver and then inviting the young man for talks. Well, at least that's the legend in Warrington and, apocryphal or not, he signed for the Wire. By 1905 he was a legend and in the semi-final against Bradford he twice outpaced Fred Cooper, the 1898 sprint champion, to score long range tries.

In the final, which had attracted a disappointing 19,468, the first half became a stalemate as both sets of forwards slugged it out. Fish, who had missed a penalty shot at goal, came closer to scoring a try when he set off in full flight as the half drew to a close. The chance, however, was lost when the Warrington winger lost his footing in the greasy conditions and he injured his thigh.

Three minutes into the second half Fish had recovered from his injury sufficiently to score the first try after a long run. Rovers went on the offensive in an attempt to prevent the game slipping away from them but Fish finally put the game beyond their reach with a second try.

Scrum half Dai Davies initiated the move, centre D. Isherwood drove hard towards the Rovers line before sending Fish away to score between the posts. The excitement must have disturbed even the great man because he missed the conversion to his own try and, shortly after, a penalty. Nevertheless, he had the satisfaction of taking a winner's medal while Tich West had to be content with his amazing record.

CHAPTER 6

FAREWELL FIFTEEN

By 1906 the initial rush of interest in Northern Rugby Union had subsided and the break-away code, just like Rugby Union, was suffering a decline in interest. Spectators were being attracted to the more easily understood sport of Association Football and this caused great concern, especially to the Northern game, because they relied on spectator appeal to raise the cash to pay the players.

The situation was reaching such a state that even the seemingly unacceptable was being considered. Hull even put up a proposition to the Northern Union that they should consider amalgamation with the Twickenham version of the game so that the handling codes could withstand the challenge, but too much had been said and done to make that kind of 'U-turn' a viable propostion.

Northern Union was still basically Rugby Union being played under another name with slight variations and, for the start of the 1905-06 season, they shed the two-division format in favour of a 31-team single division. Clubs were allowed to construct their own fixture list and the league table decided on a percentage basis.

The Challenge Cup, however, retained its high-profile place in the programme and continued to draw big crowds. Warrington, the 1905 winners, were early victims when they were beaten 6-5 in the first round by the Gallant Youths of Batley in a repeat of the 1901 final. Again the importance of Fish to the Wire was emphasised. He did not play because he had broken his leg playing for England against Other Nationalities in the annual international fixture.

Bradford, one of the most important clubs in Yorkshire, reached the semi-finals after wins over Wakefield Trinity, Leigh and after a third round replay near neighbours, Halifax. Throughout their campaign, the Bradford wing pair of J. Dunbavin and former Hawick Rugby Union club player James Dechan had proved vital with their healthy try contribution.

Bradford arrived in the last-four with a major injury problem because Dunbavin had suffered a serious ankle injury in a league game against Oldham a week earlier. Their only other recognised winger, Mosby, was also *hors de combat* and they faced the prospect of a compromise; using a non-specialist winger. A flash of inspiration, however, produced an answer for Bradford and added an amazing piece of folklore to the Challenge Cup.

In 1904 Scotsman Bill Sinton had retired after three years regular service to the team. He left to concentrate on his job and still lived in Bradford. He was asked to consider playing again and coaxed out of retirement in time to play in the Cup match.

Bradford, with an orthodox team line-up, were able to withstand the determined assault by Batley, who were seeking their fourth final appearance in ten years, and two late tries by scrum half and captain George Marsden saw Bradford through to their first Cup Final since 1898!

They faced Salford, who had reached the final for the fourth time, and had beaten Rochdale Hornets in the first round, junior club Egerton and their neighbours Broughton Rangers in a third round tie that needed two replays.

In the first ever semi-final played at Warrington's Wilderspool Stadium Salford played Keighley and the tie attracted 8,500, the smallest crowd for a last-four game. Atrocious weather and a minimum admission charge of one shilling (five pence) were blamed for the low attendance.

Keighley's preparations were hampered when several players left the agreement of match terms until a few days before the game and, eventually, Salford scraped through 6-3.

The final on 28 April 1906 was played at Headingley and, such was the status of both clubs in the game, that record of 32,507, set in 1903, was thought to be in danger. Showers of sleet on the morning of the match diminished that possibility and kept the attendance down to 15,834.

Tension was the keynote to the

Contemporary cartoons celebrating Bradford and Warrington victories.

whole game. At half-time there was no score. Salford centre Jimmy Lomas provided the main threat to Bradford for whom Marsden was inspirational. Mid-way through the second half the game boiled over when Salford back row forward Silas Warwick and Bradford forward Harry Feather were sent off for fighting.

Eventually Bradford broke the deadlock when stand-off Brear went over for the try although Marsden failed with the conversion. Shortly before the end of the game Alex Laidlaw, the former Scottish Rugby Union hooker, kicked a penalty after Salford scrum half John was penalised for being offside.

It was Bradford's first trophy for 22 years and, strangely, it was to be their last before the club decided to switch to Association Football. Disenchanted with the Rugby code, the following season 1906-07, they became Bradford Park Avenue and moved into Association Football.

For Salford it was their fourth defeat in seven Challenge Cup final appearances but the 1906 final was notable because it was the last played

under fifteen-men-per-side laws. The most significant move away from Rugby Union came at the Northern Union's 1906 annual meeting when it was decided that their fifteen men-per-side teams should be reduced to thirteen-a-side with two forwards eliminated. Besides opening up the game more as a spectacle, the reduction also had the added attraction of cutting clubs' wage bills by up to £100 per annum!

As well as that complete break from Union law, the Northern Union also introduced one of the most distinctive skills that still exists in the modern game; to play the ball. This is executed after a player has been tackled; he puts the ball down in front of him and propels it backwards with his foot. It is, effectively, a two-man scrummage to restart the game.

Falling attendances and poor finances were forcing the Northern

Union to consider their position and the Northern League was reduced from 31 clubs to 27 by club resignations.

Warrington must have known what they were doing when they proposed the change from fifteen to thirteen men per side because they were among the first to benefit from the reshaped game. In the first three rounds of the 1907 Challenge Cup they accounted for Batley, Hull and Huddersfield.

A 21-0 semi-final cruise over a poor Swinton side gave Warrington a fourth final appearance in ten years, reflecting their importance to the Northern Union.

Oldham, winners of the Cup in their only previous appearance of 1899, accounted for Runcorn, Halifax and Wakefield Trinity before they beat the previous season's beaten finalists Salford in the semi-final at Rochdale.

Jack Fish was now captain of the Warrington team having recovered from the broken leg which ruled him out for half the previous season. Like the modern professional players, he clearly believed in thorough match preparation and, prior to the 1907 final, he spent some time with a professional sprint coach adding an extra edge to his pace.

The all-Lancashire final was played at Broughton Ranger's Wheater's Field Stadium on 27 April 1907.

While Fish's talent with the ball in his hands was legendary he was also a skilled kicker. Nevertheless he missed a couple of shots from penalties and succeeded in hitting the target just once in the first half. This helped the Wirepullers, or Wire, as they are now more widely known because of their connection to the town's leading industry, to stay in touch with a powerful Oldham side who led 3-2 at half-time thanks to a try by second row Bert Avery.

Warrington, however, switched winger Ernie Brooks with stand-off Ted Hockenhull for the second half and cruised the rest of the way to their second final victory in three years, winning 17-3 including a spectacular second half try by Fish, who dribbled the ball along the ground from inside his own half before touching down.

The size of the 18,500 crowd which packed the Broughton ground, proved that the Northern Union's decision to reduce the number of players per side had indeed proved worthwhile and provided a much more open, attractive type of Rugby.

CHAPTER 7

THE GLITTERING GOLDTHORPES

It is a fact of sporting life that certain games have a special attraction for particular families and that success can attach itself to the dynasty. The Goldthorpes of Leeds were perfect examples. They were a recognised Rugby football family even before the establishment of the Northern Union, and four of the five brothers were to become players of varying proficiency.

In order of their arrival in this world there were: William, James, John Henry, Albert Edward and Walter.

James and John Henry played occasionally for Leeds Parish Church while James also played Association Football before becoming secretary to

Halifax's 1906–07 team. Beaten in the second round of the Cup by Oldham, they went on to win the championship.

the Leeds club. In fact four of the brothers, James, John Henry, Albert and Walter shared the distinction of playing in the same Hunslet team together twice during 1892.

It was, however, the two youngest brothers who found lasting fame as Hunslet moved from mainstream Rugby Union into the Northern Union. The club, which was based in the work-a-day southern suburbs of Leeds, became a major force in the Yorkshire section of the game even before the split and they remained so as the independent code struggled to find its feet. Yet they were never major trophy winners. In 1899 they reached the Challenge Cup final only to fall at the finishing line as Oldham's cosmopolitan team emerged as victors.

By 1908 they had built a team that was feared and respected throughout

the game. That year the Northern Union decided that, because of the cumbersome operation of the league system, whereby not all clubs played each other throughout the season, the championship would be settled by a play-off between the top-four clubs. Hunslet qualified by finishing second in the table.

Earlier in the season they had won the Yorkshire County Cup beating Halifax 17-0, with Albert playing a leading role, scoring a try and kicking two goals, and were also the Yorkshire County League champions; the latter competition was run in conjunction with the Northern League programme – matches against clubs from your own county counted in a separate league table.

So, by the time they arrived at Huddersfield's Fartown ground for the Challenge Cup final against Hull on 25 April 1908, they were well aware that they had a chance of winning the four major trophies available to them.

They fully realised the potential of the situation because two days before the Cup final they were fined £10, a substantial sum of money at the time, for fielding a weakened team in a league game prior to the final. Even now, however, that seems a reasonable price to pay considering that the week after the final they would contest the championship play-off.

The weather was determined to

make it as difficult as possible for Hunslet because, deep into April, the final was hit by a snow storm, and it remains the only final to be affected by such a phenomenon.

Hunslet, who had beaten Leeds, Oldham, Barrow and Broughton Rangers to qualify for the final, faced Hull, who had accounted for Swinton, Salford, Wakefield Trinity and Leigh. Like so many of the best teams of either code Hunslet had built an impressive pack of forwards and that was the base on which the team was founded. This mountain of powerful human flesh was known to the Northern Union world as 'The Terrible Six'. They were Tom Walsh, Harry Wilson, Jack Randall, Billy Brookes, Bill Jukes and John Willie Higson. Reports of the time relate that they were the ideal blend of youth, experience, strength, skill, mobility and defensive tenacity.

It was from the quality of possession that they created that Albert Goldthorpe and the rest of the back division were able to dictate the tacti-

An influential figure in Oldham's Northern Union history, Joe Ferguson.

HUNSLET C.F.& A. CLUB. 1907-8.

Hunslet's legendary four trophy winning side of 1907–08.

cal flow of their matches, and the 1907-08 season was the highpoint of the Six's powers.

Opposing teams had to contend with more than the Goldthorpe brothers because Hunslet had acquired a three-quarter line of real pace. Cumbrian Billy Eagers, the young, talented Billy Batten about whom much more was to be heard over the years and a fleet-footed former Bramley winger Fred Farrar. This combination created more than 50 tries in 1907-08.

It was an all-Yorkshire final for the first time in ten years and Hunslet had enjoyed a statistical advantage going into the match. It was the 40th meeting between the two clubs and the Leeds-area side had won on 26 occasions. The Fartown ground was used for the final for the first time and 18,000 people saw the game.

Eagers gave Hunslet the lead with a drop goal and, encouraged by that success, Albert set up their first try when he burst past a couple of defenders to ensure that scrum half Fred Smith was able to make the touchdown. To rub salt into the Humberside wound, Albert kicked the conversion. Hunslet held their 7-0 lead

until half-time and Hull looked a beaten side.

Albert, who had landed his 800th goal for the club in the semi-final win over Broughton Rangers, kicked his second goal of the match after a 'mark' by Smith. The mark was made by a player with the heel of his boot on the ground after making a clean catch and, in those days, a kick at goal was still permitted from such a situation. Hunslet's second try came when Farrar went over after a crossfield kick by centre Eager. Albert kicked the goal; giving him a total for the season of 96.

What an incredible kicker the Hunslet captain must have been, bearing in mind the weight of the leather ball used in those early years, the length of time he had played and the primitive playing conditions those early pioneers had to endure.

Hunslet ran out 14-0 winners but it cannot have exhausted them because they then went on to win the championship play-off by beating Oldham. The final at Salford was drawn 7-7 but Hunslet won the replay 12-2. In the first match Albert scored all their points with a try and two goals, while in the decider he added two more goals and Walter scored two tries.

It gave Hunslet the four trophies – they couldn't play in the Lancastrian competitions – and they remain one of three sides to achieve that feat in Rugby League history. As far as Albert was concerned it had been another record-breaking campaign. After the two championship play-off games they beat Broughton in the semi-finals, and he became the first player in Northern Union to kick 100 goals in a season.

Albert's long career had reached its zenith and, two years later, he retired; he had been a player for 22 years. A kicker of note, he was best known for his drop goals and it has been calculated that he landed 220 during his distinguished career.

His memory was revived during the 1980s when an Australian television company produced a film called 'The First Kangaroos' about the inaugural Australian touring team. Actor Dennis Waterman of 'Minder' fame was chosen to play Albert and portrayed him as a foul-mouthed character. His interpretation of the Hunslet hero was not appreciated by the Rugby League world and it remains a heated subject.

A contemporary cartoon marking Hunslet's win over Oldham on the way to winning the Cup in 1908.

CHAPTER 8

VALE OF TEARS

One of the attractions of the Northern Union's Challenge Cup was the possibilities offered by David v Goliath encounters; senior v junior club. British sport is characterised by the underdog principle, in which the lesser of two sides is favoured by many spectators because pomp may be punctured and position overturned.

During 1908 the Northern Union had attracted a measure of support from that bastion of Rugby Unionism, Wales. Two clubs, Merthyr Tydfil and Ebbw Vale, had been admitted to the professional Northern Rugby League.

In their first season 1907-08 Merthyr had finished 23rd with eight wins while Ebbw Vale finished second from bottom, 26th, just above bottom club Bramley with six victories. Encouraged by this initial return, four more Welsh clubs – Aberdare, Barry, Tre-herbert and Mid-Rhonnda – were admitted to the League.

By the time the 1908-09 season had started, the division between the Northern Rugby League and the junior clubs had grown to such an extent that, on the pitch at least, they were virtually incompatible.

Merthyr, a club who joined the Northern Union after they were expelled by the Welsh Rugby Union on suspisicion of professionalism, and Ebbw Vale were teams to be reckoned with and achieved a good measure of success against the established north of England sides. The other four found life more difficult.

Ebbw Vale and Mid-Rhondda were entered in the first round of the Challenge Cup. Their luck was out from the start because they were both drawn away from home. Of the two, however, it looked as though Ebbw Vale at least had a chance to make the second round draw; they were drawn to play Humberside-area junior club Beverley while Mid-Rhondda had to face the holders Hunslet. The form book was followed to the letter as Hunslet gained a 25-5 win but the unfortunate Ebbw Vale's journey ended in Rugby League's record books with probably the least wanted entry of all.

Their tie was undoubtedly an attraction in the picturesque East Riding town of Beverley. A record number of people for their Northern Union club, 2,000, paid a total of £30 to see the game and they went away elated by the fact that their heroes had beaten the professionals 7-2. It remains the last time a junior club eliminated a professional club in the Challenge Cup.

There were instances of amateur teams winning in two-legged Challenge Cup matches against professional clubs during the 1946-54 period but they never actually succeeded in winning the ties. In fact it stood as a feat unparalleled in Rugby League history until the 1980s when amateur clubs Cawoods and Mysons, both from Humberside, overcame Halifax and Batley respectively in the John Player, now Regal, Trophy.

Beverley's moment of glory was brief. In the second round they travelled to play Halifax and were sunk without much trace in a 53-2 defeat.

In the mainstream of Northern Union life, the Challenge Cup was producing its traditional fayre of close matches between recognised protagonists. Wakefield Trinity, a name associated indelibly with Rugby League, had been growing in reputation. They collected a fearsome pack of forwards and were nicknamed 'The Dreadnoughts' after the lumbering, armoured battleships used by the Royal Navy during that period.

This incredible Rugby machine was steered by two intelligent halfbacks, skipper Harry Slater and Tommy Newbould, and they gave notice that they were were to be a force in the 1909 competition by beating a reconstituted Bradford side 13-7 in the first round.

The original Bradford club had run into difficulties and they had opened negotiations with the Rugby Football Union for readmission. The Union were not prepared to have them back at any price and, rather than continue in Northern Union, they switched codes for the second time to become Bradford Park Avenue Association Football Club.

There remained a residue of support for the 13-a-side game in Bradford and, days after that decision, a new club was established known as Bradford Northern; the link was emphasised, i.e. Bradford Northern Union.

In the second round Trinity had to travel to Leigh and emerged with their first ever victory over that Lancastrian club in an away game. Their 9-3 triumph was assured only after they had broken Leigh's resistance eight minutes from time.

In the third round they were given the slight advantage of a home draw against holders Hunslet and the game was a classic confrontation between two mighty packs of forwards; the Yorkshire Post newspaper recorded Trinity's 19-0 triumph: 'The fact was that the Terrible Six quaked before a set of forwards who were more terrible than they'.

Just 24 hours before their semi-final against eventual champions Wigan they both had to play league games. Both fielded weakened teams. Trinity lost 53-0 against Salford while Wigan's reserves were more impres-

The popularity of the Challenge Cup: Barrow v Hunslet 28th March 1908.

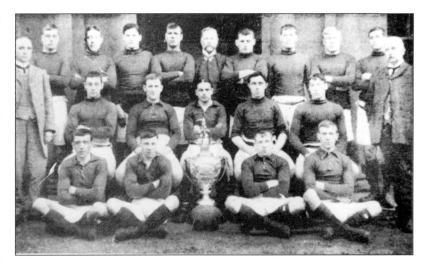

sive losing 8-5 to their bitterest rivals St Helens. They were both fined £25 by the Northern Union.

The Yorkshiremen surprised the neutral followers of the game by reaching the final, defeating Wigan 14-2. They qualified to meet the previous season's beaten finalists Hull.

The Humbersiders' journey to the final had seen them beat Normanton, Runcorn, Oldham and Halifax and like Wakefield and Wigan they too had been fined £25 for playing a weakened side in a league match before their semi-final while Halifax, who did not risk the fine, paid the penalty for trying to play a full strength side in two successive days.

For the final, which was played at Headingley on 24 April 1909, nine

Wakefield Trinity's Cup winning team of 1908–09.

special trains came from the East Riding fishing port. On one of the first was the Hull side. They arrived at 11.30 and were packed off to bed after their arrival at their hotel headquarters. Wakefield were followed by a dozen special trains as well as 'electric cars' or trams from the Wakefield Light Railway.

Hull had reinforced the team beaten by Hunslet the previous year by signing Scottish winger James Dechan from Bradford who had played in their 1906 victory.

West Yorkshire's Wakefield were clearly the more powerful side and by half-time the 23,587 crowd saw Trinity leading 6-0 with tries by Newbould and winger Bennett. As hard as the Humbersiders tried, they could not turn back the tide of play and, by the final whistle, they had conceded five tries without registering a single point.

It was disappointment again for Hull; two finals played and not a point to show from either occasion. Wakefield, on the other hand, left for home on a tram bearing the motto; 'It's 22 years sin' which, roughly translated, meant that it had been 22 years since Trinity's last success in the Yorkshire Cup.

CHAPTER 9

THE EMPIRE STRIKES BACK!

Internationally, Northern Union had been launched in 1907 when a touring team from New Zealand came to Britain to play Northern Union-style Rugby. The word that the split with Rugby Union had taken place was taken across the world by a 1905 'All Black' New Zealand Union international called George Smith and, two years later, a team led by a post office official, Albert Baskerville, arrived to play in England.

They had been nicknamed the 'All Golds' by the New Zealanders because they were going to play for money. Their journey to Britain brought them via Sydney and as well as inspiring the formation of the Australian game, they also set sail with an Australian guest, Dally Messenger, one of the great names of Rugby.

The tour, together with the subsequent arrival of the first Kangaroos in 1908, established the importance of touring to the Northern Union and, subsequently, Rugby League. In 1910, the Northern Union accepted an invitation to send a side to both Australia and New Zealand. This had a knock-on effect for the Challenge Cup because, in order to give the party time to reach the southern hemisphere, they had to bring the domestic competition forward in the fixture list.

Hull reached the final for the third successive year, while Leeds made it

through for the first time. The Humberside team had needed a replay to beat York in the first round and then disposed of Batley, Halifax and Salford to ensure that they became the first club to complete such a hat-trick. Leeds, on the other hand, beat Hull KR, Rochdale Hornets, Keighley, after a replay in the third round, and Warrington.

The final was played at Fartown, Huddersfield on 16 April 1910 and it was to distinguish itself as an unusual game. In those days travel over any discernible distance was restricted to one mode of transport, railway, which was at the height of its power as a public carrier. For the final the railway companies, and there were many prior to the grouping of 1923, arranged five special trains from Leeds and 14 from Hull.

Neither club anticipated that there would be such a problem reaching Huddersfield and, by the time the kick off time arrived, there was no sign of either set of finalists. Both had been held up in a glut of rail traffic.

Eventually, both sides arrived at the ground and the game kicked off at 4.20pm. Hull had been *en route* since noon and it had taken them two hours to make the journey from Leeds to Huddersfield; they had even seen the Leeds team on the platform waiting for their train to the game.

Hull must have entertained high

hopes of breaking their Cup final duck, after failure in the previous two seasons, and as taking the Cup to Humberside for the first time because they were leading 7-2 at half-time. Leeds had suffered what appeared to be a mortal blow when their scrum half J. Sanders was carried off and took no further part in the game. In fact he suffered so badly from the effects of his injury that they took him straight home! Leeds had to rearrange their team with F.Webster being withdrawn from the pack to replace Sanders in the three-quarter line.

Hull captain and stand-off half Willie Anderson was also injured when he dived to make a brave save. He was kicked on the leg and spent the rest of the game as a virtual passenger on the wing. There were no such things as substitutes and Leeds simply played on with 12 men while Hull adapted their game to cope with Anderson's indisposition.

Veteran Walter Goldthorpe became the hero for Leeds. He had been transferred from Hunslet to Headingley and it was his vast experience which kept Leeds in the game when Hull threatened to overrun them.

Walter had been playing at top level for 18 years but he still had enough spirit for a chase. Hull's Wallace misfielded the ball near the halfway line, Walter scooped up the ball and raced off towards try line. The spirit was willing but his legs less so, he passed to winger J.Fawcett and this drew the Hull tacklers across to the flank. Once their attention had been diverted, the wingman slipped the ball back to the veteran who crashed over for a try. Fred Young's conversion attempt failed but at least Leeds were back within reach at 7-5.

Ten minutes from time, Young found the target with a penalty kick to level the scores and he even had a chance to win the game with another shot at goal. This time he missed and at 7-7 it produced the first drawn final in the history of the Challenge Cup.

There must have been some consternation in the Northern Union hierarchy because one section of the tour party had already set off for the six-week sea passage to Australia and several players from each side were required to complete the party. It had been agreed that all clubs involved in important games like the Cup final should each release one player for the tour party and that the rest should follow at the completion of the programme.

The replay was arranged for Fartown on Monday, 18 April 1910, two days later, and it was agreed that it should be played to finish with extra-time added on, ten minutes each way, if required. The final had been seen by 19,413 people and the replay brought an attendance of 11,608.

Hull must have been badly affected by the swing against them in the final because they virtually collapsed in front of a revitalised Leeds, who had finished sixth in the league; seven places higher than the Humbersiders.

Sanders was not fit for Leeds and winger Fawcett stayed at scrum-half but the deciding factor for Leeds was their full-back Fred 'Bucket' Young who kicked five goals in the first half as the Loiners, as Leeds are nicknamed, surged into a 16-0 half-time lead.

Rowe and Goldthorpe scored second half tries for Leeds while Young added two more goals to create a seven-goal record which stood until 1973. Despondent Hull earned a measure of respectability with two late tries and three goals but they left with a hat-trick of final defeats.

Throughout Northern Union and Rugby League history crowd behaviour has always been counted among the best in professional sport. The replay produced one of the game's rare lapses. Five minutes from the end the spectators surged onto the pitch. The referee, Mr J. Priestley of Broughton, was cautioning two players when a spectator interfered with him. Other spectators became involved in the unseemly incident and there were reports that at least one player was struck. Nevertheless once the police had restored order the referee blew his whistle to end the match.

At least one commentator believed that the crowd had gone on to the pitch simply to see the medal ceremony but the real facts were that police had to restore order.

CHAPTER 10

THE FOUR JUST MEN

One of the attractions of the professional code is the transfer movement and recruitment of players from outside the game. Wigan, in particular, have never been afraid to back their judgement of a player with cash.

When the schism with the Rugby Union took place Wigan were not one of the biggest names in the game. But they developed quickly, won the last Lancashire Senior Competition in 1901-02 and, gradually, worked their way up division one in the inaugural two-division system and then established themselves as a major power in the single division.

In 1906 they finished sixth, won the championship in 1908-09 and, by 1910-11, had reached a peak in the club's history. Their investment in players had clearly brought its reward but they had also gone much further than that.

The three-quarter line they had put together became a legend, a thing of beauty that is recognised as outstanding, even today. The four stars were winger Jimmy Leytham, centre Bert Jenkins, centre Lance Todd and winger Joe Miller. It was a case of mix and match. All of them came from different areas and backgrounds combining to become a lethal rugby combination.

Miller was the local boy made good. Raised in the Wigan suburb of Pemberton, Joe joined the club in

1906. After waiting a year to make his senior debut, he went on to become one of the greatest wingers of his generation. He established a Wigan record of 49 tries in a season when he finished as the league's joint top-try scorer in 1908-09 and helped the club win two Lancashire Cup finals.

He played in just one Test match and that was against the first Australian touring team at St James' Park, the home of famous soccer club Newcastle United.

Jenkins, as his name suggests, came from Welsh Rugby Union. He joined Wigan from Mountain Ash in 1904 accompanied by the sound of wailing and gnashing of teeth as critics bemoaned his failure to play for Wales.

His move to Wigan and Northern Union was exceedingly successful and Bert became one of the finest centre three-quarters of the pre-First World War period, winning more than 20 caps for the Northern Union's Welsh national side and Great Britain. His introduction to the professional game could have been more happy because he made his debut for Wigan against Runcorn on an awful pitch and looked like a fish out of water. The result was inevitable and he was dropped. The miserable Jenkins retreated to Wales with a heavy cold which sidelined him for six weeks. Fortunately, he returned to Wigan and had to wait until the end of the

1904-05 season for his next first team game. With his apprenticeship served he became a master craftsman who toured down under in 1910 and 1914 and played in 12 Tests.

Lance Todd arrived in Britain as a member of the inaugural New Zealand touring team and stayed to become a Rugby League legend whose name will be forever linked with the Challenge Cup. He signed for Wigan the day that the New Zealanders sealed a three-Test series against the Northern Union by winning the third and decisive Test at Cheltenham, and 20,000 Wiganers went to see his debut against Oldham which Wigan lost 7-3.

He was not a big man but his skills and passing elevated him to dizzy heights. During his first season with Wigan, they won the League – Lancashire Cup double and his partnership with Joe Miller was one of the great double acts of the time.

Jimmy Leytham came from Lancaster and the story told in Wigan is that he joined the club for £10.00 in December 1903. He partnered Bert Jenkins and became a prolific try scorer and goal-kicker; a testimony to which was the 1,000 points he had scored for the club by Boxing Day 1909.

Known for his athleticism, the Wigan crowd nicknamed Leytham 'Gentleman Jim' and he was the

Northern Union's top try scorer three times between 1906 and 1910 as well as being a member of the first British Lions team to tour Australia. He scored five tries in the Test matches including a record four in Brisbane. He also scored four in one match for England against Other Nationalities in 1905.

All four were in the Wigan team which reached the 1911 Challenge Cup final at Salford's Weaste ground on 29 April when 8,000 – the lowest gate for a final – saw them play the City of Salford's other professional club Broughton Rangers.

Wigan arrived at the final after eliminating Huddersfield, Warrington and Leeds in the qualifying rounds. They faced Batley in the semi-final at Fartown, Huddersfield and it proved to be a major struggle for the Lancastrians. They led 2-0 until three minutes from time when former Hull player Willie Anderson kicked a drop goal for Batley.

A replay at Rochdale looked inevitable but from the restart Batley forward Jim Gath was involved in an incident and sent off. Their chances of victory ended when Wigan fullback Jimmy Sharrock landed the penalty for them to win 4-2.

Rangers accounted for Normanton St John's, Dewsbury and Bradford before eliminating Rochdale Hornets in the semi-final in front of an 18,000 crowd.

The final was greeted by a weather pattern traditionally associated with the Manchester region...torrential rain. Wigan had been heavily tipped to win the Cup but the cloying Weaste mud brought disaster to one

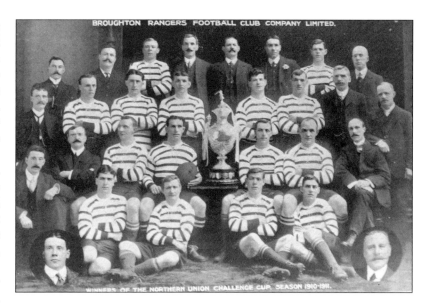

Broughton Rangers' Cup winning side of 1910–11.

of the greatest Rugby teams of any era.

Rangers, magnificently led by Welshman George Ruddick, closed the game down to such an extent that the much vaunted Wigan back division could not pull away from them out of the mud. A newspaper reporter provided one explanation for Wigan's failure when he wrote: 'Had the Wigan forwards gone into the fray with the same zest as their opponents they would have done much better than they did … credit must be given to Broughton Rangers for adapting themselves so well to the conditions.'

Sharrock was Wigan's only hero and the same newspaper recorded: 'Sharrock never made a mistake and a finer exhibition of full-back play under adverse conditions has never been seen in a Northern Union Cup final.'

Two penalties from centre Billy Harris gave Rangers a 4-0 lead at half-time and they carried that advantage all the way to the final whistle. Wigan's massive talents had been

frustrated and it was to be an honour that was to evade this team forever since the First World War was now on the horizon.

Leytham was killed in a Morecambe Bay boating accident in 1916, Miller served with the Welsh Regiment in France only playing twice more after the war – incidentally he was the last of the quartet to die, passing away in 1959 – Jenkins completed a 16 year career with Wigan in 1920-21 while Todd was surprisingly transferred to Dewsbury in 1914. He went into team management at Salford and created a legendary side. He died in a road traffic accident on his way home from Oldham in 1942. He had been the expert behind the microphone for BBC radio and his life is commemorated in the Lance Todd Trophy, the prestigious Cup final man of the match award.

CHAPTER 11

STUFF OF LEGENDS

By 1912 the Northern Union peer groups were well established with some clubs certainly more equal than others. Dewsbury had been involved in the original decision to split away from the Rugby Football Union and shied away from actually leaving Twickenham's influence although they eventually joined the Northern Union ranks in 1901-02. Their life in the code could hardly be described as spectacular; a case of solid performance in the middle of the Northern Union range.

In 1911-12 Dewsbury were enjoying one of their better seasons; they eventually won 18 of their 32 league fixtures to finish in a very creditable eighth place. For the Northern Union it had been a memorable season following the second tour by the Australians while the domestic game continued to thrive.

The uncertainty of the Challenge Cup competition was demonstrated in the first round tie between junior club Normanton St John's from the coalfields of West Yorkshire and Warrington, one of Lancashire's biggest and most successful clubs. Normanton succeeded in holding the Wire to a 6-6 draw at home although they crashed to a 75-0 defeat in the replay at Warrington.

Coincidentally, both of the previous year's finalists, Broughton Rangers and Wigan, were second-round

victims. Halifax accounted for Broughton; Wigan went down 12-8 at Oldham.

With clubs like Broughton, Halifax, Hull KR, Hunslet, Oldham and Wakefield Trinity all well placed in the League competition and fancied to transfer that form into the Challenge Cup, little or no pressure was exerted on Dewsbury, in spite of their fairly lofty Championship table position.

Their first-round tie with junior club Lane End United produced the expected victory, they emerged with a creditable 9-8 win at Salford in the second round and took a semi-final placing after winning the all heavy woollen district third round meeting with their closest neighbours Batley, the first ever winners of the Challenge Cup. Their semi-final with Halifax attracted 18,271 people to Huddersfield and Dewsbury won 8-5.

The term home-spun could be fairly applied to Dewsbury but the same could hardly be said about Oldham whose team was simply bursting with big name players, both British and overseas.

In the side that contested the 1912 final on 27 April at Headingley they had such players as centre Jimmy Lomas, whom they had purchased from Salford for £300, and Australians, centre Syd Deane and stand-off Alec Anlezark.

Oldham had already contested and lost the Lancashire Cup final when they were beaten by their rivals Rochdale Hornets, and finished as runners-up to Wigan in the Lancashire League and fifth in the league table.

The pre-match predictions were all

F Richardson, captain of Dewsbury's 1912 winning team.

The full line-up of the Dewsbury team who won the Cup in 1912.

totally ignored by the teams on the day. Oldham, who had beaten Coventry, Wigan, Huddersfield and Wakefield Trinity on the way to the final, established a 5-2 lead with a try by winger G. Cooks and a goal by prop Joe Ferguson.

Dewsbury's scrum half J. Neary registered his team's first points with a penalty. The heavy woollen team simply refused to roll over and be beaten, remaining three-points down until the closing ten minutes of the game. Then, amazingly, Oldham contributed to their own downfall. Their hooker Bert Avery was sent off and with the extra-man advantage Dewsbury winger W. Rhodes pushed them into the lead for the first time in the game with a try.

The 16,000 crowd must have been 'on the edge of their seats' as the final reached its climax. Two minutes from the end Oldham were defending desperately near their own line; a scrummage was ordered, Dewsbury took the heel and sent Rhodes roaring in for his second try.

Dewsbury won 8-5. It remains the joint pinnacle of Dewsbury's entire history. They were destined to win the Challenge Cup again during the dark days of the second World War in 1942-43 and reached the historic final of the 1928-29 season. More of that, however, later.

For Dewsbury it remained their only major Rugby title outside county restricted tournaments until they lifted the League championship in 1972-73.

CHAPTER 12

ALL HAIL TO THE PRINCE!

Throughout its history Rugby League has thrown up the kind of player that has captured not only local imagination but that of the whole sport. Such a man was Harold Wagstaff who became Rugby Royalty because he was, and still is, known as 'the Prince of Centres'.

He became a player of such legendary status that even today his

Huddersfield of 1913–14 with Harold Wagstaff in the white jersey (centre of the middle row).

name is mentioned in hallowed terms and he was one of the nine original entrants in the British Hall of Fame opened in 1988 to enshrine the game's greatest names.

He will be forever associated with Huddersfield and their famous 'Team of All Talents' that flourished in the balmy days just before and after the Great War of 1914-1918. It was, however, a matter of good fortune for the Fartown club that they were able to put any kind of a claim on him at all.

As a 15-year-old he was making a

name for himself with one of the game's most illustrious amateur clubs, Underbank Rangers, who recruited their players from the Holme Valley hills around the village-cum-market town Holmfirth which has found lasting fame among television audiences as the setting for the popular comedy series 'Last of the Summer Wine'.

Although, geographically, Holmfirth is seven miles to the south of Huddersfield it was the interlopers from Halifax, the Fartown club's close West Riding neighbours, who cast

their gaze over the blossoming Wagstaff talent but, in one of the all-time great sporting blunders, they decided not to pursue their interest with their committee saying: 'We want men, not boys.'

Huddersfield official Joe Clifford was more astute even though his club were running slightly behind their rivals. He pursuaded Wagstaff to join his closest professional club and gave the youngster five gold sovereigns for putting his name to their register.

Such was Harold's command of the game that Huddersfield threw him straight in at the deep end. He made his debut in their famous claret and gold colours at Bramley on 10 November 1906 when he was just 15 years 175 days old. His feat was such a rarity that it's veracity was challenged many times and the Huddersfield club could only settle the argument by printing his birth certificate in the club match programme at a later date to prove the point.

Original members of the Northern Rugby Union, Huddersfield's power grew as they started to assemble one of the classic teams of the game's history. Besides Wagstaff, who was a master of his position and the game, they had acquired winger Albert Rosenfeld who was a try-scorer of great renown, from the first Australian touring, former Welsh international Union forward Ben Gronow, the first man to kick off a game at the newly-opened Twickenham in 1910; forward Douglas Clark who was also a world champion wrestler; New Zealander Edgar Wrigley the youngest All Black in history; Australian centre Tommy Gleeson and Stanley Moorhouse, a rare local boy in the side.

In 1911-12 Huddersfield had won three of the four major competitions failing, narrowly, to emulate the 1908 Hunslet team. They won the league championship as well as the Yorkshire League and Cup while the Challenge Cup evaded them; they were third round victims at Oldham.

In 1912-13 they were denied the Yorkshire Cup but succeeded in winning the county league and the league championship while they also reached the Challenge Cup final for the first time, facing Warrington, who were playing in their fifth final and seeking their third victory. Huddersfield had reached the last stage of the 1913 competition by accounting for St Helens, Batley, Wigan and Wakefield while Warrington, last winners in 1907, marched through, putting Keighley, Hull KR, Salford and Dewsbury out on their way.

The final was played at Headingley for the second successive year. It had been predicted that Huddersfield's fast, free-flowing approach would leave Warrington trailing but in the first half the Wire surprised many people by taking a 5-0 lead through a try by winger Bradshaw and a massive touchline goalkick from full-back Jolley.

They held that lead in spite of everything that the wonderful Huddersfield team could throw at them. In the second half they found the strain too much to handle.

Huddersfield snatched a one point lead at 6-5 thanks to two tries by winger Moorhouse, who not without coincidence played outside the majestic Wagstaff. The previous season Moorhouse had scored 55 tries, a record for an English-born winger. It was equalled in 1926-27 by another all-time great, Alf Ellaby.

The final was now tipped in favour of Huddersfield. They quite clearly had the measure of Warrington and the Lancashire team were beginning to labour under the pressure that Huddersfield were inflicting.

Inevitably Wagstaff had a say in the decisive score of the game. He shared a passing movement with Moorhouse which ended when the wingman crossed his line for the try which made him the second player to score a hat-trick of tries in a Challenge Cup final following Broughton Rangers' Bob Wilson in 1902.

Huddersfield went on to take the championship the following Saturday when they beat Wigan in the play-off final at Wakefield. Their failure to win the county cup prevented them from taking the classic all four combination but their time was yet to come. They were the major force of the era.

CHAPTER 13

PATIENCE REWARDED

J ust three months before the shot that felled Archduke Franz Ferdinand rang out and started the First World War, the Rugby men of Hull were embarking on a campaign to set the Challenge Cup record straight as far as the game on Humberside was concerned. Hull Football Club, which is situated on the western side of the River Hull and plays in the famous, distinctive irregular black and white hoops, had appeared in three successive finals between 1908 and 1910 and lost them all.

The other professional team in the city, Hull Kingston Rovers, which is based on the eastern bank of the River Hull, was the first side from the area to battle their way through to a Challenge Cup final in 1905 and they too had to endure the bitter taste of defeat.

On 25 April 1914 Hull FC had reached the final for the fourth time when their opponents were Wakefield Trinity but, for this attempt, Hull had recruited somebody from outside Humberside to give their play that little bit extra touch of class.

That man was Billy Batten. The big, black-haired centre had achieved a god-like status in Northern Union. By the time he arrived on Humberside he already had one Challenge Cup winners medal, having been part of the famous all-four cup winning Hun-

slet team in 1908. Born at Kinsley, a little village near Fitzwilliam in South Yorkshire in 1889, he was soon recognised as a player of considerable talent and potential.

He used his bulk to simply power would-be tacklers aside. The direct route was always available to him and it was this sheer brute force, allied to his size, that brought him many of his tries. He also used the now banned tactic of jumping over his opponents.

Batten's move to Hull came in April 1913 and he was paid £14.00 per match. That was a staggering sum of money when it is considered that the average man's wages could still be counted as little more than a £1 and that, even after the Second World War, some top players were still earning little more than £20 for a win.

Until his move from Hunslet, the biggest transfer fee that had existed in Northern Union was that of £300 paid by Oldham to Salford for Jimmy Lomas and the fact that Hull were prepared not only to top that fee but double it, indicates how highly Batten was regarded.

Billy was an established international and it was hardly a coincidence that, a year after his move across Yorkshire, Hull should have reached the Challenge Cup final and were riding high in the league championship, destined to finish fourth.

Meanwhile Wakefield too had made an important signing in 1913. A

Hull KR, beaten by Warrington en route *to the 1913 Cup final against Huddersfield.*

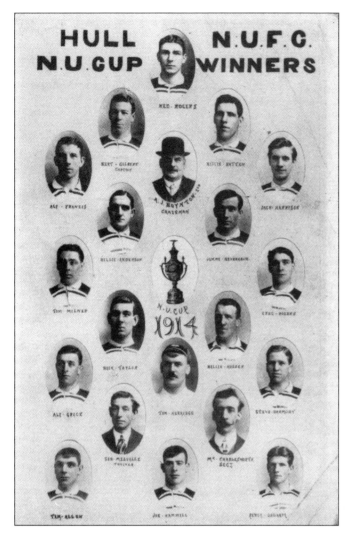

Hull KR who were beaten by Huddersfield in the second round of the 1914 competition.

end Hull put the result beyond any doubt when stand-off Jimmy Devereux and centre Bert Gilbert created a try for their other winger Alf Francis.

Neither try was converted but Hull had finally broken their dismal run of failure in Challenge Cup finals and took the trophy back to their East Yorkshire Rugby stronghold, buoyed up not only by the 6-0 victory but revenge for that 1909 defeat.

For winger Harrison there were two kinds of glory to come. The following season he became Hull's record try scorer with 52 in a season, a bench mark that remains in place even today. Like many Rugby players he joined up once the war started to gain momentum and became a second lieutenant in the East Yorkshire Regiment.

In 1917 he gave his life in action fighting at Oppy Wood and was posthumously awarded the Victoria Cross for his gallantry, the only Northern Union or Rugby League player to receive the United Kingdom's highest award for supreme gallantry in the face of the enemy.

Huddersfield did not reach the finals but they still had an impact on the Cup and its history. In the first round they played junior club Swinton Park from the Manchester area.

They simply ground the unfortunate juniors into the mud 119-2. It was a record score for the tournament and it remains so to this day. One of the main tormentors of the unfortunate Swinton Park side was the Huddersfield full-back Major Holland. He scored a club record 39 points including 36 points from 18 goals. No Huddersfield player has ever remotely challenged that return.

month before Batten had signed on the dotted line for Hull, Trinity had acquired the services of 15-year-old Jonty Parkin. The teenage stand-off half from coal-mining village Sharlston had joined the professional ranks for the princely sum of £5 and was destined to become just as influential in Rugby League as Batten.

Wins over Salford, Featherstone Rovers, Halifax and the mighty Huddersfield in the semi-final had taken Hull to the final while Wakefield beat Swinton by the smallest possible winning score of 2-0 in the first round and then gained a single point 9-8 win over Leeds.

They battled to beat Wigan 9-6 and needed a replay to beat Broughton Rangers 5-0 in the semi-final after tying the first game 3-3.

It was a repeat of the 1909 final and, for the first time, the game was staged at Halifax's Thrum Hall. It was played earlier than normal because a tour team was due to depart for Australia on 18 April and, for the second successive year, a dismissal played a decisive role in the destiny of the Challenge Cup. The game remained scoreless until the 72nd minute when Trinity's second row forward H. Kershaw was sent off. Within seconds Hull had taken the lead through a try by winger Jack Harrison who forced his way over. Two minutes from the

CHAPTER 14

TALENT BLOSSOMS

By the time the 1914-15 season was a reality men were bleeding and dying across the English Channel. The Northern Union agonised about whether to start the season and, on 11 August 1914, the Union's committee met to discuss whether or not to play on. They decided to go ahead.

On 26 September the Lions team who had toured Australia returned home with a two-one series victory. Two members of the party were reservists, Huddersfield's Fred Longstaff and Rochdale's Walter 'Rattler' Roman and they were ordered to join their units on their return although

Longstaff was allowed to return to playing.

For the two previous seasons Huddersfield had won three of the four competitions for which they were eligible to enter. The Northern Union struggled on through the opening year of the war; crowds dwindled, players joined the military services and transport around the country became increasingly difficult.

Nevertheless, by the time the climax of the season came in April and May 1915, there was still sufficient interest to provide a historic climax to the campaign.

Huddersfield won the Yorkshire County League at a canter and trounced the previous season's Challenge Cup winners Hull 31-0 in the Yorkshire Cup final at Headingley. They added the League championship when they overcame Leeds 35-2 in the play-off final and that brought them to the Challenge Cup final at Oldham's Watersheddings ground on 1 May 1915 as they sought to emulate Hunslet and become the second side

The "Team of all talents"; Huddersfield after their historic four trophy triumph of 1915.

to perform the feat of winning all four cups.

Wins over Leigh, Widnes, Salford and Wigan took them through to the big day and they faced St Helens, the beaten finalists in the first tournament back in 1897. The Saints had finished eighth in the league and they had endured a difficult path to the final. All of their three qualifying matches had been played away from home – at junior club Featherstone, Swinton and Keighley after a replay with extra-time. They also had to replay their semi-final. In the first match they drew 3-3 with Rochdale Hornets but succeeded in winning the replay at Wigan 9-2.

The rugby correspondent to the St Helens Newspaper must have been a cynic because he wrote: 'I wonder what would have been the fate of any prophet who foretold this year's events.

'If such a prophet had begun by declaring that Germany would be fighting England in 1915, he might have been believed.

'If he had said Germany would have been fighting England, France, Russia and few more – he might have stood a chance of saving his skin, provided he could run.

'But if he had said the Saints would win every round of the Cup up to the final, away from home – he would probably have been extinguished on the spot as a dangerous lunatic at large.'

As if St Helens had not had enough problems actually qualifying for the big day they then experienced even more trauma on Cup final day itself.

The St Helens team had performed their Cup miracle for a bargain pay packet of ten shillings (fifty pence) a game. It was traditional in the game to increase match terms when a team succeeded in progressing to one of the major finals and the St Helens players were certainly expecting a bonus. In the dressing room prior to the game the club chairman, Tom Phillips, was asked about the payment and the players were staggered to find out that there was to be nothing extra for them. Club funds would not stand the strain, they were told.

A strike was threatened but the situation was saved by a remarkable man, the St Helens captain Tom Barton. He was a 34-year-old winger who had been one of the fastest men in Lancashire, having won the professional sprint championship over 100 yards (98 metres) in 10.2 seconds in 1910. He was at home in any back position possessing superb tactical appreciation, personal skills and tackling ability.

He was also brave. He had broken his ankle which did not heal well and, even in those days of risky surgery, he returned to hospital, had it rebroken and set rather than give up playing the game.

So when the St Helens players were preparing to quit the dressing room it was Barton who quelled the mutiny. He has been quoted as saying: 'Never mind the bonus. There's a medal waiting there – win or lose for every man. Each medal is worth at least three pounds, and I am not going back without mine – even if I have to turn out and play Huddersfield myself.

'Listen to those people out there. Some of them must have travelled miles to see the match. We may have had what seems like a raw deal, but we can't let them down. Come on.'

Brave words and they had the desired effect too because the St Helens players did decide to play, giving the 8,000 crowd a game to watch. Sadly for the Saints supporters who had made the trip that was where the fairy tale ended, because Huddersfield's incredible team of all talents gave St Helens a 37-3 hiding to create a record widest margin of victory in a Challenge Cup final.

The claret and golds from Yorkshire led 21-0 at half-time after tries by Gleeson, Harold Wagstaff, Albert Rosenfeld, who had posted a world record 80 tries the previous season – a best unattained ever since, Wagstaff and Gleeson with three goals by Gronow.

The avalanche continued through the second half. More tries came from Holland, Moorhouse, Gronow and Rogers while the Welsh forward collected one more goal. St Helens prevented the whitewash when prop forward Sam Daniels crashed over for an unconverted try five minutes from time.

Huddersfield, after two seasons of being so close, finally achieved the four cup feat and earned a place in Rugby League folklore. The shroud of war had, by the end of the 1914-15 season, become too heavy a burden for the Northern Union to carry and, in June, competition was suspended for the duration of hostilities.

Huddersfield were in their pomp. Although they were to remain a powerful force when peace returned to Europe, the four years of conflict took with it a large chunk of the Fartown club's prime lifetime.

For at least one Huddersfield player, their international forward Fred Longstaff, it was to be a glorious finish to his free sporting life because he never returned from military service. He was killed in action during 1916.

CHAPTER 15

STRANGLEHOLD ON RUGBY

Douglas Clark survived the First World War to pick up the threads of his interrupted professional Rugby career. He had been a player of considerable standing even before the 1914-18 hostilities began and returned to his club Huddersfield with his powers miraculously intact. Clark was, however, more than just a good player, he was a great player who had been an international with five caps for appearances against Australia.

Clark was an amazing athlete, yet another import from Cumberland, and he was the archetypal example of why the professional game came into existence. The son of a Ellenborough coal merchant, he left school to join the family business delivering bags of black diamonds – even on Saturday, which had a detrimental effect on his Rugby ambitions.

Young Clark was, however, determined to succeed and he often paid his friends to undertake his Saturday delivery work. Sometimes the price was high and it would cost him the best part of his week's wages to find stand-ins so that he could play Rugby.

His father clearly did not approve and, according to a testimonial booklet issued on Douglas's behalf many years later, when retribution came it was a memorable event. The Chronicler records: 'The interview and subsequent proceedings made an impres-

sion upon the young delinquent which is still vivid in his memory.'

Whatever Clark senior was trying to impress upon his son, it did not put him off his sport. At the age of 15 he joined the famous Cumbrian junior club Brookland Rovers to play in the under 18 age group team and, in his first season, he picked up a medal as Brookland won the competition, beating Cleator in the final.

He stepped up to the under-21 level the following season and, with Douglas playing at half-back, they won every game. That season yielded three medals and this was followed by three more the following season when he played in the senior team.

Such success had to attract attention even from outside Cumberland and in April 1909 the impressive Huddersfield official Joe Clifford, who also unearthed Harold Wagstaff, invited Douglas to join them at Fartown. His decision to move to Yorkshire brought more discord in the household for Clark senior thought that his son was not strong enough for first-class Northern Union.

Discretion prevailed and Clark junior made his debut for Huddersfield in the reserve team where it was quite plain that the young Cumbrian was more than strong enough to hold his own. He made his senior debut against Hull Kingston Rovers on 23

September 1909 and that marked the start of a long and illustrious career with the Huddersfield club.

His impact was immediate and he did sufficiently well to be selected for Cumberland to face both Lancashire and Yorkshire the following month.

When the First World War broke out Douglas Clark, like many other players, joined up and he served in the same unit as his Huddersfield teammates Harold Wagstaff and Ben Gronow.

Tales of their service life grew, apocryphal or not we are not sure, but Clark distinguished himself in at least one such tale.

While on convoy duty near Windsor a halt was called and a gentleman approached their lorry. At the time Clark and his colleagues were trying to open a tin of bully beef from the wrong end. The gentleman said: 'Don't you think sonny, you'd do better if you opened the other end?' Other questions followed, Clark ran out of patience and said to their questioner: 'Look here sir, we're busy.'

The gentleman smiled and walked away. Clark's feelings can only be imagined when it was revealed that the gentleman had been none other than the reigning monarch, King George V!

Douglas was a war casualty. He was blown up near Paschendale and filled with shrapnel. The doctor who operated on Douglas told him that it was only his strong constitution which pulled him through. He was also awarded the Military Medal. A mark of the man was that when he was recuperating back in England he succeeded in winning the Army wrestling championships. He was a Cumberland and Westmorland wrestler of note and later became a world champion at freestyle wrestling!

During his war service Clark was gassed twice, one attack of which left him blind for nine days, and he was given a certificate of 95 per cent disability. He protested against the certification to such an extent that he was sent back to his unit less than four months later.

There was no doubt about his return to Rugby and, by 1919 when the Northern Union resumed on a limited basis, Clark was back in Huddersfield's Claret and Gold.

For 1918-19 Huddersfield did not field a league side because so many of their players were still in the forces but they entered the Yorkshire Cup. Even in their weakened state they won with Douglas Clark playing at prop forward.

Huddersfield were back to full strength in 1919-20 winning the Yorkshire League and Championship play-off and heading for the Challenge Cup final with another four trophy attempt in prospect.

The Fartowners beat Swinton, Wakefield Trinity, St Helens Recs after a replay, and Oldham in the semi-finals to reach the first Challenge Cup final of the new found peace. They played Wigan who had virtually rebuilt the team that had given them so many glories in the pre-war period.

Wigan, with Welshman Sid Jerram at scrum half and George Hesketh at stand-off half, had finished 14th in the Northern League table. Their progress through the qualifying rounds saw them dispose of junior club Healey Street Adults, York, Bramley and the powerful Hull in a semi-final at Salford that attracted 22,000 people.

The final, restored to Headingley on 10 April 1920, was not nearly so popular as it had been in pre-War years with 14,000 paying customers coming through the turnstiles. The first half was at least competitive, Wigan were trailing 8-5 at the interval, but Huddersfield took complete control of the game in the second half to win 21-10.

Douglas Clark was one of their try-scorers. Left-winger Hubert Pogson scored two while right winger George Todd and scrum half Robert Habron crossed for one each. The reliable boot of Gronow added three goals.

Wigan's total comprised of a try each from Jerram and winger H. Hall together with two goals from full-back Bill Jolley.

Huddersfield moved on to play Hull in the championship final knowing that victory would give them a second four-trophy haul. In the play-off final two weeks later, again at Headingley, Huddersfield were under a handicap because five of their best

Douglas Clark... a Cumbrian strongman who found fame with Huddersfield before and after the First World War.

players were on a ship with the Great Britain team heading south for a tour of Australia.

It was, to paraphrase the Duke of Wellington, a close run thing. Huddersfield, led by their Australian winger Albert Rosenfeld, who scored a world record 80 tries in 1913-14, took a 2-0 lead with a Major Holland goal, but a try by Billy Batten ensured that a 3-2 victory went to Hull and the Huddersfield four-trophy feat was dashed. Nevertheless, in four successive peace-time competitive seasons Huddersfield won three of four trophies and in the other all four. No wonder they are still revered as the 'team of all talents'.

CHAPTER 16

RED ROSE REVIVED

Leigh were one of the original breakaway rebels in 1895 and the club from the Lancashire cotton town, which lies between Wigan and Manchester, had always been sturdy competitors without being among the consistent trophy winners. They took the league championship in 1905-06 – the first under the re-introduced one-division system – and were runners-up twice in the Lancashire Cup.

The club directors clearly decided that it was time for them to make a serious attempt to join the highest echelon of the game because, by the time the 1920-21 season started, they had assembled one of the finest teams to grace their red and white colours.

They had depended heavily on dis-affected Welsh Rugby Union players such as Neath's centre or scrum half Emlyn Thomas, whose brother Johnny played with distinction neighbours Wigan, Wyndham Emery, a centre from Bridgend, Pontypool forward Jack Prosser and Llanelli centre Dai Price, who arrived at the club via Batley. They also raided English Rugby Union outside the north of England bringing Moseley winger Cyril Braund into the side.

During the season Leigh used 37 players for their first-class games and 19 of them were new to the club! They came close to glory early in the campaign when a massive crowd of 18,000 saw them beaten by Broughton Rangers in the Lancashire

Cup final but they were not able to translate that form into league matches because they finished a disappointing 20th in the Northern League.

Challenge Cup matches were, however, a totally different proposition. They had a tussle at York in the first round, eventually winning 3-0, and that must have been enough to convince the town's sporting public that their team stood a chance of winning the Cup because, for their second round home meeting with Warrington, there was a ground record attendance for the time of 21,000. They

Leigh stage a formal dinner at Sharples Hall, Bolton to celebrate their 1921 Cup final victory over Halifax.

drew 10-10 and it took a crucial try by Emlyn Thomas for Leigh to win the replay 8-3. That brought them a third round home tie against Bradford Northern and a solitary try scored by second row forward Joe Darwell proved the decisive factor as they won 7-0.

Their semi-final at Central Park, Wigan attracted 20,000 spectators and Leigh made their first Northern Union Challenge Cup final when they won 10-0.

Halifax had always been recognised as one of the Northern Union's most powerful teams and they had already won the Challenge Cup twice when they established their right to be in the 1920-21 final. The Thrum Hall team accounted for Batley, Bramley and Widnes in the qualifying rounds before meeting the West Yorkshire rivals Huddersfield at Headingley in the semi-final. The game attracted 23,500 spectators and they saw the holders beaten 2-0.

Halifax were considered to be the favourites for the final which was staged at Broughton Ranger's ground, the Cliff, which is now a Manchester United training ground, on 10 April 1921.

Leigh paid tribute to one of their players Paddy O'Neill, who had been killed in the Great War, when their team was led out on to the pitch by his son, club mascot Stanley, who also had his dog with him dressed in Leigh's colours.

The trend of the match was against all expectations as Leigh, inspired by their scrum half and captain Walter Mooney, virtually blotted Halifax out of the game.

Mooney had set up tries for centre Emlyn Thomas and prop Billy Parkinson before Halifax had realised what was happening and when Thomas charged down a kick to score his second try of the match Leigh held a commanding lead of 11-0.

Full-back Tommy Clarkson, who had kicked one goal in the first half, added a penalty in the 65th minute. That completed the scoring and Leigh shut down Halifax's attempts to rescue the match. Besides being Leigh's first Challenge Cup triumph it was also the end of a long run of Yorkshire success in the final. Leigh were the first Lancashire team to take the trophy since Broughton Rangers in 1911.

CHAPTER 17

HORNETS GO WEST

While Welsh Rugby Union has always provided the northern professional clubs with a plentiful supply of very nearly ready-made players there have been spells during the history of Rugby League when other areas have been subject to attention.

Rochdale Hornets were a case in point just before and after the First World War. They established a reputation for bringing west country men into the paid ranks and it worked well for the famous Lancashire cotton town club.

The burr of west country accents held its own as the Hornets went into the 1921-22 season and it enriched a dressing room vocal mixture already featuring players from St Helens, Wigan, Wales and even of Italian descent.

Hornets succeeded in reaching the Challenge Cup final for the first and only time in their peace-time history in 1922 and, of their six-man forward pack, three came from west country rugby union.

In the team they fielded for the final at Headingley on Saturday, 6 May 1922, the open-side prop Tommy Harris was imported from Redruth in 1920 after he had represented Cornwall seven times; Hornets were impressed by both his tackling prowess and scrummage ability. The blind side prop Dicky Padden originally turned professional as a winger

from Newton Abbot in 1910 but the former Devon county player successfully made the transition from the backs into the forwards in Northern Union.

Tommy Woods the second row forward had joined the trek north in 1909. He played for Bridgwater Albion and was an England international with 30 games for Somerset to his credit before deciding to turn professional with Hornets. He became a dual international playing for the Northern Union against the Australians before the First World War.

Rochdale Hornets had been one of Northern Union's eternal bridesmaids. Their collection of honours could hardly be described as impressive. In the early days they provided stiff opposition without actually making the big breakthrough themselves. Either side of the Great War they enjoyed their golden age winning the Lancashire Cup twice in three appearances over five years.

They had reached the Challenge Cup semi-finals in 1911 and 1915, falling at the final hurdle, but by 1922, however, they had assembled one of the finest teams to grace the club's famous red, white and blue colours.

Their determination to have a worthy team was demonstrated in January 1922 just before the start of the Cup campaign when they signed centre Eddie McLoughlin, the St He-

lens captain and Lancashire three-quarter.

The build up to the Cup games provided ample evidence that they were in the mood for a meaningful attempt at the game's highest honour. In the first round they were drawn against Cumbrian amateur side Broughton Moor and they won 54-2 with winger Joe Corsi grabbing five tries to establish a club record for one game that has been equalled just twice since.

The Corsi family played an important role in the Hornets development of the time. There were six brothers in a Cardiff-based family of Italian descent and four of them went to Northern Union Rugby.

Jack, the first Italian to win a Welsh schools international cap, went to the Athletic Grounds in 1914 as a centre and stayed for eleven years before being transferred to York. He was an incredibly talented man. Besides his Rugby career, he was a boxer securing the Italian national title during the 1914-18 War, and a water polo player. At the end of his career he toured the music halls as an accordian player with his dancer wife!

Brother Louis went to Rochdale in 1921 and was the loose forward of the time. He returned to Rochdale after the final sporting two trophies – his winner's medal and a shining black eye. He too moved on to York in the

December after the Cup final joining his brothers Jack and Angelo at the Yorkshire club.

Joe Corsi had joined Rochdale in 1920 and was one of the noted wingers of his era. Like his brother Jack, he had played for the Crumlin and Cardiff clubs and three years later he moved over the hill to Hornets' nearest and deadliest of rivals, Oldham.

In the second round Hornets faced Leeds at home, they won 15-7 and their victory was aided by a massive goal-kicking feat from one of their all-time great players Ernest W. Jones, the stand-off half from Somerset, who had joined Rochdale in 1910 at the age of 19, who hit the target from an amazing distance.

Reports of the time suggest that he was at least five yards inside the Hornets half and that it was one of the greatest efforts seen on the ground. He was, however, destined to miss the final. Injury is believed to have taken its toll although Hornets ensured he had a specially struck medal.

Their third round encounter was against Oldham. This derby game rivals any other similar kind of game for intensity and pressure. Local pride is at stake and a Joe Corsi try boosted Rochdale to a 5-2 victory in front of a massive crowd of 26,664.

Widnes were swept aside 23-3 in the semi-finals and Hornets faced Hull, who were seeking to improve in their amazingly unsuccessful return of one win from seven appearances, in the final.

The Humbersiders were clearly the pre-match favourites. The match programme stated: 'The Hull team are reported to be in splendid condition and are popular favourites … Hornets' backs are generally supposed to be weaker than the men from Hull.' Prediction is, however, an inexact science and the underdog still had a powerful bite.

Hull had not had an easy route to the final. All their opponents came from the top half of the league. In the first round they had to contend with Halifax, then a derby clash at Hull KR, a third round trip to Dewsbury and a semi-final win over Wigan, who had finished second in the table.

Billy Batten was still the darling of the Boulevard crowd and he scored the second of their two unconverted tries in the first half. The first had come from centre J.E. Kennedy. Winger Tommy Fitton had registered a try for Rochdale while Paddon landed two goals to keep Hornets in front 7-6 at half-time.

Fitton struck again to extend Rochdale's lead to 10-6 but Hull second row forward Bob Jones put the Humberside team back into contention at 10-9 with a try. Hull needed the conversion to take the lead but winger Billy Stone's kick curled wide leaving Hornets to win by the narrowest possible margin.

The Lancastrians were ecstatic about upsetting the odds and when they returned to Rochdale there was a crowd of 40,000 to meet them.

A Rochdale diarist catalogues the highlights of the final, as far as Hornets were concerned, as follows: 'Hughie Wild's tackling on Batten … Jack Bennett's hooking … Dai Woods' shadowing of the mighty Taylor … Heaton led Caswell a merry dance … the magnificent work of all the Hornets forwards … and the way Frank Prescott at full-back played courageously for the greater part of the second half with his right arm practically useless because of injury.'

The only Rochdale Hornets to win the Challenge Cup, in 1922.

CHAPTER 18

THE LEAGUE OF FRIENDS

After pressure from Australia and New Zealand, the Northern Union were eventually persuaded to change their name and they became the Rugby Football League in 1923. The Challenge Cup's title was changed accordingly and, to match the new look, the final was played at Wakefield Trinity's Belle Vue ground for the first and only time while Joe Thompson completed a 'Boys Own' first season in the professional game.

Joe was a recruit from Welsh Rugby Union with a difference – he was English. Born at Hambrook near Bristol in 1902, Joe's parents emigrated to live at Cross Keys in South Wales during his infancy. He showed little or no inclination towards the handling game and was a more than adequate Association Football player. In his late teens he fell out with the round-ball game switching, instead, to Rugby. He adapted to his new sport like the proverbial duck to water and joined his local club Abercarn; but the 19-year-old miner was to remain with them for just a matter of weeks.

His burgeoning talent was recognised by the district's senior club, Cross Keys, and in his first full season at Pandy Park they won the unofficial Welsh senior club championship. Just a month after his 20th birthday in January 1923, he was selected to play for Wales against his native England at Twickenham.

Such talent could not be hidden from the professional scouts and just

The Leeds team who beat Hull in the 1923 Cup final.

ten days after his impressive debut on the international Rugby Union stage, he was heading north to join Leeds Rugby League club as a man of substance with £300 compensation for the loss of his amateur status.

Thompson was hardly a reluctant recruit. He had been a pit worker since the age of thirteen and eagerly took the chance to put the industry behind him. He was so quick to turn professional that he did not wait for the delivery of his Welsh international cap and, such was the attitude to players who took the paid ticket, the Welsh Rugby Union were not in any hurry to send it on to him. In fact he had to wait until times had changed to see the cap when, through the good offices of Leeds Rugby League club official Bill Carter, they eventually awarded it to him in 1975, eight years before he died aged 81.

Back, however, to 1923. He was soon to make his mark among the professional ranks. His debut in the 13-a-side game was against Huddersfield at Headingley on 10 February 1923 when Leeds won 6-3. No sooner had he put that experience behind him than he was faced with his first Challenge Cup campaign.

Leeds were drawn at Leigh, the 1921 winners, in the first round and Joe scored a try as they won 11-5. They beat Huddersfield in the second round to earn a third-round placing against York where Thompson demonstrated his prowess with the boot landing two goals in their 10-2 victory.

His immense strength was tested to the full in the run up to the semi-final against Barrow when Leeds had to play six sapping league games in nine days. Joe, however, came through with flying colours because, after a tense 0-0 draw, he landed five goals in their 20-0 replay triumph.

Leeds faced Hull in the final. The Humbersiders were playing in their seventh Challenge Cup final and one victory was scant reward for that fine achievement. This time, however, they were without the immaculate Batten. He had been transferred to Wakefield Trinity and the Hull fans had recorded their appreciation for his valuable 11-year spell with the club, in which they had won every concievable honour, with a £1,000 benefit.

The final at Belle Vue on 28 April 1923 attracted 29,335 spectators. It was turning out to be an amazing debut season for Joe Thompson. The final was his sixteenth professional game and, three months earlier, he had played for Wales at Twickenham.

And he was still looking forward to his 21st birthday!

In the eleven weeks he had been at Leeds he had established a fine second row relationship with Bill Davies who, co-incidentally, was also a west countryman; he had come north from Gloucester. They made a fine pair in the Leeds pack and the *Leeds Mercury's* correspondent recorded: 'Bill Davis and Joe Thompson were the two giants of the game in the second row. Certain dribbles of theirs in the first half were among the outstanding incidents of the match. They were equally clever in their running and handling, and their combined vim and persistence, perhaps did more than anything else to undermine Hull's confidence. Davis scored a characteristic try. He and Thompson were truly great forwards.'

A fine testimony indeed. Thompson also made a fine individual contribution to Leeds comfortable 28-3 win with five valuable goals which complemented the tries of Walmsley, Harold Buck, Bowen, Brittain, Davis and Ashton.

For Thompson it was to be the start of a ten year love-affair with Leeds and their fans.

CHAPTER 19

JIM AND WIGAN'S RING OF CONFIDENCE

Two births, separated by three years and 40 miles of South Welsh coastline, provided the key to Wigan's success in the 1923-24 Challenge Cup competition.

On 13 November 1900 in Port

The first Wigan team to win the Cup, in 1924. They initiated a long relationship with Rugby League's top trophy for the Central Park club.

Talbot, Welsh sprint champion Cornelius Ring became the proud father of a son, John, and three years one month later in Cardiff James Sullivan entered the world. Both were to have a profound effect on Rugby League although it is a fair assumption that it was something that none of their parents could have forseen.

Johnny Ring inherited his father's speed over the ground. He progressed

from the junior Aberavon Harlequin team through to the senior club side, Aberavon. His talent blossomed and, in the three seasons he played for Aberavon, he produced an amazing 196 tries, including a club record 76 in 1919-20.

Wales was inhabited by a generation of talented wingers and Ring's solitary Welsh cap had to wait until 1921 while the two previous Welsh

international wingers, Wickham Powell of Cardiff and Brinley Williams of Llanelli, went north to Rochdale Hornets and Batley respectively.

Ring was selected to face England at Twickenham but he lost his place for the following game against the Scots in spite of scoring a try; the only Welsh points in an 18-3 defeat. He was replaced by Llanelli flier Frank Dafen Williams who, ironically, moved north to Swinton the year before Ring turned professional.

England went on to win the home international Grand Slam and Ring's try was the only one scored against them in that campaign. In spite of his popularity among the Welsh Rugby public of the era Johnny clearly did not enjoy the support of the international selectors. He did not play for Wales again. Ironically, two of Ring's team mates in that beaten Welsh side, centre Jerry Shea and Pontypool forward Wilf Hodder, were to play with Ring again but not on the muddied pitches of the principality. That was, however, for the future.

In August 1922 Welsh Rugby had to relinquish its hold on Ring. Wigan Rugby League club paid him £800 to turn professional and he made his debut against Salford. The pressure of his first appearance as a paid man must have been eased by the fact that his centre three-quarter was another Welshman, former Ebbw Vale man Tommy Howley.

Wigan returned to Wales six months later to sign Ring's former Aberavon centre partner Tommy Parker. While both men were to emerge as excellent signings for Wigan, Ring was exceptional; the stuff of legends.

In his first four seasons as a professional, he posted returns of 44, 49, 54 and 63 tries, ending each of those seasons as top of the league list. In fact he is one of only three men to perform

such a feat; the others were South African Tom Van Vollenhoven who played with St Helens after the Second World War, and Quentin Offiah who played with Widnes and Wigan.

Jim Sullivan was already a great Rugby player before he turned professional. Although he was just 16-years-old he played full-back for the top Welsh club Cardiff. He was, however, to assume an even greater significance for not only Wigan, but for Rugby League. His was a precocious talent; at 9 years old he played for St Albans School. But the First World War put a temporary hold on his Rugby career and he played soccer for the duration of hostilities.

After the world had finished with the Kaiser's war, Sullivan returned to rugby. With his schooldays behind him, he enjoyed his game with the St Albans Old Boys club. His ascent up the Rugby ladder started when he was spotted by London Irish in an Old Boys game at Aberavon. In spite of the fact that he was just 15-years-old he was asked to play full-back for the exiles at Abertillery. The young Welshman did not need to be asked twice and grabbed the chance gratefully.

The Irish connection was not as far fetched as first appeared because Jim's father, a Cardiff butcher, was from the Emerald Isle and it brought a debate about which country he would represent in the home international series. Not that there was any doubt in young Sullivan's mind that he would play in none other than the Scarlet of Wales.

He successfully trialled with Cardiff and, after just a handful of reserve games, he went into the famous Welsh club's first team as full-back; all this before he was seventeen. He made his debut against Neath and played 35 games that season.

Sullivan never won a Welsh cap – he was once on stand-by but missed

out because the reserve was fit in time – and times were hard in South Wales for young apprentice boilermakers.

Sullivan later explained: 'The Cardiff club would have done anything to keep me, but it just had to keep within the rules, and when I broached the subject, officials said that I could have been given a job on the ground, but that would have meant me being classed as a professional. Then, the day after I had attached my name to a form for Wigan, they did offer me a job, but it was too late.'

He had been chased by many Rugby League clubs, Huddersfield, Hull and Wakefield Trinity among others, but Wigan landed him while he was still a 17-year-old on 18 June 1921 for £750, which equalled the previous highest given to a Rugby Union man when Rochdale Hornets signed Wickham Powell from Cardiff.

His contract was for 12 years and guaranteed him £5.00 for a win, £4.15s (£4.75) for a draw and £4.10s (£4.50) for a defeat. In those days the average wage was £4.00 per week.

He arrived at Central Park to find an amazing array of talent including former All Black forward Charlie Seeling, and Welsh compatriots Danny Hurcombe, Sid Jerram, Fred Roffey and Percy Coldrick. He made his debut on 27 August 1921 against Widnes and helped Wigan to win 22-3 by landing five goals. Rugby League had its own Welsh national team in those days and, for the game against Australia at Pontypridd in December 1921, the captain and full-back Gwyn Thomas had pulled out. Sullivan accepted an invitation to join the team and kicked a goal in their 21-16 defeat.

The 1923-24 Challenge Cup had started badly because the first round draw had been mis-handled. At the draw, which was made behind closed doors, the thirty two cardboard discs, the size of an old five-pence piece, had been placed in the bag. Hunslet's was drawn out by mistake stuck to the bottom of Swinton's disc and it was not until the end of the draw that it was obvious one disc was missing.

When it was discovered what had happened Hunslet were placed last as the away team against Salford, the last club to be drawn from the bag, but that did not satisfy the club from south Leeds. They wanted the whole draw made again.

The Cup Committee considered the situation and their decision was that the draw should stand. Hunslet appealed to the Rugby League Council, the game's ruling body, and the overlords also ruled that the draw should stand, asking Salford if they would toss a coin with Hunslet to decide home advantage. Although Salford refused they could have been forgiven if they wondered whether they had made the right decision because, subsequently, they lost the tie 8-6.

Hunslet, ironically, beat Swinton in the second round but their luck ran out in the third round when they were beaten 13-8 at home by favourites Wigan, who were, surprisingly, still seeking their first Challenge Cup final win.

With the approach of the 1924 tour to Australia, the Challenge Cup final was, once again, brought forward to accommodate the departure of the tourists for their long sea voyage. Wigan had reached the final for the third time after beating Barrow in the semi-final.

Wigan were to face Oldham in the first all-Lancashire final since 1911 when, coincidentally, Wigan were the beaten finalists to Broughton Rangers.

Oldham included winger Joe Corsi from the triumphant 1922 Rochdale team and they arrived at the final on 12 April 1924 seeking a second win in four final appearances. They had despatched Rochdale, Dewsbury, Wakefield Trinity and the still mighty Huddersfield.

The Challenge Cup was clearly still gaining in popularity. In 1923 the Leeds v Hull game had attracted 32,596 spectators but 1924 took the final into a new era with 41,831 people packing into the Athletic Grounds, Rochdale to see this clash between the Lancashire giants. The sheer size of the crowd clearly took everybody by surprise. Spectators spilled on to the sides of the pitch and mounted policemen had to keep them away from the playing area. The scene was reminiscent of the previous year's first ever FA Cup final at Wembley. At one stage it was doubtful if the game would start but the referee Reverend J.H. Chambers, who had played for Huddersfield at the age of 16, and the players helped persuade the crowd to take their positions.

With nine of the summer's tour party on display, the game took some time to warm up and Oldham, who had won two of their three clashes with Wigan earlier in the season, took the lead through full-back Ernest Knapman who put over a penalty.

Wigan hit back with a try by Welsh second row Fred Roffey and then an amazing second try by South African winger Adrian Van Heerden, who rounded a mounted policeman, before touching down. Sullivan converted.

Oldham cut Wigan's lead with a penalty from their Cumbrian second row forward. Alfred Brough conceded when Jerram was caught offside, but from that point Wigan were unstoppable.

Seven minutes into the second half Hurcombe sent Parker in for a try and in the 55th minute Parker crossed for Wigan's fourth touch down. Sullivan missed with both the conversions but landed a penalty to put Wigan 16-4 up.

The Welsh double act delivered the score of the final when Ring intercepted a pass to score a try and Sullivan added the goal. Wigan's long run of Cup final success had started – at last.

CHAPTER 20

THE TEAM THAT BILLY BUILT

Billy McCutcheon was a trend setter. In 1888, before the Northern Union was even a germ of an idea, he moved from Welsh Rugby Union to play for one of the north's leading clubs, Oldham. As an international three-quarter he was the holder of seven Welsh caps and a member of the team which won the first Triple Crown.

His arrival at Oldham was one of the reasons why people pointed the finger at them accusingly when it came to the inducement argument.

Oldham, winners in 1925, the Challenge Cup's silver jubilee year.

Nevertheless, McCutcheon was destined to play a major role in Oldham and Northern Union-Rugby League developments.

He joined the Watersheddings club in December 1888, represented Lancashire in their county championship win of 1890 and played right the way through the schism with the Rugby Union until March 1897. Following his retirement as a player he moved on to become a leading administrator with Oldham and a referee of standing within the Northern Union. He took control of the Tests against New Zealand at Cheltenham in 1908 and against Australasia at

Newcastle in 1909 as well as five international matches, three Yorkshire Cup finals, one Lancashire Cup final, the championship finals of 1913 and 1914 and one Challenge Cup final in 1906 when he sent off Salford's Silas Warwick and Bradford's Harry Feather.

By the time the Silver Jubilee of the Challenge Cup had been reached in 1924-25, Billy McCutcheon had been installed as president of Oldham. They had been a power in the Rugby world at the time of the split with Twickenham and that had attracted players of quality.

They were doubly fortunate be-

cause many who came to them as good players remained with the club after their playing days and their ability to spot good players was invaluable. Thus when the First World War was behind them they were the leading administrators at Watersheddings. With the arrival of the 1920s their team rebuilding was in full swing. Their qualification for the 1924 final against Wigan was confirmation of that status.

They brought full-back Ernest Knapman up from Torquay Rugby Union club and, while he fulfilled all their expectations, he was unfortunate to arrive in the professional game at the same time as Wigan's Welsh wonderman Jim Sullivan, and his appearances in international football were strictly limited because he was generally accepted as the Central Park star's understudy.

Evan Davies, the former Llanelli and Wales centre joined Oldham in 1911 and was one of the few players to span the War years. Centre Reg Farrar was signed from Halifax and his centre partner Alf Woodward from Bath Rugby Union club, halfback George Hesketh came from Wigan while forwards prop Rothwell Marlor and second row Bob Sloman were signed from Plymouth Albion; Welsh scrum half Billy Benyon was a dual rugby-soccer international and there was the majestically named loose forward Herman Hilton, who often captained the side.

For 1924-25 Oldham were recognised as one of the best teams of the era standing comparison with the team who beat them the previous season, Wigan. That status was confirmed in the Challenge Cup during the period because they were to reach four successive finals.

The first two rounds had not been easy for Oldham. They beat Leigh 5-0 and then overcame Warrington 12-7. The pressure was relieved in the third round when they beat Featherstone Rovers and, in the semi-final, they beat 1922 winners and neighbours Rochdale Hornets 9-0 at Wigan to reach their second successive final.

In the final at Headingley on 25 April 1925, they played Hull KR, the winners of the Yorkshire League, who had reached the final for the second time. Their first appearance had been in 1905 when they were beaten by Jack Fish's Warrington and on their way to the showdown with Oldham they had ousted Bramley, Wigan Highfield, Keighley and Leeds.

Oldham approached the match with the Lancashire Cup already shining proudly on the boardroom sideboard. The popularity of the Challenge Cup remained and, although the attendance failed to reached the 40,000 plus heights of the 1924 final, the encounter still attracted 28,335 paying customers.

The final proved to be a disappointment. Oldham were kept in check by Rovers for most of the first half. Farrar scored their only try in the first period in the 33rd minute and he also kicked the conversion.

In the second half Rovers crumbled and fumbled. Oldham stepped up the pressure which brought tries for second row forward Albert Brough, winger Joe Corsi and veteran centre Davies. Farrar added another goal to seal Oldham's comfortable 16-3 win. Rovers prop Jack Wilkinson was their only points scorer.

Playing on the left wing for Rovers against Oldham was the amazing Gilbert Austin. He made his debut for the Humberside club against Wakefield Trinity on 25 January 1919 and then made 190 successive appearances for them lasting until 8 December 1923. It was a record that stood until it was broken by Widnes hooker Keith Elwell in 1981!

While Oldham added a second trophy to their collection and started a Cup dynasty they could not keep Wigan away from the glory. In the first round the 1924 holders were drawn against Cumbrian junior club Flimby and Fothergill. Their 116-0 victory provided another platform for Jim Sullivan. He kicked 22 goals which, besides being a Cup best performance, is a world record for one match. It nevertheless left Wigan short of Huddersfield's 119-2 romp over poor Swinton Park in 1914.

Oldham's third successive final, emulating Hull's hat-trick between 1908 and 1910, came in 1925-26. There had been changes to their line-up following their win in 1925 with Herman Hilton retiring in November 1925 after serious injury. They had also acquired back row forward Ambrose Baker from Neath Rugby Union, forward Jack Read from Gloucester, S.V. Fairfax from Newport, H. Wallace from Jedforest Rugby Union in Scotland and centre Abe Johnson from Leigh.

Johnson had joined Oldham in December 1925 for £650 after establishing and breaking a new points in a season record for Leigh. He was to play a big role for his new club while Baker was, reputedly, so keen to sign professional that he walked all the way from South Wales to Lancashire to sign.

It was Swinton's first appearance in the final for a quarter of a century and they too had built up an impressive team. It had an important Welsh influence. The right wing partnership was former Llanelli and Wales winger Frank Evans and his centre was Wilf Sulway from Talywain. Left winger Jack Evans and scrum half Bryn Evans were sons of Welsh international Jack Evans, who came north to play for Swinton in the early years of the code, while stand-off half Billo Rees was from Llansannan.

The 25th Challenge Cup final was staged at Rochdale's Athletic

Grounds on Saturday, 1 May 1926. The weather was far from springlike but not even driving rain could dampen enthusiasm for the all-Lancashire game with 27,000 people packing into the ground.

It was an evenly matched game. Swinton had won the Lancashire Cup while for Oldham reaching the Challenge Cup was their only success of the season.

Swinton had the wind behind them in the first half and made best use of that advantage to take control of the game. Second row forward Herbert Morris, who came from Coventry, landed one goal from several attempts and then hooker Henry Blewer went over for a try after the ball had rebounded off the cross bar following a Rees drop goal attempt. It was converted by Morris.

In the second half Oldham attempted to make best use of the elements but the Lions were not prepared to concede. Morris landed another goal and, although Joe Corsi pulled one try back for the 'Roughyeds' – Oldham's nickname,

Oldham's last Challenge Cup winning team in 1927.

roughly translated meaning Rough heads – they could not dislodge Swinton.

It was Swinton's second win in two final appearances while for Oldham it was their fourth defeat in six appearances. Coincidentally, it was a repeat of 1899 and 1900 when an Oldham win was followed by a Swinton victory.

The two protagonists faced each other again twelve months later but this time they had a much wider audience than the 33,448 people who had made their way to Central Park, Wigan for the final on Saturday, 7 May 1927. That was because this was the first final to be broadcast on radio.

Oldham's championship form had been little more than ordinary, they finished 13th in the league, seventh in the Lancashire League and were eliminated in the first round of the Lancashire Cup. The powers of their great team were on the wane and yet they summoned together enough strength to force their way through to their fourth successive final. On the way they picked up the scalps of Salford, Hunslet, Leeds and Wakefield Trinity.

Tosh Holliday was a major capture

for Oldham in 1926-27; he came from Cumbrian club Aspatria and was the England Rugby Union international full-back. Although he made his debut as a centre, by the time Oldham had reached the Cup final he was playing on the wing.

Although Swinton drew first blood with a try by their winger Chris Brockbank, the son of a former Swinton player Herbert Brockbank – one of the few who refused to move into Northern Union with the club – it was Oldham who took command. Morris improved the winger's score but Holliday flew in for a try and Johnson landed two goals so that the Watersheddings men led 7-5 at halftime.

Swinton emerged in the second half a man down because their captain and centre Hector Halsall could not continue. The pressure was too much for the Lions to contain and Oldham completed the rout with tries from centre Syd Rix, loose forward Alf Brough, second row forward Bob Sloman and two more from Holliday.

The completion of Holliday's hattrick established him in the record books as the third player to achieve such a feat following Bob Wilson for Broughton Rangers in the 1902 final and Huddersfield's Stanley Moorhouse in the 1913 final. Another Morris goal completed the Swinton score.

Coincidentally, of the four successive Oldham Cup final teams there were just four players who played in all of the games, scrum half George Hesketh, Rix, Brough and Sloman. It also marked the end of an era. Oldham's domination of the Challenge Cup was over and, so far, it remains as their last appearance in the final. Their pre-eminence was eventually dulled by the passage of time while for the Swinton Club immortality was just around the corner.

CHAPTER 21

LAST OF THE FOUR TIMERS

Martin Hodgson was born to be a Rugby League star. The only people who were not aware of that particular fact were his parents. The 17-year-old young giant was working down one of the Cumbrian coal mines which are now part of the north's industrial history. He was born, and lived, in the village of Egremont near Whitehaven and, like so many young men from that part of the world, was involved in Rugby football.

He, however, played Rugby Union for Egremont. They know a good player when they see one in that northern part of England and they had no inhibitions about putting the craggy teenager in with the men; he represented the county five times.

Then came the 1926 General Strike and Rugby League. Young Hodgson was not enamoured with the coal mining industry and said: 'After the Strike was settled, I didn't fancy going back and I knew a number of Rugby League clubs were interested.

'Even though I'd only seen League played once, I made up my mind to give it a try. But my parents said I was far too young.'

That did not stop the clubs making the trip to the far north west coast in an attempt to persuade the young giant to try his luck in the professional game.

Eventually the Hodgsons' resistance was worn down and Martin's mother told him that, in the interests of family peace and harmony, he had better accept the next offer which came his way. Cue Swinton Rugby League club. A masterpiece of timing saw them arrive in Egremont just in front of the representatives from Barrow, Bradford Northern and Leeds.

The six foot plus, 16 stone, rawboned Cumbrian arrived at Station Road on 2 January 1927. It was the start of a long, happy relationship. Swinton were big business in the mid 1920s. They won the Cup by beating Oldham in 1926 and, just after Hodgson's arrival at Station Road, they started a run which took them all the way to the 1927 Cup final in which they were beaten by Oldham.

In 1927-28, still teenaged, Hodgson had established himself as a first team player with the club which sits alongside the railway line from Manchester to Southport. They safely collected the Lancashire Cup and League double and headed off to the Challenge Cup final against Warrington at Central Park, Wigan aware that victory would put them within reach of Hunslet and Huddersfield's famous all-four trophies feat.

Swinton's route to the final had a lasting effect on the game. They had beaten junior club Whitehaven Recs and Halifax in the first and second rounds and played Castleford in the third.

In those days it was permissible for an injured player to return to the game without clearance from either the touch judge or referee. The Glassblowers, as Castleford were nicknamed, staged a break away attack during the game and looked certain to score. But an injured Swinton player, who had been off the field receiving treatment, suddenly appeared on the scene to tackle the breakaway player. Following that incident, the laws of the game were amended so that injured players had to receive clearance before returning to the game. In the semi-final Swinton beat Hull 5-3 earning the right to play Warrington in the final.

The Wire had not enjoyed the easiest of passages to the final. Although they beat junior club Kinsley 43-2 in the first round, succeeding rounds had produced tussles with Hull KR, Huddersfield and Leeds.

According to form, Swinton looked clear favourites because they sat proudly on top of the League table while Warrington had finished the season in 17th place. On Cup final day Central Park was swept by a strong wind and that element, combined with Warrington's resistance, to ensure that Swinton were not able to slip into their normal free-flowing style of Rugby.

Winger Brockbank gave Swinton the advantage with an opening try

which was disputed by Warrington. Then came an incident which was an object lesson to all broadcasters. Billy Kirk, the Warrington scrum half who coincidentally was the only Englishman in their back division – the rest were Welsh – was badly injured and two people, so Warrington legend has it, ran on to the field to attend to him. They must have had their collars reversed because it was assumed they were clergymen.

Kirk was lifted on to a stretcher, covered completely and stretchered off the field. It was assumed that his injuries had proved fatal and, aided by the assumptions of the radio broadcasters, it was rumoured in Warrington that Kirk was dead. It was, of course, subsequently proved not true and Kirk lived on for many years.

Welsh winger Dai Davies was brought in from the wing to play at scrum half and he transformed the game with his command of the position. Swinton could not break down the Warrington team and were fortu-nate to go in at half-time leading 3-0. In the second half Davies set up a move that utilised the whole of the Warrington back division and ended when loose forward Charlie Seeling, the son of the former All Black forward who played for Wigan in the 1910-11 final, went over for the equalising try.

The game was locked at 3-3 as it entered the final minutes and Swinton forced a five-yard scrummage near the Warrington line. Reports of the time recall that twice Batley based referee H. Horsfall had Warrington feed the ball into the heaving pack; each time it came out on their side but he was not satisfied. On the third feed it came out against the head advantage and Swinton scrum half Billo Rees whipped it back to winger Jack Evans, who landed the deciding drop goal.

With three trophies in the bag Swinton moved forward to take on Featherstone Rovers in the championship final at Oldham. It was less ar-duous than the Challenge Cup and

Swinton, the last club to achieve the four trophy feat in 1928.

their 11-0 win ensured that they completed the four-trophy sweep. They are still the last team to complete a clean sweep. Although the Regal Trophy has replaced the extinct county league it has made life slightly more problematical because of the vagaries of sudden-death Rugby.

Hodgson played a major role in the four trophy season and was to become one of the greatest players ever to grace the Station Road pitch. He played with distinction for his club and country.

In fact for him there was slightly more than four medals to pick up at the end of the season. He had also played for the winning Swinton team in the old Salford Royal Hospital Cup and represented Cumberland in a county championship winning season.

CHAPTER 22

THE ROAD TO WEMBLEY

The growth and popularity of the Challenge Cup competition was causing headaches for the Rugby League. They did not possess a suitable stadium large enough at which to stage such a prestigious fixture. Quite simply it had outgrown itself. There had been calls from within the movement to take the biggest match the code had to offer to London so that it could be shown to the British masses who were unable to see Rugby League in the normal course of events; the hope was that it might influence them to embrace the game.

Not that everybody subscribed to that particular view and debate swayed backwards and forwards for years with the pro-London lobby forever coming up against those who favoured keeping the showpiece game in the north.

By 1928 pressure for an answer to the stadium problem was building up; a decision, one way or the other, was being demanded. At the seventh annual conference of the Rugby League, which was staged at the Marine Hotel, Llandudno, North Wales, the problem came to a head and a vote was forced.

The proposal to explore the London option was introduced to the delegates in the conference's second session by Mr John Leake, the chairman of the League's Welsh commission.

The minutes record thus: 'Mr John Leake moved that it be a recommendation to the Council that the final tie for each Challenge Cup be played each year in London.

'Mr Walter Waide seconded and after a number of members had spoken for and against, the recommendation was carried 13 votes to 10.'

It does not follow, as several historians have pointed out, that it was Mr Leake's own idea to make such a suggestion, merely that he was the person who put the idea up for division. Nevertheless the irony that a Welshman should be making such a far-reaching, far-sighted move cannot be lost.

With the intent in place, League officials set about the preliminary work with three major capital venues, Wembley, the White City and the Crystal Palace, all offering suitable facilities. The White City failed to find favour so the choice lay between Wembley and the Crystal Palace.

The decision to take the 1929 final to London was confirmed at a meeting at the Griffin Hotel in Leeds on 3 October 1928 and the following morning the *Sporting Chronicle* reported:

'Rugby Cup Final for London
Council's Surprise Decision
'By a very narrow vote the Rugby League Council at a meeting in Leeds yesterday decided to play the Rugby League Challenge Cup next April in London at either Wembley or Crystal Palace. A final decision will be made after the secretary has obtained terms from the Crystal Palace and Wembley authorities.

'A circular will be sent to all clubs, district associations and supporters clubs in helping to make the final a success.'

A special meeting of the Rugby League Council was staged on 17 October 1928 at the Midland Hotel, Manchester. It was really a dinner to welcome home the touring team from Australia but several items of important business were also considered. First, they decided to play the annual England v Wales match at Cardiff on 14 November. The second item on the agenda was the Cup final: the members confirmed that League secretary John Wilson and chairman Mr F. Kennedy should make inspection tours of both venues.

Wilson was instructed to contact both stadium managements to find out what terms could be offered for the Rugby League showpiece and the visits took place. They reported back to the Emergency Committee at the Trafford Arms, Wakefield one week later and their minutes reveal: 'Mr Kennedy made a full report on his inspection to Crystal Palace and Wembley Stadium after hearing which the committee unanimously decided to play the Cup final at Wembley'.

The following day's *Sporting Chronicle* reported:-

Rugby final to be played
at Wembley
London novelty

'The emergency committee of the Rugby League Council met at the Trafford Arms Hotel, Wakefield and considered the claims of the Wembley and Crystal Palace grounds as venues. Messrs Kennedy and Wilson reported on their inspection of the two enclosures and terms offered.

'It was decided that the event should take place at Wembley. The price of admission will be: centre stand, reserved and numbered including tax and admission to the ground 10/6d [52pence], further to the side 7/6d [37pence], further still to the side 5/- [25pence]. All these seats are under cover. Terraces and front seats not under cover 3/- [15pence]. All the above can be booked. Rest of the field; admission by turnstile, no tickets required 2/- [10 pence].'

On what grounds the decision went Wembley's way is not revealed by official records but it has been suggested that the reason the League voted against Crystal Palace was that they asked for 33.3 per cent of the gate receipts and 100 per cent of the money taken before mid-day on Cup final day while Wembley were prepared to settle for seven and a half per cent of the gate.

Wembley Stadium was already the home of the Football Association Challenge Cup. It had been built as part of the British Empire Exhibition which opened in 1924 and the first FA Cup final was played at the stadium in 1923 between Bolton Wanderers and West Ham United, a game distinguished by a white police horse which helped control the huge crowd which packed the ground.

The Manchester Guardian observed: 'On April 27th the final tie of the Football Association Cup will be played at Wembley Stadium so that the authorities have only a week in which to change the ground from an Association Football arena to a Rugby League pitch.' The Rugby League final was switched to May no doubt to fit round the FA Cup's requirements.

The *Athletic News* of 8 April 1929 reported: 'With the finalists known, arrangements for the game in May are approaching completion. Lord Derby, the League president, is unable to be present owing to a prior engagement the same day in Lancashire.

'The intensive advertising campaign is being supported by many former Lancashire and Yorkshire supporters of the code now residing in the metropolis and practically every big club in the League is sending a 'special'.

'The Midlands, South Wales and Cumberland areas have also taken a considerable number of tickets and the organisers expressed themselves well satisfied with the results of the propaganda work undertaken to date.'

The 1929 Rugby League Cup final perfectly illustrated the width of Rugby League's socio-economic structure. It was to be contested by the glamour of Wigan, one of the biggest and richest clubs in the game, and Dewsbury, a home-spun side comprised of men from the heavy woollen district.

CHAPTER 23

A CAPITAL MOVE

A major attraction of any knock-out competition for the sporting public is that it offers the possibility of David sometimes slaying Goliath. Dewsbury, one of Rugby League's lesser lights, can lay claim to a singular honour. In this case David certainly landed the first blow because the heavy woollen district team were the first club to qualify for a Wembley final.

They had battled through the first three rounds taking out junior club Cottingham, holders Swinton and Warrington on the way to their semi-final meeting with Castleford which they won 9-3.

The other semi-final at Station Road, Swinton between St Helens Recs and Wigan ended in a 7-7 draw and Wigan, who had previously beaten St Helens in a replay in the third round, came through to win the decider at Leigh 13-12.

The comparisons between the two finalists present two completely different pictures. Wigan bristled with imported talent from Rugby Union and other clubs while Dewsbury presented a dozen Yorkshiremen and one solitary Welshman, Jack Davies from Ammanford, who was signed from Keighley.

As the two teams differed in make up so too their styles of game bore little or no comparison. Wigan offered the expansive approach demanded by

DEWSBURY R.L.F.C.   WEMBLEY CUP TEAM, 1929.

Dewsbury at the station before departure to London for the first Cup final at Wembley in 1929.

the Central Park faithful while Dewsbury relied heavily on a forward-orientated, no-risk policy which might not have been as aesthetically pleasing but had proved extremely effective.

Journalists of the period were clearly excited by the prospect of Rugby League going to Wembley and some were prepared to concede that Dewsbury's workmanlike style might give Wigan some problems.

Wigan's strength was, however, fully reflected in the leading scorer lists at the end of the season. In all three categories, tries, goals and points, a Central Park player was in top spot. Their former New Zealand international winger Lou Brown shared first place in the try list with Australian Ernie Mills from Hud-

dersfield both with 44, Jim Sullivan led the goal scoring list by a mile with 107 which was 30 in front of his nearest rival and Sullivan sat majestically on top of the points classification with 226.

Balanced against that, Dewsbury had just one entrant in the top section of the list – their veteran loose forward Joe Lyman. He had kicked 67 goals and was third in in the points scoring list with 176. Lyman was an extraordinary man, making his debut for Dewsbury in 1913 and playing in many positions for the club all with equal success.

Nonetheless people within League

A montage of the Dewsbury side who faced Wigan at Wembley in 1929.

T'Cup back', 'Good old Joe' (captain Lyman), 'Good old Plonk' (prop William Rhodes was known to them as Plonk) and 'Show'em how to laike!' which translated means show them how to play. The Yorkshire dialect word 'laike' is a derivative of lark as in 'lark about'.

Wigan delayed their departure for London until late on Friday afternoon, taking the 4.43pm train to the capital and captain Jim Sullivan was presented with a silver horse shoe for good luck by a Wigan farrier, John Crawshaw.

The final was to be broadcast to the nation on radio and former referee Reverend H. Chambers, then living in Southend, was the commentator.

Half an hour before the projected kick off time of 3.00, the League could have been forgiven for thinking that they may have made a mistake in going to London. A large part of the stadium was deserted but, in those last vital 30 minutes, a large proportion of the 41,500 crowd arrived to make their presence felt.

Fate and the Rugby Football League were unwittingly to conspire against Dewsbury in the historic game. Nobody has ever suggested that Dewsbury were 'nobbled' but the League, in its desire to make the move to Wembley a success, had some influence on their tactical planning.

League chairman Mr F. Kennedy visited both dressing rooms before the start of the game to stress the importance of the match to the sport and to emphasise that it was vital that the nation be treated to a good spectacle of open football. It was believed in Dewsbury for many years after that this entreaty acted as a constraint on their team's tactical approach.

It prevented them from undertaking their normal straight forward approach to the game and encouraged them to take more risks than usual, which played straight into Wigan's

were not prepared to write Dewsbury off as no-hopers especially as they had seen off previous holders Swinton on their way to Wembley. Dewsbury played their finalists part well. When they left by train for London each player was smartly kitted out in new 'plus four' style trousers and carried their belongings in a newly provided attaché case.

As their train left Dewsbury station the crowd cried out: 'Bring

Jim Sullivan holding the Cup after Wigan's win in the inaugural Wembley final over Dewsbury.

Jim Sullivan leads the Wigan team out before the game. Note the number of flat caps!

hands. Whether this theory is actual fact does not really matter any more; the simple fact is that Rugby League lore now dictates that this was indeed the case.

Wigan were never in any danger of losing. They led 5-2 at half-time thanks to a Sullivan penalty and a Syd Abram try against a drop goal by

Dewsbury captain Joe Lyman strides out with his team at Wembley.

Welshman Davies. What a sad irony. Dewsbury's only points in the match and they were scored by the only non-Yorkshireman in the side.

Brown scored Wigan's second try on the hour and Roy Kinnear, a former Scottish Union international centre, also the father of the late comedian Roy Kinnear, added the third ten minutes from the end. Sullivan converted the last try and Wigan became the first winners at Wembley.

Sullivan had the pleasure of receiving the trophy from Lord Daresbury while Dewsbury had to be satisfied with that place in history

and, to date, they have never reached another peace-time Challenge Cup final.

But the tradition of Rugby League playing its most prestigious fixture at Wembley had been established and the crowd had been large enough to encourage the game's administration to continue with that policy.

CHAPTER 24

A SOLITARY SPRINGBOK

George Van Rooyen was always going to be different in Rugby League. Recruited by Hull KR from South Africa in 1923, his first taste of the professional game could hardly be described as encouraging. He found life on Humberside such a trial that he wrote a letter to the Johannesburg Star newspaper appealing for help from his fellow South Africans so that he could be repatriated.

He claimed his wages were so poor that he and his family were starving. Even in those days of more primitive communications, the contents of the letter was soon back in Hull and the news was not well received either particularly when it was alleged that Rovers had broken the agreement by not helping him find a job.

The club, and the Rugby Football League, launched an enquiry but, before they could come to a conclusion, Van Rooyen was transferred to Wigan; incidentally, Rovers were exonerated of the charges.

At Central Park George found contentment and in his first season he helped Wigan win the Challenge Cup for the first time. He played a major role in the Wigan team for the next four years after which he was given a free transfer and joined Widnes.

The Widnes club, which lies a couple of good touch finding kicks from the River Mersey, was a totally different proposition to Wigan. If the Springbok thought himself isolated in the Hull KR team, which was made up of large numbers of local players, then his switch to Naughton Park put him back in the same kind of situation. Only more so.

Widnes have always relied very heavily on their own town for their main player strength, a situation that, despite some successful imports from Rugby Union, remains basically true today.

When the 1929-30 Challenge Cup campaign started Van Rooyen was the only player not born in the Widnes district but it must have been less of a problem than on Humberside because it was his second season with the club.

Widnes beat Bradford Northern in the first round, Swinton after a replay in the second and Hull in the third. They moved six miles down the road to Warrington for their semi-final win over Barrow and they qualified to meet another close neighbour, St Helens, in the second final to be played at Wembley.

St Helens were enjoying a purple spell. The arrival of three New Zealand players, winger Roy Hardgrave and forwards Trevor Hall and Lou Hutt, at the start of the 1929-30 season transformed Saints from being a good side into a very good side and, at one stage in the season, they had a chance of three titles, the Lancashire League which they won, the Challenge Cup and the League championship.

They disposed of the town's other professional club St Helens Recreation in the first round, followed by Leeds and Hunslet to earn a place against deadly rivals Wigan in the semi-final. On the Sunday before the big game their three imports dropped a major bombshell. They sent a letter to the club refusing to play in the game unless certain demands were met.

When they had joined St Helens they had received signing on fees, Hardgrave picked up £100 while Hutt and Hall £50 each. Their extra demand was considerably more substantial and their letter to the club read: 'The undermentioned are desirous of conveying the following petition and hope that the same meets with your approval. Should this petition be refused we, the undersigned, declare that we will not continue playing.

'Firstly, in reference to working wages, we desire a guarantee of £3.10s per week for the fifty two weeks of the year, regardless of football earnings. The work found for us was found to be absolutely unsatisfactory – both from a wage point of view and as a footballer's occupation.

'Secondly, we want a written guarantee of £250 each as a retaining fee. We know, as everyone knows, that

A memento of the 1930 St Helens Cup final team.

there has never been a Saints team like the present one, and we think we are worthy of consideration. We came for practically nothing, and now that we have proved ourselves, we feel quite justified in placing these claims before you. Hoping this meets with your approval.'

They completely misjudged the club and its committee in the sentiments of the last sentence of their letter. They did not approve and talks between the committee and rebel trio

were staged. They were asked to delay the matter until after the semi-final but refused, saying that they would return home unless a settlement could be reached. The committee threatened to drop them from the team in retaliation.

On the Tuesday before the match mediation arrived in the shape of the Mayor of St Helens, Mr Tom Boscow, who took it upon himself to find a settlement. He invited the Kiwi trio and the committee to his parlour for tea and talks. The Mayor was a passionate St Helens fan and he prevailed on the two warring parties. The looming prospect of a Cup semi-final against the enemy Wigan and Mr Boscow's ardour wrought concessions from both sides and it was agreed that, if the matter could be discussed after the match, the New Zealanders would withdraw the letter.

A record 37,169 people turned up at Station Road, Swinton for the semi-final. Nothing was settled after a 5-5 draw but St Helens were clear winners 22-10 in the replay at Leigh. Success brought peace to the St Helens camp. The New Zealanders were happy with the settlement which was recorded thus in the club minutes: 'Compensation be £4 per week, starting at once; that each player be paid £50 at once; £50 at Christmas and £50 each succeeding Christmas until each player had received £250. Each player be guaranteed work at £3.10s.0d per week, or work wages to be made up to this.'

The existing staff also received financial encouragement. They were offered a bonus of £10, nearly a month's salary for a working man, for finishing in the top four of the league championship which went very pleasantly with the £7.10s extra they had received for reaching Wembley. They were riches indeed when compared with the poverty of a north west industrial town in the depressed 1920s.

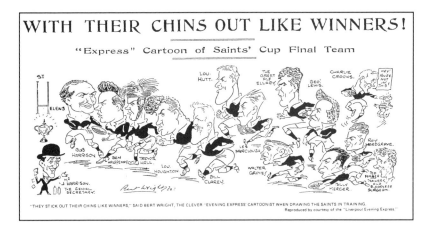

WITH THEIR CHINS OUT LIKE WINNERS!

"Express" Cartoon of Saints' Cup Final Team

Cartoon fun. The 1930 St Helens team as illustrated in a Liverpool newspaper.

Their legendary winger Alf Ellaby is on record as saying that the cheering for St Helens used to increase dramatically at three-quarter time when the unemployed were admitted!

St Helens, who took the league leadership trophy but lost in the championship play-off semi-final the Saturday before, were clear favourites at Wembley. Widnes's final league placing of 15th hardly inspired thoughts that the best St Helens team in their history was about to be unseated.

Not that life in the Widnes camp had been deliriously happy all the time in the run up to the final. The players had been unhappy with the amount of money they were to be paid for taking time off work to play but the club committee, after a one and a half hour meeting, provided a satisfactory solution.

The attractions of a Wembley final were already beginning to make themselves evident among the followers of the game. One out of work St Helens fan, miner Alfred Townsend,

To the victor, the spoils. A civic greeting at the station for the 1930 winners, Widnes.

Widnes, the 1930 Cup winners.

was so determined to see the game that he walked all the way to London.

And a Widnes fan, Abe Duffy, scaled one of the uprights just before the kick off to plant his black and white cap at the top of the post. Little did he realise the significance of his act of devotion. The attendance of 36,544 was 5,000 down on the inital year's final but the League expressed satisfaction with the attendance. Widnes captain Peter Douglas won the toss and elected to have the strong sun at their backs … and kick towards Abe Duffy's hoisted black and white cap.

Ellaby, who had scored a hat-trick of tries in the second round at Leeds, kicked through and second row forward Lou Houghton gave St Helens the lead when he chased through to touch down. Saints captain and centre George Lewis missed the conversion.

The Widnes pack inspired by Van Rooyen, now 37-years-old and over 16 stone in weight, began to exert pressure on St Helens who were found wanting. Widnes centre Albert Ratcliffe was awarded a penalty try after being obstructed by Saints full-back Charlie Crooks and loose forward Jimmy Hoey, who was to become the first player to score in every game in a season in 1932-33, kicked the goal and Widnes took a lead that they never lost.

In the 33rd minute 21-year-old winger Jack Dennett flew in for Widnes's second try and, a minute before the end of the half, Douglas notched a penalty. Widnes went in at half-time leading 10-3. There was no further scoring and the Challenge Cup went to Widnes for the first time in their history.

Van Rooyen, the only non-local man in the Widnes side, was singled out for praise for his scrummaging and powerful running, and how St Helens must have gnashed their teeth because they could have signed the veteran South African when he was released from Wigan.

It was later revealed that the committee's heavy eve-of-final programme in London took its toll on the players. A late night on the Thursday evening, a run around at Wembley and then a late night visit to the St Helens MP at the Houses of Parliament, when all their cross-London travel was done on foot, was hardly the best preparation for a big game.

One of St Helens legendary players, international forward Jack Arkwright, was injured in the semi-final against Wigan. But he didn't miss the final because he rode to Wembley on his motor bike. It must have been a long ride home.

CHAPTER 25

HALIFAX BROWN-ED OFF

In the autumn of 1930 Halifax pulled off a master stoke. They signed New Zealand Test winger Lou Brown from Wigan for £500. He had played in the first ever Wembley final when the cherry and whites beat Dewsbury and arrived at Thrum Hall as a proven match-winner.

Halifax had been constructing a top class team for a number of years and it was generally considered in the West Yorkshire woollen town that Brown's arrival was the final piece in the jigsaw. And that is how it appeared as the 1930-31 season gradually unfolded. Because of the greater number of professional clubs on the Yorkshire side of the Pennines at least one of their clubs had to play in the Lancashire League section and, for that season, it was Halifax. In the Challenge Cup they saw off Dewsbury 3-2 at Crown Flatt in the first round, battled through to a 2-0 win over league leaders Swinton at Station Road and then had to undergo two replays with Oldham before claiming the semi-final place. They won through to Wembley by overcoming St Helens, the previous season's beaten finalists, to face York.

The little team from the North Riding of Yorkshire, like so many other clubs from the country, are the backbone of the 13-a-side game and yet they have had very little glory to show for all their labours over the years. They had come into the North-ern Union circle late, delaying their entry until 1901-02, but by the early 1930s they were becoming a force in the game.

Bradford Northern, Huddersfield, Salford and Warrington all fell victim as York made their one, and as yet, only drive through to Wembley. It created the first all-Yorkshire final since 1923 when Leeds beat Hull.

In fact white rose county clubs had taken, during the 1920s, a lesser role in the Challenge Cup and only Hull KR (1925) and Dewsbury (1929) had succeeded in reaching the final – both ending up as the bridesmaids.

Halifax, however, had a problem to solve before the final. As the big game approached, the club, who were not in contention for the championship race, fielded a couple of teams that were at less than full strength, but they wanted to play their full Wembley side in the final league match of the season against Featherstone Rovers. They won, but missing from the line up was Lou Brown who was subsequently dropped from the Wembley squad as a disciplinary measure. There was no explanation for the reaction at the time but Halifax club historian Andrew Hardcastle offers the following explanation in one of his publications.

'On the same day as the Featherstone fixture, Wigan were playing Leeds at Headingley in the championship semi-final. Len Mason, a friend of Brown who had joined Wigan from New Zealand at the same time, was playing for Wigan, and Brown had a chance of a lift to the game. He decided to take it and tell Halifax he was unfit to play against Featherstone which may or may not have been true.'

'On telephoning Thrum Hall, however, he was told to attend the game to be examined and given treatment. But, saying he would attend for training on Tuesday, he put the receiver down and went to Headingley. At a committee meeting on the Monday he was suspended.'

Halifax's stand had to be admired because he was their leading try scorer for the season with more than 20 touchdowns to his credit. He was not allowed to travel to Wembley with the team and had to watch the final as one of the 40,368 crowd.

While an estimated 7,000 people from Halifax made the trip to London for the game, there was a substantial part of the club's following who could not make the trip and the final was broadcast to a large crowd gathered at their home ground, Thrum Hall. They followed events closely and it cannot have been easy for the cricketers playing close by to keep their attention on their match with such a large crowd getting involved in a Cup final broadcast.

The one person who really benefited from Brown's suspension

was Fred Adams. He was not even in the squad for the final until the New Zealander was disciplined. He had recorded just six appearances all season and in those half dozen games he had landed a total of five goals.

York, in spite of the fact that they finished eleventh, five places below Halifax, were the pre-match favourites. Their form in the run up to Wembley had been impressive and their attacking style convinced the League world that they were good enough to overcome Halifax, who used a more dour approach. At first it looked as though the critics had been correct in their assessments. York took the lead in the third minute with a penalty from prop forward Don Pascoe and increased it to 5-0 when their 21-year-old winger Harold Thomas went over for an unconverted try in the 20th minute.

It was a double blow for Halifax because it was the first try they had conceded in the whole of the 1931 competition. Halifax levelled the scores in the 36th minute and Adams was involved in the build up to the try which came when captain Dai Rees, the tactical brain in the Thrum Haller's team, went over the York line. Adams converted.

York, with the right-wing partnership of centre Mel Rosser and wing Thomas particularly dangerous, broke through the Halifax line with seconds remaining of the first half and Thomas scored his second try of the match to give the North Riding club an 8-5 half-time lead.

In the second half Halifax shook off their steady, no-risk image and produced some dazzling rugby which completely turned the final round. Adams, revelling in his good fortune landed a penalty to close the gap to 8-7 and then full-back Dick Davies kicked a drop goal to give Halifax the lead for the first time in the 65th minute.

A minute later Ivor Davies, a former Newport Rugby Union stand off half, signed from Swinton at the start of the season, was obstructed in the act of scoring and referee Jack Eddon from Swinton awarded a penalty try which Adams converted.

Halifax were in complete control and two tries from winger Laurie Higgins in the final five minutes of the match, one of which Adams improved, completed the West Yorkshire club's 22-8 victory.

The team returned to Halifax two days after the game – they had a day's rest after the match and celebration dinner in Brighton – to find 100,000 people waiting to greet them. They drove in triumph to a civic reception at the Town Hall led by the Kings Cross Band just as they had done for the triumphant 1903 team.

CHAPTER 26

THE LIONS AND A GHOST

Although there were still a number of people calling for the Challenge Cup final to be brought back to the north of England, the Rugby League Council had taken the view that they were giving the switch to Wembley a five-year trial.

The year 1932 was to be different, however, although not because the 'little northerners' had won the argument. The Rugby League selected 9 April 1932 as the date for the Challenge Cup final at Wembley but that date was ruled out because it clashed with the annual England v Scotland soccer international.

The answer looked straightforward: the final, which had to be played earlier than usual because a Great Britain tour party was leaving for the six-week voyage to Australia, had to be taken back to 16 April but that was ruled out by the Football Association who had an agreement with Wembley that no game could be played at the stadium seven days before the FA Cup; that was programmed for 23 April. Wembley could not secure a release from their agreement from the Football Association and the Rugby Football League were forced to bring the final back north. On 21 March the Council announced the Challenge Cup final would be played at Central Park, Wigan.

The Rugby authorities also said

that although the attempt to establish the Cup final as a national fixture had not been attended with the success they had hoped for, largely because of the industrial depression which prevented many people from making the journey to the stadium, it was only being brought back to the north because Wembley stadium was not available.

It's not often that a ghost has affected the outcome of the Rugby League Challenge Cup, especially one which has been imported. Nevertheless an Australian ghost, who was considerably less than spiritual, succeeded in deciding the outcome of a clash with the Lions.

In September 1930 Leeds signed Eric Harris, a winger from Toowoomba in Queensland, Australia and his devastating changes of direction and subtle sidestepping led him to be nicknamed 'the Toowoomba Ghost' by the Headingley public.

He had originally agreed to join Rochdale Hornets after failing to make the 1929 Australian tour team but, influenced by another Australian Jeff Moores who was playing centre for Leeds, Harris changed his mind, deciding to play at Headingley instead. His name is still revered by the followers of the blue and gold.

In his first season with the Leeds club he massacred the club's try-scoring record, notching 58; 28 more than

Harold Buck's record established in 1922-23, and he equalled Fred Webster's eight-tries-in-one-match feat in a clash against Bradford Northern at Headingley. But Eric cannot have scored two more valuable tries during his nine-year stay at Headingley than those in the late stages of the 1932 Cup campaign.

Leeds had marched through to the semi-final after beating Hull, Keighley and Leigh. In the last four matches at Huddersfield they had to play the holders of the trophy, Halifax, and the Yorkshire public responded to the quality of the encounter. A ground record attendance of 31,818 packed Fartown for the clash.

By the end of the 80 minutes there was deadlock with the scores tied at 2-2 and the replay at Wakefield Trinity's Belle Vue ground brought another 21,000 attendance; this time there was a decision.

It was Harris who spirited Leeds through. A contemporary report records: 'And now Harris was in the clear, apart from Dick Davies, who was guarding the touchline route. What, against apparitions? An imperceptible feathering of the accelerator...a mistimed dive...and the fullback was still gibbering in haunted disbelief as the Toowoomba ghost glided to the corner to round off a try of dazzling, unforgettable splendour.' The try helped turn the replay Leeds' way and they won 9-2, taking the path to the final.

Reigning champions Swinton, who had been the success team of the 1920s with three Lancashire League wins, two Lancashire Cup triumphs, two league titles and one runners-up spot, two Challenge Cup wins together with one runners-up spot and the one four-trophy season, had taken their form into the thirties. Widnes, Batley and Castleford had been their victims on the way to the semi-final where they beat Wakefield Trinity 7-4.

By half-time the Lions had established a grip on the game with the mighty Cumbrian second row forward Martin Hodgson landing four penalties to give Swinton an 8-2 half-time lead. Leeds prop Joe Thompson had also hit the target with a penalty.

Leeds, however, staged a second-half recovery and their deliverance came through the spiritual intervention of Harris, who repeated the same

Leeds captain Joe Thompson leaves the field at Central Park after their win over Swinton.

kind of solo success he had shown against Halifax in the semi-final.

This time it was Swinton full-back R. Scott who was left clutching at thin air as the Australian crossed for the decisive and only try of the game. Thompson added three more goals and Leeds won 11-8. For the second time in ten years, the Challenge Cup was on its way to Headingley.

Defeat would have been even harder to bear if Swinton had been able to look into the future. Although they had been one of and, perhaps, the team of their generation they

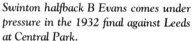

Swinton halfback B Evans comes under pressure in the 1932 final against Leeds at Central Park.

have yet to reach the Challenge Cup final again and, in spite of their illustrious history have never played at Wembley.

Just how unlucky can you be? They reached the final in the only peacetime year that the biggest game in British Rugby League was not played at the Empire Stadium and they are still seeking that particular holy grail.

The final, however, proved to be the final nail in the coffin of the lobby seeking the return of the Challenge Cup final to the north. An attendance of 40,000 had been predicted for this meeting of two attractive footballing teams. In the end the gate return for this third Challenge Cup final played at Central Park showed a disappointing 29,000.

The depression that gripped the working people of Britain, the high admission price of 1s 6d (seven and a half pence) and the fact that the final was once again broadcast on radio were all blamed. Nevertheless the League lived up to its promise and for 1933 the Challenge Cup final was transferred back to what had become its accepted home, Wembley.

CHAPTER 27

THE ROYAL AUSTRALIAN TOUCH

Australia and Rugby League have been intertwined ever since the All Golds combined with a group of disaffected Rugby Union enthusiasts to establish the game in the country in 1907. Their great sporting tradition, good climate and competitive spirit made them ideal recruits as Rugby players. Huddersfield and Warrington recognised these qualities and two signings from down under helped make them Challenge Cup forces to be reckoned with in 1933.

Britain was just starting to emerge from the cold grip of depression and Adolf Hitler starting to work his political machinations as Rugby League returned to Wembley.

Huddersfield, who had twice dominated Rugby League with famous sides, had fallen from grace and while they could not be described as a lesser club, great players of the pre- and post- First World War era had departed and they found rebuilding to that same standard particularly difficult.

Mid-way, through the 1932-33 season they were comfortably placed in the League table, though not reckoned to be much of a danger to the leading clubs of the era Salford, Swinton, York, Wigan and Warrington. The arrival of Ray Markham in January 1933 was, however, to change that scenario. Not that he was their only acquisition; they also bought scrum half Leslie Adams from Leeds and

loose forward Fred Brindle from Hull KR which helped the cause.

Markham, however, provided a link with the past and the Huddersfield tradition of acquiring Australian wingers who endeared themselves to the Fartown public. An antipodean, Ernie Mills, plied his trade on the right wing and they both carried forward the mantle created by Albert Rosenfeld, the world try scoring record holder from the famous 'Team of All Talents'.

Markham came from Cessnock, New South Wales. Somebody must have advised Huddersfield well because he was a winger who possessed pace allied to the ability to utilise clever changes in direction which left defences in disarray. The respect be-

tween him and the Yorkshire public was complete and he was to spend the rest of his life in the White Rose county.

He made his debut in Huddersfield's famous claret and gold colours in January 1933, helping them beat Leeds 13-7 and his arrival seemed to galvanise Huddersfield because they went through to their first appearance at Wembley. They saw off neighbours Dewsbury in the first round and travelled to Barrow for the second. At Craven Park the wheels almost came off their Cup bandwagon because the Furnessmen, who were enjoying one

A man for the future. Australian winger Ray Markham joins Huddersfield watched by club officials and press.

H. BROOK. MR. CROWTHER ("AUTOLYCUS") R. LOCKWOOD (CHAIRMAN) F.B. HOYLE R.T. MARKHAM C.L. REYNARD SECRETARY H.G. ROEBUCK F. WRIGHT F. CLIFFORD

of their better seasons, contained the Fartowners at 0-0. In the replay Huddersfield won 2-0 with a Len Bowkett penalty.

A third-round trip to Swinton was hardly the easiest of ties but Huddersfield, with their new-found confidence returned from Station Road with a 12-5 win to qualify for the semi-final against Leeds, which they won with ease 30-8.

Warrington too had discovered the advantage of having Australian power in their side. Bill Shankland took the Australian sporting dream to its limit. Besides being a Rugby footballer of note he was an accomplished golfer, cricketer, more than average boxer and excellent athlete. It was, however, as a Rugby player that he hit the international sports scene.

He was chosen for the Australian party for the 1929-30 tour of the United Kingdom and played in the four Tests when his strong running and fierce tackling naturally attracted a number of British clubs who made him offers at the end of the trip. His ambition to become not only a successful player, but also a top-class golfer, drove him to take up the British option and in the late summer he and his Sydney Eastern Suburbs team mate Belson (Bill) Hardy joined Warrington.

His natural qualities of leadership were recognised by the Wire and they made him the team captain. In 1932-33 Warrington gave notice of their Cup prowess when they won the Lancashire Cup beating St Helens 10-9. Their journey to Wembley saw them comfortably through the first two rounds beating Leigh and Batley and then overcome Wigan after a struggle in the third. Warrington repeated the Lancashire Cup success in the semi-final when they beat St Helens in front of 30,373; Huddersfield's last-four match had also been big box office with the gate taking 36,359.

The return to Wembley came on 6 May 1933. It was notable not just because of the increasing importance of the game on the national sporting calendar but also because the final received the royal stamp of approval.

His Majesty King George V accepted an invitation to present the Cup but had to forgo the sight of his first live Rugby League game after suffering a cold. It was felt it would have put the old King to greater health risks if he had gone to the match. He was represented by Edward Prince of Wales. Nonetheless it was League's first royal final.

The prospect of the royal presence clearly introduced a note of concern for officials who were at pains to emphasise the protocol needed on such occasions. Basically they stressed the golden rule: 'Don't speak unless you are spoken to.'

Those same officials must have been close to apoplexy when, during the Prince's introduction to the Warrington team, he went into close conversation with Shankland. They could have been forgiven for not knowing that the two had met before when Shankland had been with the Kangaroo tour party and discovered that they had a mutual interest in golf. As the Prince approached Shankland it is reported he said: 'So Shankland, we meet again. How's your golf?' Bill replied: 'Fine sir, how's yours?' The conversation went on for some time before the inspection of the two teams continued.

Playing in such an important match was clearly nerve-wracking and many years later Shankland was to reveal that the Warrington stand-off half Jack Oster was so gripped by tension that they virtually had to carry him out on to the pitch. And his game was clearly affected by the tension.

The royal presence must have had an inspirational effect on the two teams because they produced what is generally recognised as one of the best finals in the history of the competition.

Huddersfield had the best of the early exchanges and before the first half hour of the match was done they led 9-0 thanks to two penalties by their centre and captain Len Bowkett, a signing from Coventry Rugby Union club, and a try by Brindle that was converted by Bowkett.

Warrington turned the game round in the last ten minutes of the first half when centre Billy Dingsdale and scrum half Dai Davies shot in for tries which were both improved by goal kicks from full-back Billy Holding, and they led 10-9 at half-time.

Huddersfield re-established control when Bowkett kicked a penalty and then Mills flew in for a 65th minute try which Bowkett goaled but a Holding penalty cut Huddersfield's lead to 16-12.

In the last ten minutes Huddersfield stand-off half Gwyn Richards leapt on a mistake by Oster to shoot over for a try which Bowkett converted. Warrington maintained the tension when Davies, who had an outstanding game, scored a try three minutes from the end. Holding's goal made it 21-17 but Huddersfield survived the last three minutes to win the cup for the fourth time.

Warrington still point to what they believe to have been a perfectly good 'try' by Dingsdale which was disallowed by referee Frank Fairhurst and to the absence through injury of their Welsh international winger Stephen Ray, who had scored 37 tries during the season, as costing them the Cup. The aggregate number of points that day remained a Cup final record until 1959 while Warrington's total of 17 remained a best achieved by a losing side until 1985.

CHAPTER 28

LOCAL BOYS MAKE GOOD

Although professional Rugby League clubs have the right to recruit players from wherever they can, as a general rule they have remained largely loyal to, and dependent upon, men from their locality to provide the team manpower. The richer clubs have recruited players from other sides and brought in the best players they could tempt across from Rugby Union. But that has not always guaranteed success as was demonstrated in 1933-34.

In 1930 when Widnes reached the final, twelve of the thirteen players in their side had been born in Widnes. On their return to Wembley four years later they went one step further because all the players in the team were produced in Widnes.

Hunslet too have a tradition of heavy dependency on players coming from around the south eastern suburbs of Leeds and, for their first visit to the stadium, they had nine players from the district in their team.

Ironically the two finalists had finished almost together in the final league table; Hunslet were sixth and Widnes seventh, separated by just one point, 47 to 46.

The fact that two clubs from the grass roots of the sport had reached the final helped put many things into perspective bearing in mind that this was the season that the French pioneer Jean Galia had first come into

Rugby League after being banned for alleged professionalism by Rugby Union and there was another glamourous tour by the Australians. It was also a year when many clubs were feeling the financial pinch with Bramley and St Helens both in trouble, and the London Highfield experiment was in deep financial trouble.

Neither Hunslet or Widnes had easy runs through to Wembley. The

Yorkshiremen won at Leigh in the first round, beat Castleford after a replay in the second and York in the third. Their street credibility was, however, fully established in the semifinal when they eliminated the holders and still powerful Huddersfield 12-7 in front of 27,450 people at Belle

Hunslet prop Len Smith scores a try in the 1934 final against Widnes.

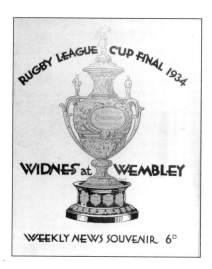

The front of a special edition of the Widnes Weekly News marking the Chemics' 1934 Cup final appearance against Hunslet.

Vue, Wakefield. The only problem created by the semi-final was that forward Jim Traill, whose son Ken was to figure prominently in the sport just after the second World War, broke his arm and was unable to play in the final.

Widnes had a good look at some of the best sides in Yorkshire in the first three rounds beating Leeds, Hull KR and then Halifax before coming up against Oldham in the semi-final at Station Road. They won 7-4 to become the first club to reach a second Challenge Cup final at Wembley.

Both clubs were in London on the eve of the final and spent the evening watching the London Highfield club play their match against Bramley. Perhaps because it was a final without any of the game's glamour sides ticket sales for this fifth Wembley final were disappointing in the north of England and yet when the big day dawned on 5 May the attendance of 41,280 was only marginally short of the previous year's 41,874 for the Huddersfield v Warrington meeting.

Hunslet were captained by one of the club's greatest ever players, full-back Jack Walkington. He had joined the Leeds area club in 1928 as a centre three-quarter and in 1933-34 he figured in the top goal and points scoring lists.

Peter Topping had started his professional career with Widnes in 1927 and already had one Cup winning medal from the 1930 final. He got his chance in a second final because injuries had left Widnes without a recognised goalkicker.

His Majesty King George V was again expected at the final but once more his health was again giving cause for concern and Lord Derby was commissioned to replace him.

Walkington won the toss and gave Widnes the disadvantage of playing into the very strong sunlight which, at a Wembley still without stand cover for a large proportion of the terracing, proved to be a major disadvantage. Widnes overcame that handicap to

Hunslet skipper Jack Walkington is hoisted shoulder high after their 1934 victory over Widnes.

The southern perception of Rugby League and its Cup final from contemporary newspapers for the 1934 Hunslet v Widnes encounter at Wembley.

establish a 3-2 lead with a Hugh Mc-Dowell try answered by a penalty from Mark Tolson, the Hunslet stand-off half.

Hunslet took the lead in the 26th minute when centre Cyril Morrell went over for a try but in the act of scoring he broke his collar bone. The extent of the damage was not evident at the time but it reduced him first to passenger status and then removed him from the action.

One of the major qualities required in the Challenge Cup is courage under adversity. By its very nature

Rugby League is a physical, body-contact sport and injuries are, regrettably, an integral part of what happens. In 1934, however, there were no such things as substitutes and, if a player was lost to a side through injury at any part of the game, then that was just tough luck. They had to soldier on without reinforcement.

Hunslet faced the second half with 12 effective players. And, as often happens, the players who remained stepped up their performance so that the gap in their ranks was hidden.

Widnes turned the screw, trying to

pull Hunslet into the centre of the pitch so that the inevitable gaps would be revealed. They scored a second try through second-row forward Albert Ratcliffe, a centre in the 1930 final, two minutes into the second half which levelled the scoreline but Hunslet maintained their resolution.

The 12-men Hunslet team regained the lead when loose forward Harry Beverley went in for a 50th minute try and, four minutes from the end, they struck the decisive blow with a try by prop Len Smith. Their courage had earned them an 11-5 victory and the Challenge Cup for the second time in the club's history.

CHAPTER 29

WIGAN TO WEMBLEY - VIA DUBLIN

Jim Croston was born in Wigan in 1911 and yet he never played Rugby League until he joined Castleford in 1933-34 season. And even then the game might never have crossed his path but for the miracle of radio.

Although he was born and had spent the first few years of his life in the County Palatine he did not stay long. His father, who served in the Lancashire Fusiliers, was killed during the First World War and his mother who was Irish took her family back to Dublin to live with her parents.

Jim went to the Royal Hibernian Military School in Dublin and then moved back to England when he joined the Royal Engineers. At that stage he was a hockey player and athlete and did not play Rugby.

One day his unit Rugby Union team was left a man short and Jim, who could cover 100 yards in 10.2 seconds was drafted into the side. His taste for the game was considerably enhanced after he scored in that initial game and eighteen months later he found himself playing for the Army against the Navy and RAF at Twickenham. That experience led him directly to Rugby League. In those days the inter-services games were broadcast and the Castleford club secretary Captain Pickles was, as a good military man, listening to the game.

He clearly took note of the name

Croston together with that of a Royal Signals corporal called Ted Saddler. Captain Pickles, an officer from the First World War, visited Aldershot to see Sapper Croston and clearly made his case well because it was agreed that he, and Saddler, should come north to play League.

Part of the condition of discharge from the Army was that employment should be guaranteed and because Jim was a joiner and carpenter there were few problems finding him a job.

Croston fitted well into the Castleford back line. He played alongside one of the finest players ever produced by the Castleford club, Arthur Atkinson who was, until the mid-1980s, the club's most capped player. In fact all four three-quarter line players, Croston, Atkinson and wingers Bernard Cunniffe and Tommy Askin were Test players.

Castleford, who had joined the professional ranks in 1926 after many years as a successful junior club, had performed well in 1934-35; they finished ninth in the League table and had been beaten by neighbours Wakefield Trinity in the Yorkshire Cup semi-final.

Just nine years after joining the senior professional ranks they were on their way to Wembley. They were drawn away against amateurs Astley and Tyldesley Collieries in the first round but the Lancashire lads gave

away home advantage in favour of better pickings from the professional side.

In the second round they won 8-2 at Liverpool, the successor to the defunct London Highfield, while they sunk 1934 winners Hunslet in the third round. Their place at Wembley on 4 May 1935 was assured when they beat Barrow 11-5 in a semi-final at Swinton.

Huddersfield were by this time back among the leading clubs in the Rugby League and they had an early indication of Castleford's power when they lost in a replay to 'the babes' in the second round of the Yorkshire Cup.

There had been a slight change of personnel since their 1933 Wembley appearance. Welshman Idris Towill had replaced Stanley Brogden in the centre, Scotsman Alec Fiddes had taken over from Len Bowkett as captain and centre while scrum half Leslie Adams had moved to Castleford. The pack too had new faces.

Adams was a particulary interesting case. He had won Challenge Cup medals with Leeds in 1932 and picked up his second with Huddersfield a year later.

With his military contacts coming into play once again Captain Pickles ensured that Castleford had the best possible training facilities for their Wembley warm-up because they

Castleford and Huddersfield walk out alongside each other before the start of the 1935 final.

trained on an Army owned pitch at Woolwich in south east London.

Castleford had finished eighth in the league table with 46 points while the Fartowners were just one place worse off with 42 points.

It was King George V and Queen Mary's Silver Jubilee year and the Rugby League marked the occasion by printing the match programme with a silver cover while the French international team flew across to London to be guests at Wembley and play a Jubilee match at Leeds.

Huddersfield came into the game without their Australian right winger Ernest Mills, who was injured, and he was replaced by Welshman Stanley Mountain, who had joined the club earlier in the season.

Although Atkinson was already a

Action from the Castleford v Huddersfield final.

legend with the Castleford fans he could hardly have enjoyed the experience of the first half. He had knocked the ball on with the Huddersfield line at his mercy twice and then slammed a penalty attempt up against an upright.

Fortunately Huddersfield had not inflicted too much damage. Towill, who came from Bridgend, had scored an 18th minute try but Castleford went in at half-time leading 5-2 thanks to an Atkinson penalty and a 29th minute try by Askin.

Action on the Huddersfield try line in 1935 as Castleford press home an attack.

Adams put one over on his former club with a 45th minute try and then 19-year-old Cunniffe crossed the Huddersfield line for their third try. Castleford then had to defend for the last half hour of the game. Huddersfield ensured that none of the disappointing 39,000 crowd left their seats until the end when front row forward Herbert Sherwood kicked a penalty with eight minutes to go and Fiddes crossed for an unconverted try three minutes from time.

Castleford's nerve held and they won 11-8 taking the Cup for the first time on their initial visit to Wembley. The unpredictable swing of fortune was contrasted by the two opposing scrum halves. For Leslie 'Juicy' Adams it was an amazing third cup winners medal with a third different club while the man bought to replace him from Warrington, Dai Davies, was suf-fering his third Cup final defeat with his second different club. And his story was still incomplete.

Croston's relationship with the Cup final and Wembley was to be re-newed eleven years later when he took Wakefield Trinity to the first post Second World War final.

Incidentally the Huddersfield trainer for that 1935 final was Chris Brockbank who had played in the final for Swinton in their four trophy season of 1928.

CHAPTER 30

A FISHERMAN OF ENGLAND

James Wasdale Brough was destined to reach a Cup final at Wembley one way or another. He could have chosen two routes, as a professional Rugby League player or as a soccer player.

Born in Silloth, Cumberland in November 1903 Jim Brough was 19 when he started on his way to that fateful moment. He was recruited by his local Rugby Union club and, such was the impact he made, that selection for the county side followed shortly after. In spite of his youth he held his place in their side on merit throughout the nine-match programme and it was his 50-yard drop goal that saw them through a nervous semi-final against Leicestershire to play Kent in the final which the Cumbrians won 14-3.

To be part of a county championship winning team in his first full season of Rugby was not a bad start for young Brough, who was a fisherman by trade, but better was to follow in his second season 1924-25.

Seven more county appearances followed and then he was selected for England, making his debut at Twickenham in a match against the All Blacks when New Zealand's Cyril Brownlie was sent off. And he returned to Rugby Union headquarters two weeks later to play against Wales.

His close proximity to Rugby League – although in those far off days

Carlisle, Whitehaven or Workington Town were not in the professional game – and his impact on the Cumberland and England Rugby Union sides soon had the professional clubs beating a path to his door with offers of contracts.

Although he maintained that he wanted to stay in the amateur game the pressure to take him into the professional ranks was building up from two directions, Rugby League clubs and Liverpool soccer club.

For a while it looked as though young Brough was to be lost to the oval ball game. He signed amateur forms for the Anfield club and was set to trial as either a goalkeeper or fullback. The Merseyside soccer giants actually wanted him to understudy for their well-known goalkeeper, Elisha Scott.

Speculation about his future was growing all the time, especially when he lost his England Rugby Union place for the three remaining internationals of the season to a boy from further down the Cumbrian coast, Tom Holliday of Aspatria who was also destined to become a professional and win a Cup winners medal with Swinton.

In the end it came down to money. Before his second England appearance against Wales, Swinton had been making overtures to him and he had rejected their offer in favour of that

second cap. Soccer lost out on his signature too. He recalled: 'If I had signed for soccer, under the Football Association's rules I was only entitled to a signing on fee of £10.00. I was paid almost £1,000 cash by Leeds to play Rugby League.'

He joined the Headingley club in June 1925 with just two years Rugby Union experience under his belt. He took to his new sport well and he became one of the leading players of his era with all the skills in both attack and defence. Although his game consisted of far more, he was the master of tactical kicking.

In just one area did his luck desert him. He played Rugby League at the same time as the immortal Jim Sullivan and that kept his list of representative honours to a minimum. Their meetings on the field were legendary and their kicking duels kept the crowds enraptured for many years.

Brough picked up his first Challenge Cup final winners medal in 1932 when the game was switched away from Wembley, but one of the finest players in Rugby League history finally paraded his talents at Wembley in 1936.

In Yorkshire terms the club was very successful during that part of his career, winning the county cup five times and the county league six times; but the 1932 Challenge Cup win was the only thing they had to show on a wider scale, in spite of being one of the game's leading clubs.

Leeds' route to the final was slightly longer than usual. Not because they had to play any more games than was usually expected in the Cup, but because after their first round win over Dewsbury at Headingley they had to travel to London to play Streatham and Mitcham where yet another attempt to establish the code in the capital was being made. Leeds, however, made their visit to London pay with a 13-3 win.

A close third round win at Hull put them into the semi-final against Huddersfield at Wakefield and the Loiners claimed their Wembley debut by winning 10-5.

Warrington reached a Wembley final for the second time in three years and third final in nine years. Their progress had been more traditional with victories over Barrow, Halifax and Wigan followed by a semi-final struggle over an emerging Salford at Wigan. The meeting attracted a record attendance for a Challenge Cup final with Wembley – the final was again brought forward to accommodate the departure of a British tour party to Australia – packing in 51,250 people on 18 April 1936.

The incentive to win was there for both sides but more so for Warrington who were making their eighth final appearance with just two wins, in 1905 and 1907, on their record sheet.

Controversy hit the game in the eighth minute when Eric Harris's crossfield kick was collected by Welsh loose forward Iorwerth Issac to go over for a try. Warrington claimed passionately that the Welshman was offside but the referee, Mr. A.S. Dobson from Featherstone, was unmoved by their protests, allowing the score to stand. Evan Williams, the Leeds scrum half who had played for Wales against Brough's England at Twickenham, kicked the goal.

Brough's kicking and the hard-working Leeds pack gradually wore the Lancastrians down. The Wire's full-back and captain Australian Bill Shankland kicked a penalty but they fell further behind when Leeds centre Fred Harris went in for their second try and Williams kicked a penalty.

Toowoomba Ghost Eric Harris marked his second Challenge Cup final with a try (he also scored one in the 1932 final) in the 66th minute which Williams converted and five minutes from the end centre Gwyn Parker crowned the Leeds effort with their fourth try.

Proud captain Brough collected the Challenge Cup from the Lord Derby. He had led his team to a record-equalling fourth victory, bringing them level with Huddersfield, and

Warrington's souvenir of the 1936 Challenge Cup final.

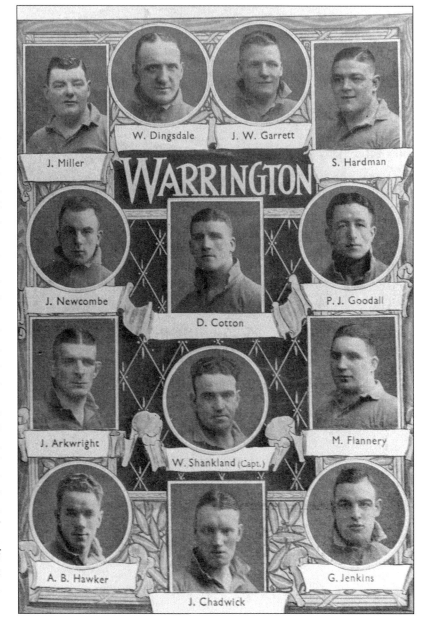

seen them establish the widest margin of victory in the six Wembley finals.

For Warrington captain Shankland it was the end of his Wembley dream but his sporting ambitions were already taking a different direction. One of the reasons he agreed to leave Australia for England was to further his golfing career.

While he played at Wilderspool, he became assistant professional at West Lancashire Golf Club and then professional at Haydock near St Helens. He moved to play at Temple-newsam near Leeds and, in 1939, he finished third in the British Open Championship which was staged at St Andrews.

In 1947 he had a chance to win the British Open title when the championship was played at Hoylake but a bunker disaster at the 16th hole, when he took a six on the third round saw him finish third for a second time. He completed a hat-trick of third places behind winner Max Faulkner in the 1951 Open at Portrush in Northern Ireland.

He might not have been able to win the Open himself but he did have a hand in creating a British victory because when he was professional at Potters Bar in Hertfordshire one of his 16-year-old assistants was Tony Jacklin who won the 1969 Open and the 1970 American Open.

The Wembley dream remained alive for Warrington's Welsh winger Griff Jenkins. He was to enjoy further visits as coach to both Wigan and Salford.

CHAPTER 31

CHEMICS FIND RIGHT FORMULA

There is a proverb within Rugby League which has been cited on the launching of many a hopeful career. Basically the tenet is: 'If you're good enough, you're old enough'. In 1937 a young Welshman called Reginald Waller Lloyd was living proof that the theory worked.

Although Rugby League football has always had a warm place in the life of the farm workers and townsfolk of Yorkshire's Craven area, success can hardly be described as a constant companion of the Keighley club. They have ploughed their furrow sometimes from financial crisis to financial crisis and enjoyed the occasional liaison with glory.

Not that Keighley were afraid to go outside the bounds of their picturesque boundaries to recruit players. They favoured Welshmen and for the 1936-37 campaign they had built up a substantial collection of players from the Principality.

Lloyd was a 16-year-old born in Neath, who had reached the senior club at The Gnoll in the time honoured Welsh fashion. He played for village side, Resolven, before moving into the famous all black jersey of Neath.

His Union career was nipped in the bud by Keighley. His potential must have been spotted by a scout and they played the 16-year-old in a trial game under the name of 'Johnson'. It

was a pseudonym much favoured by the Keighley club for Union players trying their hand at League.

Reg must have impressed them sufficiently because he signed professional forms for the Lawkholme Lane club aged sixteen in August 1936. He must have felt at home in the Keighley back division because three of the four three-quarters were Welsh; only right winger and goalkicker Joe Sherburn was English. He was born in Hull and joined Keighley from York and Halifax.

Keighley's investment that season saw them bring in New Zealander Len Mason, who had played eight seasons with Wigan, and former Coventry Rugby Union club back Len Bowkett, the six-goal hero of Huddersfield's 1933 Wembley winning team.

In the first round Keighley made club history. They beat Hunslet for the first time at the Parkside ground, with Lloyd scoring the crucial try in the 5-2 victory. The second round brought them victory over Broughton Rangers, the Yorkshiremen's first in 13 meetings between the clubs, and a third round win over Liverpool Stanley took them through to the semifinals for the first time in 31 years.

Their league programme gave them just three days of respite before their semi-final and they spent some time recuperating in the envigorating air of Lancashire seaside resort, More-

cambe. Their opponents Wakefield Trinity had fielded a team with 13 reserves against Huddersfield at the same time and were fined £25 by the league.

The semi-final attracted a massive 39,998 gate to Headingley – it was later amended to 40,038 according to at least one authoritative source. Tension was the order of the day with the match ending as a 0-0 draw but Keighley won the replay at Huddersfield 5-3 for the biggest day in the club's history; the Challenge Cup final on 8 May 1937.

When Reg Lloyd stepped out on to the hallowed turf he made history. He became the youngest player to appear in a Challenge Cup final. He was 17 years, seven months old. It was a record which stood unbeaten for 47 years.

While Keighley were battling their way through to the biggest game in the club's diamond jubilee year, across the other side of the Pennines Widnes were adding even more to their growing relationship with the Challenge Cup.

At the heart of things for the Chemics that season as they were for some time was one of the all time great halfback partnerships of Tommy Shannon and Tommy McCue. The double act came together for the first time in November 1931 when they lined up against Broughton Rangers

Peter Topping, a third Wembley final for Widnes in 1937.

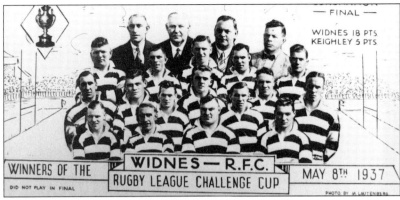
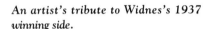

An artist's tribute to Widnes's 1937 winning side.

and they went on to terrorise defences all over the Rugby League for the remainder of the 1930s. They even guested for Halifax in the wartime competitions in 1942-43.

At the time of Widnes's 1934 Cup final appearance the partnership was still in its formative years but by the 1936-37 season they were in full bloom.

Keighley had finished 18th in the league table with 38 points while Widnes were two places lower in 20th with 35 points. When it came to the Cup the Chemics like the Craven he-

A rare picture of the Keighley team who reached the 1937 final against Widnes.

roes put their league form to one side.

In the first round they set Oldham-area amateur club Higginshaw aside while their second round game against Dewsbury was abandoned at half-time when Widnes were leading 8-0, fog intervened, and they won the rerun 12-7.

Swinton were their third-round victims and they disposed of the mighty Wigan in the semi-final to become the first team to play three times at Wembley. Their previous visits were in 1930 and 1934.

The final itself was a disappointing, one-sided affair with Shannon and McCue running the show. In fact Shannon scored the first try in the seventh minute and centre Peter Topping, playing in his third Wembley final for Widnes, kicked the goal. McCue broke Keighley down again in the 28th minute to take Widnes's second try and the Chemics led 8-0 at half-time.

Sherburn gave Keighley their first points of the game with a penalty in the 42nd minute but tries from centre Ken Barber and their 33-year-old former international prop Nat Silcock extended Widnes's lead still further. Topping, who converted Barber's try, then added a penalty to give Widnes an 18-2 lead.

The game was well beyond Keighley but Lloyd still had another entry to make in the Challenge Cup history book. Four minutes from time he flew in for a try to make himself the youngest try scorer in Cup final history; that record still exists.

That try gave Reg 15 for his initial season as a professional with Keighley. His stay at Lawkholme was brief and he was transferred to Castleford in October 1938 still aged just 19. He remained with Cas until 1951 when he went to Manchester to join Belle Vue Rangers – the former Broughton Rangers who had moved to play at the once famous Manchester fun-park centre.

Although most of the Keighley players' pain at losing at Wembley was acute it must have paled into insignificance compared with that of their Welsh scrum half Dai Davies. Four finals with three different clubs … and defeat each time.

CHAPTER 32

THE RED DEVILS

Salford had been one of the power clubs in the initial years of the Northern Union and they had reached three finals in 1902, 1903 and 1906 without actually having their name engraved on the Cup. Gradually their power base faded and they dropped out of the game's first echelon.

In 1929 they started the climb back to the top and the catalyst was a remarkable man, Lance Todd. He was a member of the pioneer 1907 All Gold touring team from New Zealand and was a former All Black. After that initial tour he stayed in Britain to become a great player with Wigan and, when he was transferred to Dewsbury in 1914, the storm of protest that hit the Central Park club from their fans was enormous. He remained at Crown Flatt for the rest of his career and after his retirement he was appointed as secretary of Blackpool Golf club. He returned to professional Rugby in 1928 when he took over as manager of Salford, the starting point for a golden era in the inner city club's history.

Under the guidance of the Kiwi master they started to accumulate players for a side that was to dominate the game for large tracts of the 1930s.

They won the Lancashire League in 1932-33, 1933-34, 1934-35, 1936-37 and 1938-39; the Lancashire Cup

in 1934-35, 1935-36 and 1936-37 and the League championship in 1932-33, 1936-37 and 1938-39 while they were beaten championship play-off finalists in 1933-34.

One of the secrets of Salford's success was Todd's recruiting policy. He built a team that contained some of the finest players of their generation.

Toddy's Toddlers, as they were known, grew into something much bigger. Because they played a particularly attractive brand of Rugby they were exported to France in 1934 to help encourage the growth of League across the Channel. While preparing for one of their games they noticed a poster proclaiming their presence and they were christened 'Les Diables Rouges' or the Red Devils and that is how they acquired their nickname. They had it before their close soccer neighbours Manchester United, who also lay claim to the title.

Salford were a team of all stars. Their names still roll off the tongue; Harold Osbaldestin, Barney Hudson, Emlyn Jenkins, Alan Edwards, Billy Watkins and Jack Feetham. They are enshrined in League lore and the jewel in Todd and Salford's crown was Welshman Gus Risman.

Rugby League must be thankful that Augustus John Risman left school in the dark days of 1928. He was another product of Cardiff's noto-

rious Tiger Bay area and at the age of 17 he emerged to manhood to find Wales gradually sinking beneath the black tide of an industrial depression and himself as one of thousands who could not find work.

He started playing Rugby with Dinas Powys. As with most Rugby Union players he paid for the privilege of playing but finding free funds to continue his sport was hard. When the offer came to switch to Cardiff Scottish he jumped at the chance because they paid their players' expenses.

And it was just before his first game for Cardiff Scottish at Stroud in Gloucestershire that he first came into contact with Rugby League. He explains in his autobiography *Rugby Renegade*: 'Just before the match a man called Frank Young, who represented many Rugby League teams in the South Wales area, stopped me in the street and asked what I thought of Rugby League.

'I was shocked! To talk about Rugby League was a sin comparable with blasphemy in the chapel. In the public house, which served as the changing room at Stroud, there were notices which warned us of dire penalties if we even so much as talked to a Rugby League scout, and we youngsters were left in no doubt that serious as theft and murder may be, the greatest crime of all was to let the words 'Rugby League' pass our lips, or thoughts of the game enter our minds.'

Although Gus did not feel that he had played well at Stroud, he found Young persistent. The pressure of unemployment was there all the time and, eventually, Risman conceded interest in League. Young's first offer of a trial with Leeds did not materialise but a similar move to Salford did.

Such was the fear of discovery that he used deception, telling people that he was going to England in search of work rather than admit that he was connected with the evil Rugby League. He didn't even leave a forwarding address. That was another stroke of fortune for League because, while he was away in England, two important invitations arrived. First came an invitation to play from Cardiff Rugby Union club.

There was also an invitation from London soccer club Tottenham Hot-

spur. He had enjoyed some success with Barry West End soccer team and Spurs heard of his talent and were ready to give him a chance; that too was allowed to lie.

He underwent a month's trial at Salford but they were not convinced. He agreed to another month's trial but chipped a bone in his ankle in the first match. Eventually he completed his approval period and returned to his home in Barry to await the verdict.

Salford made a wise decision. They offered him a contract. He received a signing on fee of £52 payable at a £1 per week and playing terms of £3 for a win and £1.15s (£1.75) for losing. And if he didn't play there was no pay.

Although he made his professional debut on the wing he was moved to full-back for his second match against St Helens. By the time the 1937-38 season was underway Risman was accepted as an all time great player. He

had been part of the 1932 and 1936 tours to Australia and had won 14 caps. Salford had become the team everybody wanted to see and it was Risman who made them tick on the field while Todd pulled all the strings off.

Salford had not been to a Cup final since the move to Wembley nine years before. Even though they had been the predominant force in Rugby League throughout the 1930s they had always failed to make it through to the big game of the season.

With all the power at their disposal it had to happen eventually and 1937-38 was to be their year. They beat Hull, Liverpool Stanley and St Helens Recs on their way to the semifinal where they were drawn against their closest neighbours Swinton. That fixture shares the same passion and ferocity as Hull v Hull KR, Wigan

Albert Gear's crucial try for Salford in the 1938 final against Barrow.

Captain Gus Risman is carried shoulder high by his delighted team-mates after the 1938 final.

v St Helens, Manchester City v Manchester United, Everton v Liverpool or Celtic v Rangers. Much local pride is at stake.

The other Rugby League ground in the Manchester area at the time was Belle Vue Stadium, the new home for the re-housed Broughton Rangers. The Hyde Road stadium was better known as the home of Belle Vue speedway team and was placed right next to a world famous zoological garden and fairground. The game caught the public's imagination and 31,384 saw Salford win through to Wembley for the first time by beating the Lions 6-0.

While Salford were celebrating the Wembley miracle and their first Cup final appearance since 1906, Barrow won through to play their first ever Challenge Cup final.

In the first three rounds Barrow were drawn at home. Amateur club Maryport were sunk 83-3 followed by Bramley and Leeds. In the semi-final they battled to beat Halifax 4-2 at Huddersfield.

Barrow had been beaten in the Lancashire Cup final by Warrington and were determined to take something back to the Furness area that season. On a very hot 7 May at Wembley they pushed the glamourous Salford every inch of the way. Two Risman goals, a penalty and drop goal, were matched by a Fred French penalty and Billy Little drop goal.

A replay was looming when, in the last minute, Barrow skipper Alec Troup's pass went to ground and Salford centre Albert Gear, who had been concussed earlier in the game, gathered it up to go over for the only try of the game. Risman missed with the conversion and then referee Mr F. Peel from Bradford blew the whistle for the end of the game.

Salford's magnificent era was crowned the moment that Gus Risman received the Challenge Cup from the hands of immortal Australian cricketer Donald Bradman.

The final was seen by 51,243 which just failed to match the biggest ever crowd for a Rugby League match in Britain of 54,112 for the Championship play-off between Hunslet and Leeds in the all-Leeds area final at Elland Road stadium the previous week which Hunslet won 8-2.

CHAPTER 33

THE ROCHDALE DISASTER

Rugby League has always been very fortunate in its safety record because many of its best games have attracted immense crowds with little or no serious problems. One of the reasons that the final was moved away from the north was that its popularity was growing and the grounds were not able to cope with the numbers of people who wanted to see the game.

The Athletic Grounds home of Rochdale Hornets was a case in point. It had housed the Challenge Cup final in 1902 (15,006 attendance), 1924 (41,831), 1926 (27,000) as well as numerous semi-finals. The stadium was ideally situated for games of such importance because it was close to the Manchester conurbation which offered neutral ground status for local derbies and centrally placed on the railway and road networks for inter-county clashes.

The problem was that it could not cope with the bigger crowds generated by the increasing popularity of the game and the situation came to a head in the 1939 semi-final between holders Salford, the undoubted team of the 1930s, and their Lancashire rivals Wigan, last winners of the Cup in the first final at Wembley in 1929.

Salford had been favoured with home ties in the first three rounds where they had beaten St Helens, league champions Hunslet and Bramley. Wigan, on the other hand, had an

easy 33-0 first round win over Leigh before tougher wins over St Helens Recs and Bradford Northern.

Their semi-final was to be played at Rochdale. The game proved to be a major attraction. A massive crowd squeezed itself into the Athletic Grounds. The official gate was 31,212 but, so many people gained illegal entry, that the size of the crowd is estimated at being closer to 40,000.

There were people in every nook and cranny even spilling on to the greyhound racing track which surrounded the pitch. To gain a better vantage point some spectators climbed on to the roof of the stand that was built parallel with the embankment of the Rochdale to Oldham railway line.

Newspaper reports of the incident report that twice police had ordered people down from the lofty vantage point but, as one set of spectators obeyed the instruction, their places were taken by a fresh set.

The start of the game had been delayed by the number of spectators encroaching on to the playing area and hardly had the game started than five minutes later the stand collapsed. The players helped carry away the casualties.

The splitting sounds of the pillars and woodwork had been heard all over the ground and, as it collapsed under the weight, the stand spilled

fans down on to the heads of the people underneath.

Remarkably only 17 people had to be taken to Rochdale Infirmary but that, unfortunately, included two fatalities. Joseph Howles, 41, a textile worker from Rochdale died of his injuries while 51-year-old Annie West from Monton, Eccles died in another part of the ground which was bursting to capacity.

It took seven minutes to clear the injured from the scene and then a conference was staged involving the two clubs, the referee and officials from the League. It was decided to continue but the crowd was still packed around the playing area. One fan was slightly injured after colliding with a Salford player, who was tackled into touch.

As a matter of record Cup holders Salford won through 11-2 and became the first club to reach Wembley in successive seasons. This time they played 1933 winners Halifax. The Yorkshire team started well by knocking the 1938 finalists Barrow out in the first round and then Hull KR in the second.

Their third round meeting with Wakefield at Belle Vue attracted a big crowd and the kick off had to be delayed by five minutes so that some 24,800 people could squeeze in. They saw a 5-5 draw and, in the replay, 22,830 spectators packed themselves

An aerial shot of Bradford's Odsal Stadium for the Halifax v Leeds Cup semi-final on 1st April 1939 when the attendance was recorded at 66,308.

into Thrum Hall. In the excitement a wall collapsed at the Hanson Lane end of the ground and two men were injured.

But Halifax qualified for the semifinal when they won 15-12. All roads led to Odsal for that last-four meeting with Leeds. The game attracted a record Rugby League gate of 64,543 beating the previous record set at the 1938 Wembley final. After a tremendous game the Thrum Hallers went through to their second Wembley appearance winning 10-4.

Halifax's victory was not greeted warmly in every quarter. The *Sunday Chronicle* newspaper opened: 'Rugby League hopes of a classic Cup final struggle between Leeds and Salford have not materialised!'

Salford, who were to end the season as league champions for the third time during the 1930s, were still believed to be the favourites to retain the Cup they had won at Wembley in 1938.

The Halifax team was not without Wembley experience. Second row forward Jack Cox had played with

Leeds in the 1932 final, George Todd and captain Harry Beverley with Hunslet in 1934 and Jack Goodall and John Chadwick with Warrington in 1936 while trainer Bill Bennett had been in charge of both 1933 and 1936 Warrington teams.

Halifax left for London on Friday morning and settled into their hotel but the Salford preparations had taken a turn for the worse after an unorthodox training routine. Risman explained in his book that manager Lance Todd had thought up a scheme where he had taken the team out training in the country in the week leading up to the final. But it all went wrong when the barn he had hired for the players to use as training accommodation lacked baths and a number of players caught colds which were still with them when they walked out to face Halifax at Wembley.

Cup fever had struck Halifax with 8,000 people going south for the game and one company in the town, Pratt's Engineers, not only gave their workforce the morning off but paid their fares to London. Another party lunched in Halifax and then drove to Yeadon Airport near Leeds to fly down to Croydon on Cup final morning 6 May 1939.

Halifax's forwards took control of

the match early on and by half-time the Yorkshiremen led 10-0 with their Maori centre Charlie Smith and former Northampton Rugby Union club centre Jack Treen both scoring tries which were converted by full-back Hubert Lockwood, a future chairman of the Rugby Football League.

Four minutes into the second half Risman pulled back a try for Salford but Halifax proved too powerful, running in two more tries from stand-off Todd and Welsh winger Jim Bevan. Lockwood completed a satisfactory afternoon's practice by adding both conversions to win 20-3.

It had been a victory against the odds. Salford had been pre-final favourites but Halifax's superb teamwork, based on the forwards led by Beverley, had taken them through to the club's fourth Challenge Cup triumph in front of 55,453 spectators.

It was a new record Cup final attendance. But more important matters than Rugby League saw the Challenge Cup put in storage while Europe and most of the free world fought in the Second World War.

Halifax celebrate their surprise win over Salford in the 1939 final.

CHAPTER 34

WARTIME FINALS

The cobwebs were not allowed to rest for long on the game's best silverware. After missing the 1939-40 season the League decided on 15 January 1941 to run a Challenge Cup competition at the end of the 1940-41 War Emergency League season. John Wilson, the League secretary, revealed that he was hoping 22 clubs would be available to take part.

As a concession to the hostilities it was decided that instead of medals the League could give War Savings Certificates. Four each would go to the winners and three to the losers. It was also settled that 20 per cent of the gates would go into a Cup pool while half the remaining receipts would be paid over to the League and the other half to the competing clubs. The draw for the first and second rounds was seeded so that Hull would not have to play outside Yorkshire and Barrow could remain within Lancashire.

Guest players were allowed but they could not play for more than one club in the competition. There was also a provision for 20 minutes extra time if it was necessary and, if at the end of that time it was still a draw, the first team to score would win the tie.

There was an example of playing to the death in the Castleford v Featherstone in the first round. It was a draw at the end of normal time as well as extra time so they played on

and Castleford scored the decisive try in the 117th minute.

Halifax, the winners of the last peace time final at Wembley, reached the first of the war time Challenge Cup finals in which they faced Leeds at Odsal Stadium.

Halifax had played in the first round beating Broughton Rangers while Leeds received a bye. In the second round of matches Leeds beat a Dewsbury team for which Eddie Waring, later of television commentator fame, was acting as manager and had assembled some of the best players from non-operational clubs as guests, while Halifax despatched York.

Places in the final came after Leeds had beaten both Hunslet and Bradford Northern while Halifax eliminated Huddersfield and Wakefield Trinity. The semi-finals were played over two legs.

Halifax's ground, Thrum Hall, came close to suffering air raid damage. The only bomb to hit Halifax throughout the whole war landed against a building in nearby Hanson Lane damaging several buildings which had to be demolished including the West Hill Hotel of former Halifax player Clem Garforth.

Centre Charlie Smith and Arthur Bassett returned from war duties and the Halifax team was reinforced by guest players such as Tommy McCue

and Harry Millington from Widnes and F. Osbourne from Salford. Leeds used guest players Eric Batten from Hunslet and Johnny Lawrenson from Wigan.

The final attracted an attendance of 28,500 which was excellent considering wartime travel restrictions. Australian centre Vic Hay and Lawrenson each scored two tries for Leeds while scrum half Dai Jenkins went in for one and full-back C. Eaton scored two goals. A Mel Meek penalty was all that Halifax could muster.

In the 1941-42 Challenge Cup the same two clubs, Leeds and Halifax, reached the final again. Each of the qualifying rounds was split into two-legged affairs. Holders Leeds collected a bye in the first round and then progressed to the final by beating Wakefield Trinity, Hull and Oldham while Halifax qualified on the basis of a bye and wins over Huddersfield, Bradford Northern and Wigan.

Both clubs called on guest players again. Leeds were able to select two of Salford's biggest names, Gus Risman and Alan Edwards, while Halifax picked up three Widnes players, McCue, Millington and hooker Glyn Jones. The game was closer than in 1942 but Leeds ran out winners 15-10 in the final at Odsal.

Edwards claimed two tries and Risman three goals while scrum half

Oliver Morris added the third try. Hubert Lockwood hit the goal target five times to compile the Halifax total by himself. By this stage in the War the crowd was reduced to 15,250.

On 14 November 1942 Rugby League suffered a terrible blow when Salford manager Lance Todd was killed in a road accident in Oldham and in February 1943 a prominent group of Rugby League men met in Manchester to discuss a memorial to the New Zealander.

It was agreed to open a fund in Defence Bonds and use the interest each year to buy a trophy to be awarded to the outstanding player in the Challenge Cup final. And from the first meeting £60 was subscribed for an award which is still administered by the Salford ex-players organisation, the Red Devils Association.

Dewsbury, twice peace-time finalists, winners in 1912 and beaten finalists in 1929, found wartime conditions to their liking and they reached the final in 1942-43 when it was played on a two-legged basis. Waring had assembled an impressive Dewsbury team built up of guest players whose clubs were not functioning during the hostilities and existing Crown Flatt staff.

They qualified to play Leeds with wins over Hull, Huddersfield and Oldham and, for the final played on Saturday, 24 April 1943 and then Monday 26 April, he had recruited five Salford players including Edwards, George Curran and Barney Hudson and two from Castleford one of which was the former Keighley player Reg Lloyd.

Leeds accounted for York, Wakefield Trinity and Keighley and imported as guests Hunslet's Jack Walkington and Eric Batten, son of the former Hunslet and Hull great Billy, who played in the second leg. This time Leeds, winners of both wartime finals were beaten 16-15.

By mid-1943 the War was turning in favour of the Allies and the Rugby Football League felt confident enough in their long term future to conclude an agreement with the owners of Wembley Stadium for Challenge Cup finals to be staged there for the first five years after peace was achieved. The Stadium were to receive 20 per cent of the receipts for each final.

Salford's Gus Risman returned after serving with the forces in Italy in January 1944 and wanted to play for Dewsbury with whom he had guested earlier in the War. But the Crown Flatt club already had six Salford players as their guests which was all that the League would allow. Even though two of those half-dozen were no longer able to play they were refused clearance for Risman to be made a seventh guest.

For the 1943-44 Challenge Cup competition the League decided that entry would be restricted to just 16 clubs. The previous year they had allowed Barrow to play in Cup without them having played in the Emergency League competition.

Clubs had to endure peculiar problems during the War. No football kit could be bought without clothing ration coupons – including boots. The Board of Trade gave each type of football club an allocation to help ease the situation, allowing each club to appeal to its supporters and players to donate any odd coupons they might have for disposal.

While War raged around the world an amnesty was declared between Rugby League and Union. There were even games between teams raised from either code and they played each other – at Rugby Union, of course – at grounds like Headingley and Odsal. The end of the war saw hostilities revived between the two codes. In one of the fixtures two former secretaries of the Rugby Football Union, Bob Weighhill and Robin Prescott, played for the Rugby Union against the Rugby League.

For the 1943-44 final, again played over two legs, Bradford Northern played Wigan and won 8-3 with each club failing to score in their away leg. In the last Wartime Challenge Cup final Huddersfield beat Bradford 13-9 over two legs.

CHAPTER 35

TRINITY'S DRY WEMBLEY

Wakefield Trinity, one of Rugby League's most famous clubs, had never been to Wembley when Rugby League emerged into the peace-time world which was still traumatised after six years of the Second World War.

They did, however, possess a slight advantage because of their geographical position as a mining town. Very few of their players had been called up because they had been all vital workers in the coal industry. Mining is a tough industry, it breeds tough men and it has been connected with Rugby League since the moment the vote to split with the Rugby Union was taken at the George Hotel, Huddersfield in 1895.

Trinity, after the war, were under the wing of player-coach Jim Croston, the Wigan born centre who had been to Wembley with Castleford in 1935 and they were reaching the height of their powers.

In the re-introduced Challenge Cup the first round was played on a two-legged basis. Wakefield were drawn against Huddersfield, winning both at Fartown and Belle Vue. Halifax were their victims at Belle Vue in the second round and then they made history by eliminating Workington Town, who had been admitted to the League at the start of the season.

In fact the Cumbrians had survived a nasty shock in the Wakefield

area in the first round when they were beaten by amateur team Sharlston 12-7 in the first leg but Town won the second leg 16-2 to survive and thrive. Wakefield's Wembley dream finally came true when they beat Hunslet 7-3 in the semi-final at Headingley.

Herbert Goodfellow was the Trinity scrum half of the era. Like so many of his clubmates he worked underground at the pit. He lived right next to the Sharlston ground where Workington had suffered the fright of their lives. He recalled: 'We were a good team in the true sense of the word. There were no stars.'

The same could not be said of their opponents Wigan whose side was packed with famous players. Their coach was the great Jim Sullivan. He had appeared in his last game as a player against Batley in February 1946 after he had been appointed as player-coach in 1932. The moment his playing career ended he remained as the coach at Central Park.

Included in the Wigan team of the era were New Zealand international winger Brian Nordgren, Test centre Ernie Ashcroft, international half-back Tommy Bradshaw, brothers Jack and Bill Blan and full-back Jack Cunliffe.

They put out Swinton in the two-legged first round followed by wins over Keighley, Barrow and Widnes to make sure of their place at Wembley.

Wigan were the pre-match favourites, their top-of-the-table position justified that rating while Wakefield were pushing for a top four play-off placing which made them dangerous opponents.

Wigan, however, went into the final without four key players: Martin Ryan, Ken Gee, Ted Ward and Joe Egan. Like Trinity's Harry Murphy, they had been despatched to the first post-war tour of Australia before the final. They had jumped a lift with aircraft carrier HMS Indomitable and that sailing could not be delayed.

Nevertheless Wigan, for whom forward Frank Barton was drafted in after bringing his leave from the Lancashire Fusiliers forward by 28 days, still held the mantle as favourites.

In the lead up to the final Trinity stand-off half Johnny Jones fractured his collar bone and it was a race against time to get him fit for the final. It appeared that he had won that battle because he declared himself fit to play at Wembley.

After 15 minutes of the final his shoulder, to use Goodfellow's words, 'went again'. From that point the 12 other Wakefield players were forced to carry him as a passenger.

Wigan soon established a grip on the game. They were leading 6-0 after 19 minutes after tries by Jack Blan and Nordgren. The big New Zealand winger had missed both conversions.

Wigan's George Banks makes a tackle while the Wakefield Trinity attack tries to drive away from their own line in the 1946 final at Wembley.

Wakefield hit back with a try by centre Billy Stott and he cut the Wigan lead to just one point at half-time with a 35th minute penalty.

The Lancastrian team started the second half in a similar manner with a try after 50 minutes by left winger Stan Jolley but again Nordgren missed the conversion and that was a worrying trend for Wigan. Stott, who had scored all Trinity's points up to this point, added his second try seven minutes later but missed with the goal kick.

There was a second try for Nordgren in the 65th minute but the goal touch continued to elude him and six minutes later player-coach Croston forced his way over for an unconverted try to leave Trinity trailing 12-11.

There were just 90 seconds left to play when Wigan were caught offside just in their own half and everybody in the ground was staggered when Stott sent the ball sailing between the posts to give Trinity the lead 13-12.

Billy Stott's match-winning penalty for Wakefield in 1946.

Wigan were handed a chance to save the game when they won a scrum penalty just inside their Trinity half in the last minute. But Yorkshire cunning had engineered the situation. Goodfellow recalled: 'I told the boys that I would feed their feet at the scrum.

'There was so little time left that if Wigan took the ball we would have tackled them out and if they got a penalty it didn't really matter. If Nordgren couldn't kick them from in front of our posts, he had no chance from near the halfway line.'

And the half-back, who had served Trinity since he was a 16-year-old back in 1932, was spot on with his assessment. The New Zealander, who had failed with his previous six kicks, was short with this attempt and ironically it was Goodfellow who caught the ball and he was virtually in touch

when the referee Mr A. Hill of Leeds blew the final whistle.

Nordgren was distraught because he knew just one success from those seven kicks would have given Wigan the Cup on their first visit to Wembley since 1929. Stott, who landed that important goal – 'He'd never hit one like that before' said Goodfellow – was named as the first winner of the Lance Todd Trophy as man of the match.

If the Trinity players thought that they would celebrate their victory in style back at their London base, the Waldorf, they were sadly mistaken. Goodfellow recalled: 'We were told 'No drinks tonight boys, you're playing Warrington on Tuesday.

'But they couldn't stop us, we simply split up and Wakefield players could be found celebrating all round London.'

And the day after they got back

from Wembley they beat the Wire to earn third place in the league. Again Goodfellow turned back the history book pages. He said: 'We got £15 for winning at Wembley. That wasn't bad money but I lost £7.10s in four days' lost wages. And worse than that I almost lost my job.

'I was supposed to have gone back to the pit on the Tuesday after Wembley but because of the Warrington game I didn't make it until the Wednesday.

'I had to appear before the tribunal for missing the day but I escaped with my life because the manager spoke up for me. He said that he'd been at Wembley for the game and I deserved to keep my job because it had been great entertainment.'

Wakefield Trinity, the surprise winners against Wigan in 1946.

CHAPTER 36

ODSAL TO WEMBLEY AND BACK... THREE TIMES

Although Trevor John French Foster was born in Wales in 1916, he was destined to make a piece of West Yorkshire his own. This son of a soldier turned publican, who played Rugby for Cardiff, was developing into a major talent in Welsh Rugby.

In his first season playing at Rodney Parade with his beloved home-town club of Newport, he was selected as a reserve for Wales but after just 35 games with the famous amber and blacks he was spirited away to Rugby League in 1938.

At one stage he looked like joining Wigan but he decided to take the £400 that Bradford Northern were offering. The fact that another famous Welshman Dai Rees, the former Abertillery and Wales centre three-quarter, was the Northern team manager did have some bearing on his decision – which must have been correct because more than 50 years later he is still serving the Bradford club as a timekeeper.

Foster was tailor made for Rugby League. The game suited his talent for powerful running and handling of the ball. He made his Bradford first team debut in October 1938 in a home defeat by Hull and, like so many other players of the generation, the Second World War robbed him of a large chunk of his footballing years and he spent the last year of hostilities far

away from Wales and West Yorkshire serving in the Middle East.

He had not been overseas all the time in the War and played a major role in the revolutionary Rugby League v Rugby Union matches as well as the Northern Command games against other areas. Demobilisation came late in February and so the first peace-time season was all but lost to him. By 1946-47 one of Bradford's all time great teams had been assembled.

Apart from Foster they had acquired such as winger Eric Batten from Hunslet to add to their existing stars, centre Ernest Ward, stand-off

W.T.H 'Willie' Davies and huge Welsh prop Frank Whitcombe.

The two-legged first round ties were still in operation for the 1947 campaign and Northern sustained a 5-2 defeat at Salford in the opening match of the campaign but they turned it round by winning 10-0 at Odsal.

Huddersfield were next to fall in the second round and League new-boys Workington who were third-

The Duke of Gloucester shakes hands with Bradford Northern's Jack Kitching before the start of the 1947 final against Leeds.

round victims to Wakefield in 1946, fell at the same stage to Bradford in 1947. Bradford assured themselves of their first trip to Wembley with a 11-7 semi-final win over Warrington at Swinton. It had been a long time since Northern had reached this stage in peace time. The last occasion had been in 1906 when they had triumphed over Salford in the final. The omens were good.

Another record crowd for Rugby League of 77,605 was attracted to Wembley on 3 May for the final against Leeds who were a star-studded team with the incomparable New Zealander Bert Cook at full-back and Australian forward legend Arthur Clues in the second row. They had beaten Barrow and Hunslet in the first two rounds and it had taken a stupendous 50-yard goal in the mud at Central Park to beat Wigan in the third. They set up the showdown with Northern by hammering the 1946 winners Wakefield in the semi-final 21-0.

It would have been easy to understand if Northern had been unnerved before they reached the stadium. On their way to the game the coach driver who was taking them became hopelessly lost and just could not find his way to the stadium.

Northern were running late. It needed a man with nerves of steel to find a solution and Northern had one in giant prop Whitcombe. He held a heavy goods vehicle licence and the bus driver was eased out of his seat to be replaced by Whitcombe, who had driven heavy lorries during the War. And he got them to Wembley Stadium although admittedly they were running 30 minutes behind their schedule!

Both sides fenced for an opening in the early minutes of the game and it took 27 minutes for the first points to arrive when Cook landed a penalty. The game failed to live up to its pre-match expectations and it was Northern who claimed the first try in the 49th minute. Ward, one of the classiest centres to be produced by League, provided the opening and Welsh winger Emlyn Walters crossed for the touch down.

Two minutes later Leeds regained the lead through another Cook penalty. Ernest Ward – there were two Wards in the Bradford side, the other being scrum half Donald Ward – pulled Northern into a 5-4 lead with a drop goal and then Trevor Foster pounced on a tragic mistake by Cook to score a match-winning try just a minute from the end.

The financial rewards for winning at Wembley were not there for the clubs in 1947. Both finalists received £750 each from total receipts of £17,500. And, thus, Northern became the first team in the history of the game to win the Challenge Cup having lost a game; remember they were beaten at Salford in the first round, first leg in February. Willie Davies, their Welsh stand-off born in the same year as Foster, was the winner of the Lance Todd Trophy.

When it came round to the Challenge Cup in 1948 Bradford relished the defence of the Cup. Again they lost the first leg of the first round. This time they went down 6-2 at Hud-dersfield but the return match at Odsal brought them overall victory with a second leg win 15-3.

The second round was arduous too. They drew 3-3 with Wakefield Trinity at Belle Vue and had to rely on a 9-2 replay victory to clinch a third round place against Oldham which they won easily 30-0. Wembley came into view for a second time when they beat Hunslet in the semi-final at Headingley.

Wigan collected their third Wembley placing when Castleford were sunk without trace in the first round followed by wins over Leeds, Warrington and Rochdale Hornets.

The 1948 final was the first to be attended by a reigning monarch when His Majesty King George VI presented the Cup while, for the third successive final, the attendance of 91,465 was yet again a world record for the sport.

Wigan had finished top of the league having beaten Bradford, both home and away, during that run. Northern had, however, beaten them in the semi-final of the Championship play-off the week before Wembley and that was perceived as a psycholog-

Bradford Northern captain Ernest Ward (left) and Wigan skipper Joe Egan (right) lead their teams out for the 1948 final.

ical advantage. Yet the media and the bookmakers still made Wigan the favourites to win. The final was billed as the 'Battle of the Giants', and not without reason.

Both clubs had dedicated followers, none more so than 48-year-old Wigan fanatic Alfred Townsend, who walked all the way to Wembley repeating the feat he had first completed for the first ever Wembley final in 1929 when Wigan beat Dewsbury.

Rain had fallen for the two days before the final and again on the morning of the match. That made conditions for the game difficult and it was Wigan who adapted their game first.

A Bradford blunder brought the first points. Wigan winger Jack Hilton charged down a Batten kick, dribbled the ball forward over the line and went in for the try; Ted Ward converted.

Bradford responded with a try four minutes after through Alan Edwards but they still trailed Wigan because Ernest Ward missed with his goal attempt.

Heavy rain and wind took a great deal of the gloss off the first royal Wembley which was, incidentally, the first Challenge Cup final to be televised. Not that either His Majesty or the small television audience must have been impressed with Rugby League. The poor conditions made handling difficult.

In the last minute Bradford drop kicked from under their own posts and the ball fell at the feet of Wigan's second row pairing Len White and Bill Blan. They dribbled it back along the floor to the Bradford line where prop Frank Barton took it over for a try. Ward's goal kick failed but Wigan had won the Cup for the first time since 1929.

Although the Northern team was beginning to be affected by the ravages of time, when the 1948-49 season

Wigan full-back Martin Ryan is tackled by Bradford's Welsh star Trevor Foster while Bill Hudson moves in to help in the 1948 final.

got under way they were still a potent force as they demonstrated by beating Castleford to win the Yorkshire Cup.

It was as if they could not keep up their high standards for the pressure of week-to-week League Rugby while the heady adrenalin of knock-out Cup Rugby provided a sip of the elixir of life. The merest scent of Wembley seemed to put the side back on their mettle and, once the competition had started, they became very difficult to beat.

St Helens, Castleford, Belle Vue Rangers – the successors to Broughton Rangers – and Barrow all tried to stand in their way but Bradford succeeded in becoming the first club to reach Wembley in three successive seasons. An amazing feat.

It was another all-Yorkshire affair because Halifax, winners of the last peace-time final before the War in 1939, had qualified for their third visit to Wembley.

While Bradford had been enjoying a heady period of success, life just across the hills at Thrum Hall had not been so easy following the end of hostilities. Their team, which had threatened to dominate Rugby League in the years before Hitler's war, had now broken up.

• Their rebuilding scheme took time

to implement. They even had the mortification of seeing one of their players, 37-year-old international prop forward Hudson Irving, tragically die on the touchline after suffering a blood clot during a game at home to Dewsbury.

The transformation, when it came, stunned Rugby League. In 1947-48 they finished 18th in the 28 strong league and their dismal form spilled over into 1948-49. They still had not found a cure when the Challenge Cup came around but they were taking the right kind of medicine.

In 1946-47 they had acquired a young scrum half, Stan Kielty, from Wakefield Trinity followed by a host of other signings including forwards Frank Mawson and Don Hatfield from junior clubs in the area. Even though they were under the cosh in the league Halifax continued to invest and recruit. Home crowds remained buoyant with their average attendance for League games still up at 9,916.

As they moved towards the Cup they bought in 20-year-old Working-

Bradford Northern, winners on their third successive visit to Wembley, in 1949.

ton Town hooker Alvin Ackerley, Swansea Rugby Union club prop Michael Condon, a massive South African second row forward Jan Pansegrouw and, unusually, a pair of Irishmen. There was forward Des Healy and threequarter Paddy Reid who moved from Huddersfield.

Two local lads Ken Dean and Jack Wilkinson had fought their way up through the ranks and all that was needed was the final catalyst which came in the shape of 30-year-old centre Gareth Price from Leeds. He cost Halifax £2,750 but he proved to be a tremendous investment. He was a superb tactical player who, most importantly, had the talent of making other people play to the best of their ability.

Price was signed in the nick of time, literally just before the Cup signing deadline expired, and he missed the first leg of the first round

tie at Hull when Halifax were beaten 4-0. His impact on the side was instant because they went through to the second round after winning the return leg 10-0.

Keeping in mind their lowly league position it was a surprise of major proportions when they disposed of, first,

Swinton, one of the top sides of the season, and then Oldham. The joy of their Cup success was, however, flawed because amazingly, in a body contact game where fatalities are

Halifax, beaten finalists in the 1949 final with Bradford Northern.

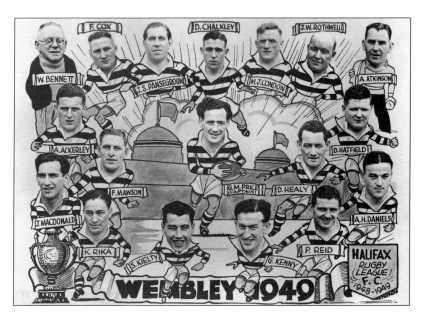

Wembley groundstaff put the finishing touches to the posts while Halifax's Dennis Chalkley and George Kenny get the feel of the turf prior to the 1949 final.

thankfully very rare, Halifax had to endure another tragedy. Winger Peter Craven died in hospital after injuring his neck in a collision with the shoulder of Workington Town forward Bill Cavanagh a week before their second round tie against Swinton. Craven had only signed for Halifax that season from Blaydon Rugby Union club in County Durham.

Their semi-final meeting with their rivals from over the Ainley Hills, Huddersfield, at Odsal certainly packed them in with an attendance of 64,250 to see the all-West Yorkshire meeting. Halifax were the underdogs. That was the opinion of their directors who felt that victory was that unlikely that they could offer a healthy winning bonus of £30; big money just after the War and their cash looked safe as Huddersfield romped off into a 10-0 lead.

Three goals by full-back Dennis Chalkley gave them some hope and in the last few minutes Kielty dropped on a Huddersfield mistake to score a try which Chalkley converted to give them the lead at 11-10.

The Fartowners hit them with everything but Halifax held on to become the club from the lowest league position to reach Wembley. They ended that season in 25th position with just four clubs below them.

The all-Yorkshire final proved to be a massive attraction as Britain's sports-starved public gorged themselves on the feast being offered to them. Wembley was packed to capacity with yet another world record crowd of 95,050 but the final proved to be a disappointment.

Bradford controlled the game completely. Eric Batten had dived in for a tenth minute try even though he was suffering with a broken shoulder – substitutes were still a thing of the future – and Ernest Ward converted.

Halifax, who had defended well through the rest of the first half, went further behind on the hour when Ward hit a penalty and Northern delivered the coup de grace in the 72nd minute.

Suitably it was Trevor Foster, by consent one of the finest forwards of his generation, who delivered the final blow with the try which Ward converted. Halifax's league form had come home to roost and they became the first team not to score in a Wembley final.

Foster played 13 first class games against Halifax in his career, scoring just two tries – including that Wembley winner.

More Halifax training with (left to right) John Rothwell, George Kenny, Stan Kielty, captain Gareth Price and Dennis Chalkley.

CHAPTER 37

THE PRODIGAL RETURNS

Harold Palin found fame with his home-town club Warrington after they had rejected him. Signed as an amateur in 1936 he made a quicker than expected acquaintance with the Challenge Cup after first choice Wire full-back Billy Holding broke his leg.

The teenaged Palin was introduced to the team for the second round at Halifax. The clash at Thrum Hall ended in a 2-2 draw but Harold had clearly done enough to stay in the side which won the replay at Wilderspool.

Then the Wire team management lost faith and he was replaced. In fact in the three remaining rounds right the way through to the final Warrington used three different full-backs finishing up at Wembley with Australian Bill Shankland in the number one jersey.

Palin's career, meanwhile, was on hold. The club did not offer him professional terms and when Swinton did produce the necessary professional contract, he had little hesitation in moving to Station Road.

There he blossomed as a player, winning Lancashire county honours as both a second row and loose forward. Then Wilderspool realised their mistake and had to hand over cash to Swinton to bring him back to Warrington; an irony often repeated in professional sport.

He did not play much before the Second World War but once Warrington resumed in peace-time they found Palin at the height of his powers. They won their first league championship in 1947-48, were beaten championship play-off finalists the following season and won the Lancashire League in each of those seasons.

It was a golden era with a Kangaroo influence in the Warrington club history. Two of the biggest names in the Wire team were both Australian, winger Brian Bevan, a boney, balding, bandy man whose unlikely athletic prowess made one of the all time great wingers and earned him a place in Rugby League's Hall of Fame, and forward Harry Bath one of the greatest packmen from down under never to represent his country.

Warrington cruised through the two-legged first round against Hull KR following that with wins over Swinton and Hunslet to reach the semi-finals against Leeds. The hunger for sport was still with the nation even though the War had been over for five years and this trans-Pennine meeting at Odsal Stadium was a record breaker in its own right. The attendance that day of 69,898 has remained unchallenged ever since.

The Lancashire club came through and so were to face Widnes, their deadliest local rivals. Competitors they might have been but they were on speaking terms. They must have been because Warrington paid Widnes a record £4,600 to secure the transfer of centre Albert Naughton who was one of three brothers, Albert, Johnny and Danny, on the Naughton Park club's books.

When the Wembley final came around on May 6 Danny was on the high seas heading out on tour with Great Britain leaving his two other brothers to face each other on Wembley's lush turf. Albert had been a target for St Helens too but he preferred to play for Warrington even though the Saints were prepared to pay £5,000.

Warrington's team manager for the game was Chris Brockbank, who played for Swinton when they beat the Wire in the 1928 final and was trainer to Huddersfield when they were beaten by Castleford at Wembley in 1935, while Widnes had their former halfback Tommy Shannon, a winner and loser at Wembley during the 1930s, as coach.

By reaching the final Widnes became the first club to appear in four finals at the old Empire Stadium and in those four games they had used just five players from outside the Widnes district – three of them in the 1950 team.

One of those players was Hull-based centre Colin Hutton who was later to become chairman of Hull KR and was the team manager for the 1982 Great Britain team which lost all three Tests to the touring Australians.

From the loose forward berth Palin was able to exert a great deal of influence on Warrington's playing style and dictated the flow of their game. He gave the primrose and blues the lead with an unusual drop goal in the 15th minute. Club historian Ernie Day says: 'It was a left-footed kick. He had never used that leg for kicking before that day at Wembley and almost certainly didn't ever use it again.'

Bath, who had a pain-killing injection in an injury before the start, and their live-wire scrum half Gerry Helme had taken control in midfield and Widnes could not make an impact on the game.

Warrington piled on the agony. A Palin penalty, a Bath try converted by Palin and a Ron Ryder try virtually completed the game as a competitive spectacle before half-time.

Palin kept putting the boot into the Warrington neighbours and he found the target for the fifth time in the game with a 58th minute penalty

and the Wire completed the rout with a Bryn Knowleden try in the 67th minute. Warrington's 19-0 win gave them the Cup for the third time in their history and their first win in three visits to Wembley.

Test half-back Gerry Helme became the first Lancashire club winner of the Lance Todd award for man of the match but Palin must have run him close with five goals and a large contribution in organisation while Bath became the first overseas captain to lift the Challenge Cup.

CHAPTER 38

GEE FORCE

The Challenge Cup reached its half century in 1951. It had grown into the sport's biggest and most widely recognised asset. Exactly the same could be said of Wigan and their prop forward Ken Gee.

Wigan, who had not won the Cup for the first time until 1924, have always been associated by modern generations with the Cup and Wembley; yet it was not until after the Second World War that they really made an impact. Winners in 1923 and 1929 and beaten finalists in 1911 and 1920, they came to prominence in the 1950s when they established a vice-like grip on the thirteen-a-side game.

Ken Gee helped put them there. The balding, barrel-chested prop forward was a big man in all senses of the word and he possessed the ball-handling skills of a halfback and a cruise missile-style goal kick.

More often than not people saw him as an enforcer and scrummaging machine, who partnered the great Wigan hooker Joe Egan. He was, however, very much more than that. Born in 1916, Gee signed for his home-town club, Wigan, in January 1933 shortly after his 16th birthday, and more than two years later he gained his first team-debut in the front row of the scrummage; his sporting world until August 1954. He made 637 appearances in Wigan's Cherry and White – 636 of them at prop; the remaining one as hooker.

He was a goalkicker of note and in 1949-50 season he was joint top goal scorer in the Rugby League. He kicked 133 goals and shared the award with Warrington loose forward Harold Palin.

It was fitting, therefore, that a year after Palin had helped Warrington to victory over Widnes at Wembley in 1950 Ken Gee should be heading back to Wembley.

Gee had picked up a winners medal with them in 1948 when they beat Bradford Northern. By 1950-51 he was in the autumn of his professional career and he had just returned from a second tour of Australia with Great Britain as well as being a member of probably the most famous Wigan team of them all.

Rugby League persisted with two-legged first rounds although there were signs that interest in them was waning. In 1949-50, 200,000 people had watched the double-headers but for 1950-51 the returns were down by 35,000.

Wigan soundly spanked Rochdale 32-0 and 18-5 before being drawn at home in the second round to Batley. The draw had been slightly unusual, even by Rugby League's standards. Because so many people wanted to see the ceremony the League experimented by staging it at the Scala Ballroom, Leeds which had a capacity of 800.

But it did not make any difference to Batley who were comfortably dis-

posed of giving Wigan another home draw against Huddersfield in the third round. This was a much tougher proposition and it took a Gee penalty to provide the solution.

The prospect of the semi-final between Wigan and the holders Warrington was so attractive that moves were made to take the game to Liverpool soccer club's Anfield Stadium.

Unfortunately, the idea was not successful and the match was staged at Station Road, Swinton where 44,621 people saw Wigan win 3-2 thanks to a Brian Nordgren try; a touchdown which must have helped paper over the cracks he left by missing seven goals in the 1946 Wembley defeat by Wakefield.

Until 1950-51 the best that Barrow had managed in 50 years as a professional club was beaten finalists in the 1937-38 Challenge Cup and Lancashire Cup but the Shipbuilders were altogether a different proposition in the early 1950s.

Their player-coach Willie Horne, one of the earliest goalkickers to successfully use the soccer-style round the corner approach to goal-kicking, was one of the shrewdest tacticians of the era while wingers Jimmy Lewthwaite and Frank Castle were deadly finishers, centre Phil Jackson a powerful runner and second row forward Jack Grundy immensely powerful.

They had bounced the far-distant Welsh professional club Llanelli in the two-legged first-round before overcoming eventual League champions Workington Town at Craven Park in the second. Bradford Northern were next to fall in the third round and the line-up against Leeds in the semi-final at Odsal Stadium, Bradford was watched by an incredible 57,729 people. Bert Cook, Leeds' Kiwi full-back did his best to put Leeds through with four goals and a try but Barrow forced a 14-14 draw and went on to win the replay at Fartown 28-13.

The Furness area sent 20 trains packed with supporters down to London with many of the locomotives sporting highly decorated Wembley logos attached to their smokebox doors. It was estimated that 12,000 Barrow fans followed their side, while Wigan took 15,000.

One of the trains from that isolated patch of Lancashire left Barrow at 11.20 pm on Cup final eve. It contained the youngest member of their supporters club committee Miss Betty Brockbank and she celebrated her 21st birthday party during the overnight journey to London.

Barrow tried to prepare in the most professional way possible and Horne had his players romping around a golf course because that was the nearest he could find to Wembley turf.

The final on 5 May was subjected to heavy bursts of rain which made the ball very heavy and difficult to handle. Barrow were no match for the superb Wigan team for whom their New Zealand stand-off half Cec Mountford had been doubtful through injury, but then declared himself fit and played well enough to become the first overseas winner of the Lance Todd Trophy as the man of the match.

Gee's mighty boot provided the only points of the first half with a sixth minute penalty. Winger Jack Hilton scored a try to put alongside the one he had registered against Bradford Northern in the 1948 final and then, with ten minutes to go, Gee showed a surprising burst of speed from the Barrow 25 yard line to score the decisive try.

The exertion had had an effect on the big man and he handed the goal-kicking role over to Mountford. The man destined to become a New Zealand Test coach never wasted any time with his goalkicks and he shot the ball between the uprights.

Wigan loose forward Billy Blan, who still works for the club, had an outstanding game and many shrewd judges believe that he rivalled Mountford for the man of the match award.

Wigan's relationship with the Challenge Cup final was building. It was their seventh peace-time final and their fourth win as well as being their fourth visit to Wembley.

Wigan's Ken Gee powers his way over for a try in the 1951 final against Barrow.

CHAPTER 39

THE OLD MASTER

During the years of the Second World War the prospects of forming a senior professional club at Workington in Cumberland was explored and, by the time peace was restored, they were ready to start operations after gaining membership to the Northern Rugby League.

The man they sought to lead them into the professional world was none other than Salford's Welsh genius Gus Risman. He had been serving overseas with the British Army's first Airbourne Division and, with his playing days seemingly numbered, he decided that he would like a role in club managership, and the adventure of launching a new club appealed to him.

He had been approached by the Town consortium in January 1946 and, as Salford were prepared to release him, it was agreed that he should join them for the 1946-47 season as soon as he returned from captaining the successful 1946 tour to Australia.

When he eventually arrived in the Cumbrian steel port town he found an embryo club stuck on the western edge of the English Lake District sharing a ground with the local Football League side and their reserve team playing at the adjoining greyhound racing stadium.

He was asked how long it would take before they could compete with the major powers in the game and, vaguely, Risman said he could not promise anything sooner than five years. Town kept climbing up the league table but Workington people kept wondering whether Risman's five-year plan had any chance of succeeding.

Although Risman intended the comment as a warning not to expect a miracle, the Cumbrian people took it as a virtual commitment and it became an albatross around his neck. But the Risman magic spell did come to pass because in 1950-51, five years after he started work, against all the odds Workington Town became the Rugby League champions. An amazing feat by any standards.

He had constructed a solid side utilising the best Cumbrian talents mixed with imported players. Australians Tony Paskins and Johnny Mudge combined with former Wigan winger Johnny Lawrenson while the local hero was loose forward Billy Ivison, who was unlucky not to win international recognition.

Having won the League title, Workington had proved that they were serious contenders for any of Rugby League's top competitions; especially while Risman kept playing. When he had joined Town he had not expected to continue playing. But Town could live without him ... well almost. Risman had been seriously injured, rupturing a kidney, playing against his old club Salford and missed the first three rounds of the Cup.

In his absence Workington comfortably disposed of York and then St Helens in front of a massive 20,403 crowd; the whole of West Cumberland must have gone to the match! Then they ran into trouble in the third round when they were drawn at home against Warrington.

The soccer club with whom they shared the ground were also at home on the same day Saturday, 15 March but the Rugby League insisted that the game should go ahead because the semi-final was scheduled for 29 March.

The Workington clubs compromised. The soccer team agreed to kick off at 2pm and the Rugby League match at 4.45pm. Warrington objected but, eventually, the Rugby League insisted that the game should take place at 4.45pm. By this time the soccer club had made other arrangements with their opponents Oldham Athletic to kick off at 3pm and were reluctant to change back at that late stage.

Talks with the Football League finally persuaded the soccer club to return to the compromise plan allowing an hour between each game to service the stadium and change the pitch posts and markings. If Warrington were unhappy about the match arrangements, they must have been unconsolable on the long journey home after being beaten 14-0.

Risman, who had been detained for a couple of weeks in Salford Royal

Hospital, returned in time to play in the semi-final against Leigh at Headingley. He admitted in his autobiography that he thought long and hard about selecting himself. His decision to play was vindicated when he kicked a goal in their 5-2 win to clinch a place at Wembley.

Town were sharing their experience of a first Challenge Cup final and trip to play at Wembley with their opponents Featherstone Rovers, the little team from the pit village built on a crossroads between Wakefield and Pontefract.

Until the 1921-22 season they remained in the junior game sub-culture, emerging now and then to remind the professional clubs of their latent strength. After they joined the senior club ranks the furthest they progressed in any competition was to the championship final in 1927-28 when they were beaten by Swinton.

Rovers had acquired the veteran winger Eric Batten from Bradford Northern as player-coach and his arrival at Post Office Road transformed the club. Their Cup campaign had gathered pace when their first round, first leg produced a narrow win at Rochdale and a comfortable victory in the second at home.

They overcame Batley in the second round and faced the mighty Wigan in the third. Wigan had already collected their sixth successive Lancashire Cup and were destined to become League champions. Post Office Road was packed to its 15,000 capacity for the tie and their former Hull full-back Freddie Miller kicked four goals as Rovers stunned the Rugby League world by winning 14-11. Their semi-final against Leigh at Headingley brought 33,926 spectators; 2,000 more than Workington's last-four meeting with Barrow.

The reliable boot of 35-year-old veteran Miller was a deadly weapon and Rovers set out on the road to Wembley after he landed three penalties to Leigh's one in the 6-2 win. The final at Wembley on 19 April was historic not just because two different clubs were making their debut, but also because it was being televised nationally for the first time. Two years earlier the cameras had been at Warrington's win over Widnes but the broadcast had been restricted to the London area.

Both teams relied heavily on 'experience'. From the moment Risman set foot on the turf he set a new record because he became the oldest man to play in a final at 41 years 29 days while Batten at the age of 37 was not to play much longer. Rovers also contained ageing full-back Miller and Irish prop forward John Daly, 34. Al-

A disputed Wembley try as Featherstone Rovers' player-coach Eric Batten tries to get the ball down against Workington in 1952. Seconds later the touch judge ruled his leg to have been out of play before he grounded the ball.

though the final did not contain one of the recognised giants of the game it became one of the classics of the competition's history.

The Cumbrians set the early pace with a first-minute Risman penalty followed by a try by winger Johnny Lawrenson 15 minutes later which Risman converted.

Rovers put the brake on their slide when Miller kicked two penalties and by half-time Town led 7-4. The final came to life three minutes into the second half when Batten scored a unconverted try to equalise for Rovers. But the turning point in the match came when Workington's Australian John Mudge raced 60 yards for a try which restored their lead.

A minute later Town struck again.

Daly's pass to winger Norman Mitchell near the Workington line was intercepted by Lawrenson and he left the Rovers defenders far in his wake as he sprinted 85 yards for a try that Risman converted. He had already set up a new club try-scoring record before the final with 44 and was to finish the season with 49 for a record that still survives.

Great Britain winger George Wilson scored Town's fourth and final try in the 66th minute and, ten minutes later, Rovers scrum half Ray Evans scored a try which reports of the time put it among the 'greatest tries scored at Wembley' category. He received the ball on the Rovers 25-yard line and reached the Workington try line after a superb, side-stepping run

through the tiring Cumbrian defence.

Miller missed with the goal kick but Town's 18-10 win had given them the League championship and Challenge Cup in consecutive seasons. A wonder achievement for a club just six years old.

Town's loose forward Billy Ivison stood head and shoulders above any player on the pitch and was a clear winner of the Lance Todd Trophy and the *Sporting Chronicle* commented: 'Never has one man dominated as Ivison did.'

Even though Featherstone Rovers were beaten by Workington Town in the 1952 final they returned to a big welcome from the pit village.

CHAPTER 40

A NOSE FOR SUCCESS

In post-war Britain the old and the new often stood side by side. The contrast was particulary marked as the country emerged into a newly shaped world. His Majesty King George VI had died during 1952 and early in 1953 Princess Elizabeth was the monarch awaiting coronation. The new order was ready to move in.

While the nation mourned the loss of the King, who had seen them through the trauma of the Second World War, and looked with interest at their future monarch, Rugby League was enjoying a golden spell.

Huddersfield had manufactured another great team which stood in the same kind of light as their 1914-1921 and 1933 teams. It was a superb footballing machine but its heart was imported from Australia. After the Second World War, an international signing ban was imposed to save the Australian game from being savaged by the demands of the British clubs but before it could be fully implemented Huddersfield had signed three players who were to become legends; full-back Johnny Hunter, winger Lionel Cooper and stand-off half Pat Devery. Their names are still spoken of in awe and respect even though Huddersfield has fallen from grace in Rugby League terms.

The pulling power of Huddersfield in the early 1950s was such that they were able to sign All Black winger Peter Henderson and powerful former Scottish Rugby Union international forward Dave Valentine as a loose forward.

Their team was also constructed of players acquired from all over the United Kingdom; their scrum half was Welshman Billy Banks, captain and centre Cumbrian Russ Pepperell, and prop Ted Slevin, a creative footballer, was signed from Wigan.

Across the other side of the Pennines St Helens had left the Rugby League fraternity open mouthed in July 1952 when they persuaded Jim Sullivan to leave his beloved Wigan to take over as their first-ever full time manager-coach. Nobody could accept that Sullivan and Wigan could be separated but the offer of a seven-year contract and bonuses for Cup and top-four placings quite clearly appealed to the Welsh legend.

Huddersfield took the Yorkshire Cup early in the season by beating Batley 18-8 while St Helens were defeated by Leigh in the Lancashire Cup final. Both clubs had, therefore, established a track record in knockout cup matches for the season.

In the first round, first leg against Castleford, Huddersfield ran in eight tries in their 36-14 home win but had a much tougher 6-2 win in the second leg. At Wheldon Road their points came from two Cooper tries, one of which gave him his 1,000th point for the club enabling him to join such illustrious figures as Ben Gronow, Albert Rosenfeld, Alex Fiddes and Jeff Bawden in Fartown history books.

A home win over Barrow in the second round brought 18-year-old stand-off half Peter Ramsden into the spotlight and he scored one of Huddersfield's six tries. His scoring ability was to be a great asset to the claret and golds at Wembley.

Huddersfield had to come from behind in the third round to beat Bradford Northern while the hero of their

Huddersfield and Wigan players descend from the old dressing rooms at Bradford's Odsal Stadium for the 1953 semi-final.

Huddersfield trainer Bill Smith leads Peter Ramsden off the field for treatment to a broken nose in the 1953 final.

7-0 semi-final win over Wigan was skipper Pepperell, who had to have two stitches inserted in a head wound before returning to play a leading role in the match.

St Helens dumped Oldham and Belle Vue Rangers off the Cup trail in the first two rounds before coming up against Leigh at Hilton Park in the third round when their 12-3 win was sweet revenge for that county cup final defeat.

At half-time in their semi-final St Helens trailed 3-2 after winger Brian Bevan had scored a try for Warrington and the end of the Wembley trail seemed in sight until George Langfield, nicknamed 'the Man with the Gold Boot', surprised everybody by launching a massive drop goal to give Saints a 4-3 lead.

It broke the Warrington resistance and St Helens booked their second appearance at Wembley and their fourth appearance in a Challenge Cup final. They were, however, still seeking their first win.

Television was still in its infancy and Rugby League was clearly suspicious of the new-fangled method of broadcasting. For many years the sport

believed that the medium was a curse on its gate-taking ability but the advent of sponsorship substantially changed their stance in the late 1970s.

But that was in the future; in 1953 the League banned television cover-

age of the final allowing just match commentary on the Home Service of BBC Radio.

This meeting of giants from either side of the Pennines, however, did not need any real selling and there was a massive following from St Helens alone. In the second volume of his history of the club, historian Alex Service, reveals that the fans made their way to Wembley with the help of 13 charter trains and at least 240 motor coaches; they contributed a large proportion of the 89,588 crowd who packed Wembley.

The final will, however, carry a controversial tag as long as the game of Rugby League is played. It was the day that Saints became Sinners.

Ramsden will always have reason

Three Huddersfield players tackle a lone St Helens attacker in the 1953 final.

Huddersfield captain Russell Pepperell leaves Wembley arena with the Cup in 1953.

to remember the final because it was played on 25 April 1953, his 19th birthday, and he was to have a decisive say in the destination of the Challenge Cup although after six minutes he had to leave the field with blood streaming from his nose after a collision with Saints centre Don Gullick.

The Lancastrians had clearly chosen to take a physical approach towards the Huddersfield attacking machine. After three minutes treatment on the touch line the young stand-off pluckily returned to the game with his nose plugged and, in the 29th minute, he cut through the St Helens defence to score the opening try of the game. Pat Devery kicked the goal.

Argument about that touch down continues, even today. St Helens claimed that, before he got the ball down on the line, Ramsden had been held in a tackle by prop forward Alan Prescott. But referee George Phillips, who was right on top of the incident, allowed the score to stand.

Although the television cameras were not present, the cinema newsreel equipment was in place and their footage revealed that St Helens protests did have some substance. Nevertheless the referee's decision was final and he did not have the benefit of any replay facility so the try stood.

Langfield's boot claimed two points for St Helens with a penalty in the 38th minute and, from the kick off, Saints equalised with a try through Welshman Steve Llewellyn. Langfield's goalkick failed.

St Helens took the lead for the first time in the 58th minute when Langfield scored a try which he failed to convert and it took Huddersfield seven minutes to correct that situation.

The little man from Maesteg, scrum half Banks, scooted in for a try and Cooper, who had taken over as Huddersfield's goalkicker from Devery who had injured a thigh, landed the conversion to put the Yorkshiremen back in front at 10-8.

Langfield, the man who changed the course of the semi-final with Warrington with a drop goal, struck again eight minutes from time with a drop effort that tied the score at 10-10. But Ramsden assured himself of the Lance Todd Trophy and the Cup for Huddersfield when, after Valentine and Jim Bowden had inter-passed, the birthday boy raced in for a try with five minutes of the match remaining. Cooper tacked on the conversion points.

St Helens lost more than the final. Their 'strong arm' tactics were heavily criticised and they fuelled discussion for years to come.

But the Saints had to wait just seven days for their revenge. They faced Huddersfield in the semi-final of the championship play off at Knowsley Road and sent them back to Yorkshire with their tails between their legs following a ten-try 46-0 defeat.

And they went on to beat Halifax in the final to win the League Championship.

Centre Pat Devery sends the ball sailing between the St Helens posts in the 1953 final.

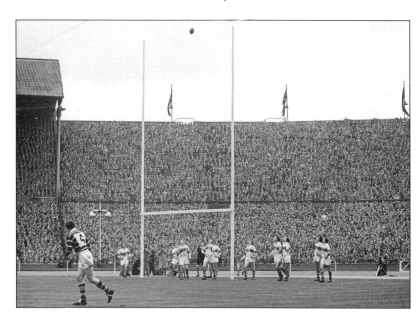

CHAPTER 41

THE REPLAY

Every generation can pinpoint a notable occasion where just about everybody can remember where they were at the time. For the Rugby League enthusiast of the 1950s only one question really mattered: 'Where were you the night of the Challenge Cup replay at Bradford's Odsal Stadium?'

It was one of those rare occasions when the whole nation took notice of something that happened in Rugby League. The like of that night had never been seen before and it has never been seen since.

It was the first time that a Challenge Cup final had needed a replay to reach a settlement since the draw between Leeds and Hull. The final on 24 April had been a major anti-climax.

Halifax had qualified for their ninth Challenge Cup final by putting out Dewsbury, Keighley, Wigan and Hunslet, while Warrington disposed of Bramley, Oldham, York and then Leeds in the semi-final.

The final was a terrific disappointment for all concerned. It ended in a 4-4 draw with former Newport Rugby Union ace Tyssul Griffiths kicking two goals for Halifax and Harry Bath, Warrington's Australian second row forward, cancelling them out with two for the Wire. Extra-time was not allowed and the replay was scheduled for Odsal Stadium, home of Bradford Northern, on Wednesday, 5 May.

Putting the game at the Yorkshire stadium put the Challenge Cup final within reach of every fan who could either finish work in time to make Bradford or take a day off.

In the early 1950s there were no motorways and, even though the vast majority of people still did not possess their own cars, the traffic built up.

Rugby League spectators are a pretty orderly but determined lot and they set off for Bradford in numbers to see this game.

Warrington, after playing in the Challenge Cup final, had returned north to overcome St Helens in the semi-final of the Championship play-off. Their success attracted a big following and the traffic snaked its way across the Pennines towards Odsal. At the same time the Halifax fans, who had the advantage of living just over the hill from Bradford, set off and the inevitable happened; a massive traffic jam.

It reached such proportions that, at one stage, the jam stretched the 20-plus miles back across the hills to Oldham. That was the main route across from Lancashire and so many people wanted to reach the game that they headed, lemming-like for the same route.

Odsal Stadium is a natural bowl built in a stream valley which had been the site of a Bradford Corporation rubbish tip. It is possible, even

today, to drive past and not know that such an impressive stadium is lurking below eye level.

The first game was played at the stadium in 1934 and, in 1951, it became the first stadium in either Rugby League or Association Football to possess floodlights outside London.

The stadium had staged many of Rugby League's biggest matches before 1954 with huge crowds and the League must have been aware that many people would want to see the game. It is a fair assumption that even they were overwhelmed by the sheer demand of people who wanted to see the encounter.

The official gate for the game was declared at 102,575, a world record for a Rugby match that stands unchallenged today, however, the unofficial gate, would be far, far more because the police and stadium officials were unable to prevent people from illegally breaking into the stadium.

The fans had been queuing for four hours before the 7pm kick-off and every available bus and private car was brought out to take people to Bradford.

The Halifax team bus was snagged up in the traffic too and it took a police escort bringing them on the wrong side of the road all the way to get them to Odsal in time to play. It is estimated that there were 60,000 people in the stadium before 6pm.

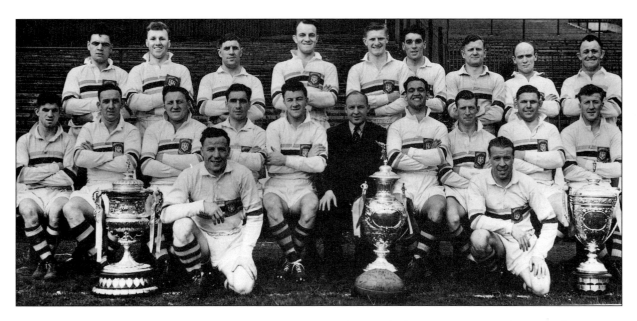

Warrington, who emerged as winners after the classic 1954 Challenge Cup final replay with Halifax.

The match traffic mingled with the Bradford rush-hour traffic and, gradually, everything ground to a halt. It was such a wretched situation and some fans from Lancashire never actually got to the game. Warrington historian Ernie Day even remembers that some people from Warrington, who realised that they were not going to gain admission, went around houses in Bradford asking to be allowed to listen to the radio coverage.

Inside Odsal there was pandemonium. While there were no reports of injuries the ambulance crews reported 200 cases of fainting and many of the people, even inside the stadium, never actually saw the game. There were simply too many of them packed inside for everybody to get a viewing point.

After the 4-4 draw at Wembley the two teams produced a close encounter of the second kind. At half-time Warrington led 3-2 and centre Jim Challinor, who was later to coach Great Britain, scored a ninth-minute try while Griffiths hit the target with a 39th minute penalty.

Warrington put on another surge in the 57th minute with a penalty by Bath but Halifax stayed in contention, when four minutes later, the accurate Griffiths kicked another penalty.

The issue was finally settled 12 minutes from time when Gerry Helme, the Warrington scrum half, went in for a try in spite of stumbling over the turf which was laid to provide the pitch over the speedway track which surrounded the playing area.

It was enough to give Helme the Lance Todd Trophy and he became the first player to win the man of the match award twice, having won it for the first time in 1950.

There was a note of controversy in the final moments of the game. Halifax winger Arthur Daniels followed a Stan Kielty kick through and dived over the line for what looked to be a try. But, by the time referee Ron Gelder arrived on the scene, the winger had been turned on his back by Warrington and Mr Gelder ruled 'no try'.

The Halifax protests went unheard and at least one source claims that the touch judge told the referee a try had been scored, but Mr Gelder was not for turning.

Warrington had won the Challenge Cup for the fourth time and they went on to complete the double beating the luckless Halifax 8-7 in the championship play-off final at Manchester City Association Football club's Maine Road ground.

It was later revealed that for the four games, the Cup final at Wembley, the championship semi-final, the Cup final replay and the Championship final the Warrington players picked up £140. Great value even in the 1950s when a man's weekly wage packet was still only worth £5-£7.

This was the last season in which two-legged first rounds were played. They were consigned to the history books in a season when Whitehaven beat Wakefield Trinity in the first round after being 11 points down in the first leg, which was believed to be a record.

CHAPTER 42

ROUND THE HORNE

Willie Horne, Barrow Rugby League club and Wembley were inextricably linked. The little master craftsmen ensured that his home-town club made it through to three Wembley finals in one of the game's golden eras, the 1950s.

The little stand-off was a Rugby League artist. In spite of the fact that he was so slight at 5 foot 9 inches and 12 stone wet through, he was a genius. His passing was superbly accurate while his round-the-corner kicking style was his trademark throughout the world of Rugby League.

For placed kicks on the ground he used to approach the ball with an arced run and the accuracy of the style has inspired many people to imitate him with greater or lesser degrees of success.

By the time Barrow had played in the 1951 Wembley defeat by Wigan, Willie had toured Australia and New Zealand in 1946 and 1950 and was an established star player under whose leadership Barrow were a force to be reckoned with in Rugby League.

If Horne was the cutting edge of the Barrow team then Jack Grundy was the bludgeon. Signed from St Helens in 1951, the balding second row forward was known for his aggressive, robust approach to the game.

He was the complete opposite to his skipper and a claimant to the periodically awarded title, the 'Iron Man

of Rugby League'. In fact his approach to the game was not appreciated by a French touch judge in a Great Britain Test against France.

The official took such exception to the Barrow forward that he took a corner flag out of the ground and brought it crashing down on Grundy's bald pate! He was a real powerhouse in both attack and defence who made 12 consecutive appearances for Great Britain during the 1950s.

Both players contributed to the balanced Barrow team. While Horne was the dancing master for a back division that contained international centre Phil Jackson and winger Frank Castle, the unmistakable figure of Grundy was part of a tough, mobile back three with Reg Parker, who was later to be a director at Blackpool Borough, chairman of the Rugby League and a manager of the Great Britain and Wales touring teams, and Bill Healey.

They took the scenic route to the semi-finals with away wins over Dewsbury, Salford and Rochdale Hornets in the qualifying ties and then they qualified for their third Wembley final when they beat Hunslet 9-6.

Workington Town returned to Wembley after a three-year absence. This time they arrived without their coach and mentor of their formative years, Gus Risman. He had left the club under a cloud and been replaced

by a man who returned to his Cumbrian roots, Jim Brough, the former Leeds and Great Britain full-back.

While Barrow had not seen anything of their Craven Park home Workington Town never had to leave their Cumbrian outpost. Amateurs Dewsbury Celtic, Leeds and St Helens all had fruitless journeys to Derwent Park before Town qualified to face Featherstone Rovers in a repeat of their 1952 final in the semi-final at Headingley and went through on a 13-2 scoreline.

While Risman was gone, Workington had remained a formidable team. Ike Southward, Australian Tony Paskins and England international centre Eppie Gibson remained the backbone of the three-quarter division while 18-year-old giant Brian Edgar was gradually taking over from the veteran Norman Herbert in the second row. He was one leg of a back three that was completed by Australian Johnny Mudge and Billy Ivison.

The Wembley final was still presenting difficulties between the Rugby League and the BBC. The Corporation wanted to broadcast the game live, either on television or radio, and the League, still believing that the attendance would be adversely affected, fought against that ambition.

Many supporters of the game complained to the League and secretary

Barrow skipper Willie Horne's moment of triumph after the 1955 win over Workington Town at Wembley.

Bill Fallowfield explained what had happened. He said: 'The BBC's original offer was £350 to televise the game or £450 plus a three-year contract. The Rugby League thought that £1,000 should be the minimum.

'The BBC then offered £1,000, but not only wanted a three-year contract for the final, but exclusive rights to any other matches in that period. The Rugby League wanted the freedom to approach the commercial television companies.

'The sound broadcast fee was usually 50 guineas (£52.50) for 80 minutes play but the League again thought it was about time that it was increased and wanted 100 guineas (£105.00) but the BBC said no.'

And, so the final, which had been televised to the London area in 1952, was to remain hidden from the television screen for another three years when the BBC paid £2,000 and then £2,500 in 1959. It has been televised live ever since.

Such was the appeal of the final that the coal mines which were still open in West Cumbria – there are no pits operating in the area today – could only find enough men to operate skeleton staffs and output was expected to slump.

Town delayed the selection of their team until an hour before the kick off on 30 April. Both Herbert and winger Bill Ivill failed to recover from injury in time and that let Edgar into the final while stand-off Ken Faulder had to play out on the wing with Bill Wookey in at number six.

Barrow's 22-year-old centre Jackson had been given special permission to leave his army unit to join Barrow for their build up to the final and they took the unusual step of announcing

The Barrow squad who completed the job in the 1955 Challenge Cup campaign.

The Cumbrian heroes. Workington Town the beaten 1955 finalists.

their team at a reserve team game against Salford when 6,000 people were present.

The two teams exchanged more than the usual pleasantries in the first half with Paskins giving Town the lead in the fifth minute and Horne putting Barrow level with a penalty nine minutes later.

The real action started in the second half. Horne hit a second penalty after 46 minutes and followed up with a drop goal a minute later. While all that was happening John 'Sol' Roper, the 18-year-old Workington scrum half, was lying on the floor with an injured shoulder and had to be stretchered off.

Workington were forced to shuffle their team and, as they were sorting themselves out, Barrow grabbed two tries, the first through veteran hooker Vince McKeating and the second by centre Dennis, both of which were converted by Horne.

Crippled Town battled back and Faulder took advantage of a Gibson pass to score a 68th minute try to which Paskins added the goal points. Nine minutes from time Barrow worked their third try of the final through winger Castle and Horne hit the goal target for the sixth time to equal the record set by Huddersfield skipper Len Bowkett in 1933.

Cumbrian grit kept Town going through those dark moments and their pride was maintained when Gibson shot through to score a try which Paskins improved. But they were still on the wrong end of a 21-12 scoreline.

While Horne's prompting and goal kicking had played its usual role in the Barrow performance, the prestigious Lance Todd man of the match trophy went to the grafting Grundy. A reward for service under the flag. His workrate had turned the game Barrow's way.

CHAPTER 43

SAINTS AT LAST

Fate brought Steve Llewellyn to St Helens and Rugby League. In 1947 Steve, or to use his correct christian name Stuart, was the Monmouthshire county right winger playing with Abertillery Rugby Union club and the professional game-was not even a consideration for him.

A chance visit by a delegation from Lancashire club St Helens changed all that when they arrived to watch another Abertillery three-quarter called Terry Cook. In a game, against unrecorded opposition, Llewellyn played a major role with his powerful running in wet, soggy conditions. The professionals were impressed and switched their interest from Cook to Llewellyn.

Saints' Welsh scout Arthur Fairfax opened the negotiations on behalf of the club and, eventually, Llewellyn was persuaded that his future lay with Rugby League and, of course, the Knowsley Road club. He joined them in exchange for £600 compensation covering the loss of his amateur status.

Coincidentally he signed on the same day as another Welshman, Newport forward George Parsons. Together they moved north and, unlike many other signings from the principality, both achieved success.

They suffered disappointment at Wembley in 1953 when Saints were beaten by Peter Ramsden's Huddersfield but the arrival of Jim Sullivan as

St Helens coach created the right kind of environment for another attempt at winning the Challenge Cup for the first time.

How ironic that St Helens, who played in that first Challenge Cup final against Batley, should still be seeking the ultimate breakthrough almost 60 years later. And Llewellyn knew how important breaking that virtual hoodoo was to St Helens.

The former Welsh Guards sergeant paved the way to Wembley. In the first round the Saints beat eventual league champions Warrington 15-6 but in the second round they ran riot hammering a weak Castleford 48-5 with Llewellyn grabbing six tries by himself.

He recalled: 'In fact I could have had nine but the referee disallowed three touch downs.'

A third round landslide win of 53-6 against Bradford Northern, when St Helens were at home for the third successive round, saw the Lancashire club break a long Challenge Cup drought against the Yorkshire club. Winger Frank Carlton scored the first try against them in six hours and ten minutes in Cup Rugby and they added ten more to make up for lost time.

The semi-final against Barrow remains one of the classic confrontations of its kind. After 80 minutes of toil and effort at Swinton's Station Road they remained locked at 5-5.

The replay was scheduled to be played at Central Park, Wigan on the following Wednesday. They did not possess floodlights in those days so the kick off was timed for five o'clock. By the appointed time there were 44,731 people packed in and, after 80 minutes of effort in the Central Park mud, there were still no points on the board.

A decision was essential. Extra-time followed and in the 89th minute of the game Llewellyn made a crucial break. He handed-off Barrow winger Frank Castle, avoided a challenge from another defender and then, after a 40 metre sprint, shrugged off another lunging challenge by Castle to go over for the first try of the game.

stand-off Austin Rhodes landed the goal and Saints had established a psychologial advantage. Prop forward Jack Grundy, who ironically had been sold to Barrow from St Helens a few seasons earlier, kept the match at fever pitch with a unconverted try but Llewellyn's touch down proved to be the decisive factor as St Helens returned to Wembley after three years for their fifth Challenge Cup final appearance.

Halifax were at a high point in their history. Their team was packed with international players, eight of them having played at Wembley in a final, and they gained their record fifth visit to Wembley by removing

Widnes, Workington Town, Leeds and Wigan on the way.

Interestingly, the two clubs faced each other in the championship play-off in the run up to the final and Halifax won 23-8 at Thrum Hall. The game proved expensive for Saints who suffered injuries to key players, stand-off Todder Dickinson, loose forward Vince Karalius and second row forward Walter Delves.

Vincent Peter Patrick Karalius, an outstanding forward of the age was a Widnes-born son of a Scottish father, Irish mother and Lithuanian grand-parents, suffered a head laceration but he was fit in time for the big game. Dickinson and Delves failed to make it through and their places went to Bill Finnan and Roy Robinson respectively.

Defeat at Thrum Hall might have been expensive but it proved invaluable at Wembley as Llewellyn explains: 'Although we lost we came away from the match knowing just what they could do and very confident that we would beat them at Wembley.'

Both of the final teams were riding on the crest of the wave. Halifax, winners of the Yorkshire Cup, after a replay with Hull, and the League, had an all-international front row of hooker and captain Alvin Ackerley and props Jack Wilkinson and Peter Henderson, while Jim Sullivan had added the steel of Karalius to the pace of Llewellyn and Carlton and power of Alan Prescott, who captained his club, county and country.

In the final on 28 April neither side gave an inch never mind a point in the first half and by half-time there

Tommy Lynch, the Halifax winger, finds the attention of Frank Carlton (left) and Brian Howard (right) too formidable.

was no-score. Then St Helens reached out to put one hand on the Cup. First Carlton shot down one wing for a try which Rhodes goaled and then Llewellyn crowned a super Challenge Cup year by streaking through for his second Wembley try (he had scored against Huddersfield in 1953) which Rhodes also converted.

Halifax full-back Tyssul Griffiths kicked a controversial penalty in the 73rd minute. There was open dissent among the Halifax players who thought that the decision to kick for goal was wrong and that it would have been better, even at that late stage, to keep pressing for a try.

In the dying seconds of the game Saints captain Alan Prescott crashed over for a try to complete the 13-2 scoreline. The burly prop's touch down must have stung Halifax because he had joined them during the War as a winger and was transferred to

St Helens for £2,500 in the early months of peace.

While the St Helens players remained in London until Monday before returning for the victory celebrations Llewellyn had gone home the day earlier.

'I was a schoolteacher,' said Steve, 'And I had to be back at work on Monday morning. But I still had a share of the Cup celebrations because I went to join the team at Liverpool and returned to St Helens in triumph on the special bus.'

There were more disappointments for Halifax two weeks later ... they were beaten 10-9 by Hull in the championship final at Maine Road, Manchester!

CHAPTER 44

WEMBLEY'S MENTAL BLOCKAGE

Some of the best players in Rugby League have never appeared in a Challenge Cup final. There is no guarantee of that privilege in a professional contract. On the same basis there are those players who have had just one shot at playing in British Rugby League's annual game of games. One such man is Lewis Jones.

The Jones boy is, without doubt, one of the biggest captures from Welsh Rugby Union in the history of such dealings. His switch to Rugby League was totally unexpected and, until that move in November 1952, he had been the golden boy of Welsh Rugby. He had been destined for stardom even in Rugby Union.

He was born in the west Wales village of Gorseinon and went to the same school as the famous Welsh half-back Haydn Tanner. Association Football had been his speciality at school while he also showed great promise as both a Rugby player and cricketer.

It was as a Rugby player that he was to make most progress. In 1947-48 he played at full-back for Welsh Schools against France and his captain that day was Carwyn James, the man destined to coach Wales and the triumphant 1971 British Lions team in New Zealand.

In January 1950 when playing for Neath he received his call to join Welsh sport's list of immortals. He was selected to play for Wales against England at Twickenham. The Welsh won 11-5 and it was only their second win over the English at the headquarters of the Union game.

Inspired by such a start Wales went on to collect their first Grand Slam since 1911 and young Jones played in all four matches; two in the centre and two at full-back. But his relationship with the Welsh selectors was hardly consistent. He was dropped from the side after a bad defeat by Scotland and brought back for the 1951 game against the Springboks. By March 1952 he had won 10 caps and was generally recognised as being one of the game's major discoveries.

His prowess had been recognised by the British Lions, although somewhat belatedly, when, aged 19, he was called out to New Zealand as a replacement for an injured player. He played in seven tour games and returned with 92 points to his credit; only six points fewer than Malcolm Thomas, the tour's leading scorer.

It cost Leeds £6,000 to tempt Jones into the professional ranks. His move sent Wales into depression and gave the Headingley followers a new idol. Although he had started as a Neath player after he had completed his national service in the Royal Navy he had moved to Llanelli and the reaction to his decision to turn professional was reported in one newspaper:

'Llanelli secretary Mr Sid Williams, had nothing to say, but decided to go to the pictures to "drown my sorrows"'.

For his first match before the Leeds public against Keighley 17,000 curious people came to see what the expensive Welshman could do and he returned seven goals as Leeds won 56-7. The downside of professional Rugby came when Jones, playing his eighth game, broke his arm in a fair tackle by John Etty of Batley.

It was to be the base line in his career. It became quite clear that the Jones boy had chosen well. Points and honours flowed his way. He was selected for the 1954 tour of Australia and, although Great Britain lost the series 2-1, it was a personal triumph for Jones. He kicked 127 goals and returned to the UK with a record 278 points to his credit.

By 1957 Jones had arrived at the highpoint in his professional career. Leeds reached the Challenge Cup final for the first time in ten years and Britain were due to defend the World Cup they won in 1954 in Australia.

The passage to Wembley was not easy for the men from Headingley. A first-round win over Wigan was followed by a more comfortable experience at Warrington in the second round. But the third round and semi-

Leeds number two Delmos Hodgkinson is the final barrier to a Barrow drive in the 1957 final.

final proved less than easy as they travelled first to Thrum Hall to beat Halifax and then endured a torrid semi-final against Whitehaven at Odsal Stadium.

Jones said: 'The semi-final was particulary difficult for Leeds. In those days there was no limit to the number of tackles for which you could retain the ball. All the acting half-back had to do was pass the ball and the next player would drive it forward.

'Whitehaven were very good at that and, for 20 minutes, all we could do was keep tackling because we simply could not take the ball away from them. Eventually they made a mistake and our scrum half Jeff Stevenson took us through to Wembley with a drop goal that saw us win 10-9.'

Barrow, who had won the Cup by beating Workington in 1955, had obviously acquired a taste for Wembley. It was their third visit of the 1950s. They hammered amateur club Wakefield Loco 53-12 in the first round and then picked their way through the rest of the rounds by beating Castleford, Huddersfield and Leigh after a replay in the semi-finals.

The scene was set on 11 May 1957 for Lewis Jones, one of the greatest ever Welshmen to play Rugby League, to take the stage at Wembley. There is, however, a aspect of the Challenge Cup final that has been known to affect even the most hardened professional...nerves.

Jones takes up the story: 'Here I was, a player who had played on all the big grounds in the world both in Union and League, and yet when we stood in the tunnel at Wembley my legs just turned to jelly. You stand down there and look out into this huge bowl. All you can see is a bright light and then you go out into a sea of

faces and a massive barrier of sound.

'It had a devastating effect on me. It was the first time that I ever thought about the effect of my game and what it all meant.

'It was all over so quickly. I know that I didn't play well and I simply cannot remember much of the game.'

Barrow had, surprisingly, opted to play second row forward Reg Parker at prop, a decision hardly calculated to please the resident of that position, 32-year-old former Wigan forward Frank Barton who was expecting to make a record-breaking fifth appearance at Wembley. He never played again.

Leeds edged ahead when their fullback Pat Quinn scored a 23rd minute try and, the effect of the occasion on Jones was clearly illustrated when he missed a conversion chance.

Jones did play a leading role in the creation of the second Leeds try a minute into the second half when he sent their 18-year-old winger Delmos Hodgkinson over the Barrow line but he still could not put his kicking game together, missing the conversion.

The immaculate Willie Horne, who was skippering Barrow for the third time at Wembley, hit a penalty to make the score 6-2 to Leeds and then controversy played its hand.

Jack Grundy, the man of the match in the 1955 final, amazingly passed the ball to Leeds forward Don Robinson. Barrow were defending their line when Grundy blundered but

he later claimed that he heard a call for a pass and thought it was from a Barrow player. It is against the law of the game to pretend to be a member of the opposing team and shout for the ball.

Robinson's 54th minute try took Leeds into a 9-2 lead, Jones failed with his conversion again, and that proved to be insurmountable for Barrow who, in spite of a 64th minute try by centre Peter Jackson and a Horne conversion, were still trailing 9-7 at the end.

Fate had decided that the former Welsh golden boy Lewis Jones was never to play in a Challenge Cup final again. Although he did not play well, by his own admission, how sad that the curse of big match tension should have robbed his memory of his only appearance at Wembley.

Lewis Jones, Leeds' Welsh star, who suffered from Wembley nerves.

CHAPTER 45

MORE WIGAN GLORY

Eric Ashton's 14-year career with Wigan started on the sacred turf of Scottish Rugby Union, Murrayfield. A tip-off from one of the Wigan faithful that a useful player was playing for one of the Army teams sent the Central Park club scouts scurrying north of the border.

They liked what they saw and in 1955 they signed the gifted, willowy centre three-quarter. It was to be the start of a very happy relationship but the fact that he signed for Wigan must have caused consternation down the road at St Helens because Ashton came from the glass-making town.

Wigan were so confident of his ability that they put him straight into their first team. He played on the opposite wing to a powerful Welshman, Billy Boston, who had made such a startling impression on the professional game when he came north the previous year. The man from Tiger Bay had played just six games of Rugby League when he was selected for the 1954 tour of Australia and New Zealand.

The two men were, however, destined to spend virtually 12 years playing alongside each other; Ashton as the creative, footballing centre who set up the chances for Boston, the explosive, powerful running winger to whom tries were the very food of life.

By the time the 1957-58 Cup campaign started they were recognised as an outstanding pair in an outstanding Wigan team. The club had dominated Rugby League from 1945 until the early 1950s when they started rebuilding their side.

In 1957 the blending process was virtually complete with Ashton emerging as a driving force in the side. Wigan were able to fully harness his leadership qualities when team captain, full-back Don Platt, suffered a serious injury and never returned to the side. Ashton dropped naturally into the captaincy role.

Under his leadership Wigan were to play at Wembley six times while he allied his inspirational qualities with his own playing ability; he was a prolific try and goal scorer in his own right.

Ashton's control of the team was complete by the start of the 1958 Challenge Cup and Whitehaven were swept aside 39-10 in the first round, Boston and Ashton both scoring two tries, while the visit to Wakefield in the second round proved more troublesome, Wigan emerging with an 11-5 victory with Ashton and Boston both among the tries.

Ashton recalls that the third-round draw was hardly kind to Wigan. He said: 'We were at Oldham and nobody wanted that one. At that time they had a wonderful side and the prospect of playing at Watersheddings did not appeal to us.'

Wigan, who had been beaten by Oldham in the Lancashire Cup earlier in the season, carried it off winning 8-0 but if they thought that they had finished with east Lancashire they were mistaken because they were drawn against Rochdale Hornets in the semi-final at Swinton.

Again Ashton, who later coached Wigan, remembered: 'We were really struggling that day. Rochdale had been the surprise team of the season and they had us on the rack.

'It was not one of our better performances and yet I suppose it is the mark of the good side that they can win even though they do not play particulary well. We came close to missing out on Wembley against Hornets and it took a great try by our international wingman Mick Sullivan in the second half to turn the game our way.'

Unusually for a Wigan club, who had recruited heavily from outside their town to maintain the strength of the team, they arrived at Wembley for the fourth time with a pack of forwards acquired from the Wigan area.

It contained players of rare talent and ability like Brian McTigue, one of Britain's most creative footballers, and sturdy second row Frank Collier, who was known to break into song during even the toughest of scrummages.

Wigan's preparations were interrupted at a vital moment when their 19-year-old loose forward Roy Evans, who had come into the side that season, was stricken by influenza which verged on pneumonia. His place in the side went to Bernard McGurrin, who had been playing in the Wigan second team.

McGurrin was a Wigan man, who had signed for the Central Park club in the same year as Ashton but without the same success, and he was plunged into the pressure of a Challenge Cup final at Wembley.

Workington Town were still a considerable force in the professional game and they worked their way through to face Wigan. They resisted a brave attempt by Leigh in the first round match at Derwent Park and were taken the full distance at Widnes in the second round where they won 8-5.

Town qualified for Wembley for the third time in their 13-year history by dumping Warrington out of the third round and Featherstone Rovers, after a titanic struggle, in the semi-final at Odsal.

The Cumbrian horde was still coached by legendary former Leeds full-back Jim Brough while their traditional forward strength was maintained by such players as prop Norman Herbert and second-row combination of 21-year-old Brian Edgar and Cec Thompson.

Like most other great Rugby teams they possessed halfbacks of craft and graft in Harry Archer and Sol Roper while their cutting edge was on the right wing in the craggy form of Ike Southward, who was one of the most effective finishers of the era.

Television returned to Wembley in 1958. After the broadcast of the 1952 final the League had rejected approaches from the television authorities for even partial coverage. The game's administrators were afraid that live television coverage would adversly effect the gate-taking potential of the Wembley occasion after all their hard work of establishing the Challenge Cup final as a national sporting event.

And those fears looked well founded because the final on 10 May 1958 attracted 66,109 people, the lowest gate return since 1946. Televising the game had clearly influenced the spectators, especially those from Cumberland. One Workington coach owner reported that he had sent eight full vehicles for Town's previous final ap-

A cartoonist's view of Wigan prop John Barton who played at Wembley in 1958.

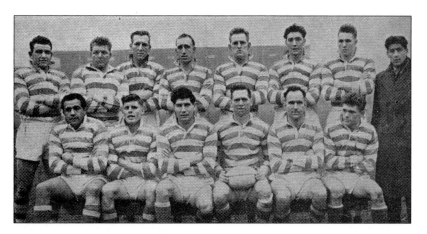

Wigan in 1958 with Bernard McGurrin, a late replacement for the Wembley final, on the far left of the back row.

pearances in 1952 and 1955 but for 1958 he had filled just two. Wigan, normally a hotbed of support, succeeded in selling 6,200 tickets while in 1951 they had sold 11,000 in one day.

Ashton, who had reached the final in his first season as captain, recalled that Wigan did not have their own way in the final.

'Workington were a tough nut to crack in those days,' he said. 'We couldn't relax at any stage in the game because they kept coming at us.'

Fortunes swayed first one way and then the other. Southward took eleven minutes to make his presence felt when he went over for a try which he also converted. Wigan restored the balance six minutes later with a Sullivan try which full-back Jack Cunliffe converted.

And then Wigan edged in front in the 28th minute when prop John Barton went over for a try which again Cunliffe improved. But, if Wigan thought that they were establishing some breathing space they were wrong, because Southward hit a penalty after McTigue had been penalised for obstruction.

McTigue atoned for that misdemeanour when he dummied and side-stepped his way for a try in the 50th minute. Still Workington retained an influence in the game and Southward, after kicking a 61st minute penalty, almost took the Cup back to Derwent Park for the second time when he raced towards the Wigan line.

Ashton again takes up the story: 'Ike was a strong finisher and he was very close to our line when Norman Cherrington pushed him into touch. It was still anybody's game at that stage and a try against us would have been the end for us.' But Wigan held on to win 13-9.

'I don't know how to explain it,' he said. 'But as soon as the Challenge Cup comes around Wigan seem to add an extra dimension to their game. The Cup has a hold on the club that it just can't and won't shake off.'

Wigan proved their former captain's theory of excitement when they returned to Wembley in 1959. They were again a leading team playing at the very top of their form.

For Ashton and his team the critical point had been their third round visit to Halifax. They had beaten Leeds and Hunslet in the first two rounds and again the Wigan team leader explained: 'Halifax were a very strong side and we knew before we played them at Thrum Hall that if we won we would probably go back to Wembley.'

That gut reaction was borne out,

Wigan trounced the Thrum Hallers 26-0 and they went on to play Hull in the final after beating Leigh 5-0 in the semi-final at Swinton with Sullivan scoring the only try and their South African full-back Fred 'Punchy' Griffiths kicking the goal.

Wigan's relationship with the final and Wembley was growing by the year. They became the first club since Bradford Northern to return in successive years and it was their sixth appearance at Wembley.

Hull, once previous winners of the Cup and five times beaten finalists, were the first Humberside club to reach Wembley.

Blackpool Borough found the long trip across the country too much in the first round while Hull needed a replay to beat Wakefield Trinity in the second. Their third round presented a much different proposition because they had to play neighbours Hull KR.

The rivalry between the two Kingston upon Hull clubs is intense. The black and whites of Hull FC occupy the east side of the city while the red and whites of Rovers count their territory as the west bank of the River Hull which bisects the Yorkshire port as it flows into the River Humber.

The tie was staged at Hull's ground and Rovers went the way of all flesh as the black and whites ran away with the tie 23-9. Jim Drake, one of the dreaded twin brother forwards, scored one try while their outstanding loose forward Johnny Whiteley went over for two more.

At half-time the game was hanging in the balance at 5-4 but the powerful Hull pack sapped all the energy out of Rovers.

For the second successive season Featherstone Rovers reached the semi-final stage but they too fell victim to the Hull roll-up and the men from the Boulevard took the final place against Wigan.

Wigan had been the very model of consistency using the same team line for all of the qualifying rounds: Griffiths; Boston, Ashton, Holden, Sullivan; Bolton, Thomas; Bretherton, Sayer, Barton, Cherrington, McTigue, Evans.

For the final they had toyed with the idea of replacing 32-year-old Welsh scrum half Rees Thomas, who had won the Lance Todd Trophy as man of the match in 1959, with 19-year-old Terry Entwistle but, finally, they decided to stick with Thomas. There was also a doubt about Ashton. He had a leg injury and he needed a pain-killing injection to play.

Hull had no doubts about going for youth and they opted to play 19-year-old Arthur Keegan instead of Peter Bateson with whom he had been sharing the full-back role all season.

On the day the Hull pack failed to hit anything like its normal form and Wigan became the first side to win the Cup five times at Wembley.

It was one-way traffic in the first half as Keith Holden, Sullivan, Dave Bolton and Boston scored tries and Griffiths kicked four goals with only a Keegan penalty coming in reply. The young full-back hit two penalties early for Hull in the second half but they could not hold Wigan who pounded on for further tries by McTigue and Boston and two Griffiths goals.

Hull had the consolation of at least one try when scrum half Tom

A slice of the action from the 1958 final between Wigan and Workington Town.

Finn crossed the Wigan line with eight minutes of the game remaining and Keegan converted.

Wigan added even more entries in the record book. Their 30-13 victory was the largest the number of points scored by a winning side in a Wembley final and it was also the largest aggregate score.

For young Keegan, who was later to play for his country in Test Rugby, there was the consolation of a place in the record book too. His conversion to Finn's try was the 100th successful goal kick at Wembley.

CHAPTER 46

FAMILY FORTUNE

The Fox family from Yorkshire mining village Sharlston were destined to play substantial parts in the history and mystique of the Challenge Cup.

Although the eldest brother Peter failed to make the final as a player, he has shared in Rugby League's day of days as a coach with Featherstone Rovers while middle brother Don played a part in one of the all time Cup final legends. It was, however, the youngest brother, Neil, who became the most recognised of the trio and the one who made it to Wembley first.

Both Peter and Don joined their nearest professional club, Featherstone Rovers, and, for a while, it appeared as though Neil would follow them to Post Office Road. A Yorkshire Schoolboy representative, he joined the Rovers' under-18 team and went on to captain the side.

The short step from there to the professional club was blocked by their close rivals Wakefield Trinity. At the age of 16 in October 1955 he joined Featherstone's rivals and so began a relationship with both club and game that was to last for four decades.

In 1957-58 Neil established himself as a first-team player and he equalled or extended every record in the club's record book. His 344-point return for the campaign easily beat any previous record while his 32 tries in the season equalled Dennis Booker's record.

And the man who played as his wing partner, former Leeds player Fred Smith, also benefitted from the room Neil created by setting a new try scoring record of 38 the following season.

In his second full season as a professional, 1958-59, the international selectors could not resist Neil any longer and he was brought into the Great Britain team to face France for the first Test in Grenoble, scoring two tries.

Besides the acquisition of Fox and several other good young players from the Wakefield region, the Belle Vue club instituted a recruiting campaign. From Oldham they bought the legendary hard-man of the professional game loose forward Derek 'Rocky' Turner and Welsh forward Don Vines, while from Halifax they acquired teak-tough prop Jack Wilkinson, a veteran of two Wembley finals with the Thrum Hall club.

'It just felt right,' said Fox. 'We could feel in our bones that we were in at the start of something good. That something special was going to happen.'

Trinity must have bought an away-day ticket at the start of 1959-60 because they were drawn to travel in all three qualifying rounds. They returned from St Helens, Widnes and Whitehaven still in contention and were drawn against Featherstone in the semi-final at Odsal Stadium.

The rivalry between Trinity and pit village club Featherstone runs deep in that part of Yorkshire and it also brought two Fox brothers face to face because middle brother Don lined up for Rovers against Neil in front of 55,800 partisan supporters. Trinity won 11-2 giving Neil the family honour of a first appearance at Wembley.

Beaten Cup finalists usually vow that they 'will be back next year' in the aftermath of the defeat. Hull, however, meant it and, after their 1959 hammering by Wigan, they had the incentive of needing to restore their reputation.

They eliminated York and Keighley in the first two rounds and then had the satisfaction of beating their Wembley tormentors, Wigan, in the third round. They travelled into Lancashire for their semi-final against Oldham and returned to Yorkshire knowing that they, like General McArthur, were certain to return.

Trinity, however, arrived at Wembley with a psychologial and physical advantage. On the Saturday before the final they had given Hull a 24-4 roasting in the Championship play-off semi-final and as Fox says: 'We came away from that match knowing just what we had to do and supremely confident that we would win the Cup final'.

Hull's drive for the Cup and Championship had cost them dear. In the week before Wembley their first-team squad was decimated by injury so that, by the time they walked out to take on Wakefield, they had just five of the previous season's Cup final side still in the team.

They were like lambs to the slaughter. Trinity tore into Hull from the kick off and the patched-up Humbersiders simply could not hold them.

Fox was in his element. He had celebrated his 21st birthday just ten days before the final and was entering a long period in which he would be recognised as one of the foremost centre three-quarters of Rugby League's history.

What reserves of energy Hull had managed to accumulate were expended in the first half trying to keep the Trinity machine in check; Wakefield led 7-5 at half-time and Fox contributed to that scoreline with two penalties.

In the second half Trinity simply stepped on the accelerator and left Hull trailing behind. Fox was supreme. Two tries, one in the 45th

Wakefield's Keith Holliday scores Wembley's 100th try in the 1960 final against Hull.

Her Majesty the Queen presents the Cup to Wakefield Trinity's winning captain Derek Turner in 1960.

minute and the other in the 72nd minute, together with five conversions ensured that he became the recognised King of Wembley. How apt, therefore, that this should be the first final to be attended by Her Majesty the Queen.

Fox had established a new record for the number of points scored by one player at Wembley. This all-time best of 20 points from seven goals and two tries still stands today in spite of the fact that Rugby League increased the value of a try from three to four points in 1983.

Fox is philosophical about the feat and reasons that his early experience of playing for Great Britain was a major factor in his performance.

'I had been really nervous the first time I had played for Great Britain,' he said. 'Nothing ever matched that experience as far as I was concerned. Of course I was nervous at Wembley but no more than I was for any other big game.

'Other players in the Trinity team were much more affected by the match and the day than me because I had experienced other major matches.

'Wembley had not been enclosed totally with stand roofs at that stage but I don't really think that made any

difference to my goal-kicking. Like the rest of the Trinity team I was just so confident that we would win the Cup and played my normal game.'

Hull's only sop for becoming the first club to lose in successive Wembleys was that their Welsh hooker Tommy Harris won the Lance Todd Trophy as man of the match but he spoke for many on Humberside when he said: 'I'd rather have had the Cup.' It was also revealed later that gritty Harris had been concussed in the first half and his vision had been restricted to just one eye.

It was also little comfort that Trinity's 38-5 win went into the record books as the biggest winning score in Challenge Cup history. And it remains there today.

Hull's Mike Smith drafted in at the eleventh hour for injured second row forward Bill Drake also had an interesting record. The 22-year-old had been playing soccer the previous season and had made several impressive reserve team appearances. His first team debut was, however, at Wembley. It was a remarkable first even by Challenge Cup standards.

CHAPTER 47

THE MAN FROM BETHLEHEM

South Africa is a country of untold riches. As diamonds have been mined from its land so its people have produced generations of Rugby players. But while the minerals are always up for sale, only a small trickle of their Rugby talent has made its way to British Rugby League since just before the First World War.

St Helens, however, struck it rich in 1957 when they signed Karel Thomas – known as Tom – Van Vollenhoven. He was South Africa's 'Sportsman of the Year' and he became a legend.

It was an unlikely development for a child who had been medically banned from 'rough and tumble' sports at school because of a chest problem. He was born in Bethlehem, Orange Free State into a five-strong family of Dutch descent and once his chest problem had disappeared in the process of growing up, he became a Rugby player.

He started as a forward and developed into a three-quarter as he progressed. The discovery that he possessed outstanding speed came by accident in his final year at the Voortrekker High School. Although he was recognised as a middle distance runner, he was asked to make up the numbers in sprint training and stunned everybody by clocking 10.5 seconds for the 100 yards.

After leaving school he joined the South African police and that saw his Rugby career develop even more quickly because at the age of 17 he was selected to play for the Northern Transvaal state side.

Two years later he became a fully fledged international, a Springbok, and played against the British Lions. In the second Test Vollenhoven became a national hero after he grabbed a hat-trick of tries against the vaunted British winger Tony O'Reilly. The following year, 1956, he was part of the Springbok touring team of Australasia. The final Test in New Zealand was the last time he wore the famous green and gold jersey.

He left the police and moved to North Rhodesia to work in the mining industry but before he left Pretoria, however, came the meeting that was to take him to the north of England and Rugby League.

Former England and Lancashire wicket keeper George Duckworth was the baggage handler-scorer to the MCC team who played in Pretoria in 1956 and he met Van Vollenhoven. They discussed English Rugby League and Duckworth told the young Springbok that Warrington would be interested in him.

The Wire's interest never materialised but word of his willingness to listen to Rugby League offers must have spread because Wigan wrote offering him £2,000 to turn professional. It failed to impress him but, encouraged by his wife Leonie, he maintained the correspondence.

St Helens also joined the chase and their progressive chairman Harry Cook was not a man to let grass grow under his feet. Now the race was on between two of the biggest rivals in Rugby. St Helens had discovered that Wigan had made an offer and that their chairman, Bill Gore, was about to fly out to see Vollenhoven.

Cook did not allow this head start to deter him. He was mandated by the St Helens board of directors to compete with Wigan for the 22-year-old South African and set about finding an agent to put their case to Van Vollenhoven.

His method was ingenious. They discovered his whereabouts in Rhodesia and then contacted a number of education authorities. They discovered that an English-born teacher was working close to Van Vollenhoven's location and asked him to represent the St Helens club. Ironically the man came from Wigan!

Nevertheless he agreed to help and was instructed to find out just how much Wigan had offered. He was also told to top anything Wigan could put before Van Vollenhoven.

News that St Helens were interested had also reached Central Park and a telegram was despatched to

Van Vollenhoven; it read : 'We will increase any offer Saints make. Signed J.B. Wood, Wigan secretary.'

But they reckoned without an act of God. St Helens' agent was on his 300-mile journey to see Van Vollenhoven when Wigan sent their telegram via Salisbury. But their race against time ran out when the telegraph boy suffered a puncture on his way to the last delivery – Van Vollenhoven's house.

By the time he had repaired the

St Helens forward Ray French, now BBC television commentator, grins up at Wigan's Eric Ashton after a heavy tackle in the 1961 final.

puncture and made the delivery, the flying former policeman had given his word to join St Helens only a few minutes earlier.

Van Vollenhoven was an instant hit in Rugby League and he became a major attraction at any ground where St Helens played. The rivalry with Wigan remained, deep, bitter and emotional. In 1960-61 St Helens and Wigan were the two biggest names in the business and they played each other four times in the season.

The first meeting was in the Lancashire Cup and Saints emerged as winners as they did in the second meeting in, a league game. The third match took place slightly before the

Challenge Cup semi-finals and, this time, Wigan won. The fourth encounter was what amounted to the dream final at Wembley on 13 May 1961.

Saints needed a replay to beat Widnes in the first round and then straight wins over Castleford and Swinton took them through to the semi-final against Hull at Odsal. They cruised through to Wembley for the fourth time with a 26-9 victory.

Wigan matched Saints in the first round when they had to go to a replay to beat Leeds and then they marched through to the semi-final with victories over Wakefield Trinity and Salford. They stepped ahead of their great rivals after their semi-final triumph over Halifax because the Central Park club had reached Wembley for a record seventh time.

For Rugby League followers it was a match made in heaven. Both sides contained so many of the best players of the period. St Helens had the incomparable Alex Murphy at stand-off half, London-born prop Cliff Watson, the long-striding second row forward Dick Huddart and fearsome loose forward Vince Karalius.

Wigan, on the other hand, were able to call upon Billy Boston, Eric Ashton, former St Helens winger Frank Carlton, scheming-forward Brian McTigue and South African full-back Fred Griffiths.

Wembley was packed with a crowd of 94,672 on a beautiful sunny day and temperatures soared into the 90 degree fahrenheit range – hardly a day for playing a physically demanding game like Rugby League. The players, however, produced the kind of game to match the splendour of the occasion.

St Helens led 5-2 at half-time. Although Griffiths had given Wigan an early 2-0 lead with a penalty, Saints had fought their way back with a 32nd minute try by irrepressible Mur-

phy and an Austin Rhodes penalty from near the half-way line five minutes before the interval.

Griffiths cut their lead to a single point with his second penalty of the match five minutes into the second half and then came a try that earned itself a place in League legend for sheer beauty and precision.

A pass from McTigue to Collier went to ground off the big second row forward's body. Huddart dropped on the loose ball and moved on to centre Ken Large; he surged through the disorganised defence and passed to the supporting Van Vollenhoven.

The Springbok accelerated away down the wing only to find his way to Wigan line blocked by Griffiths. He swapped the ball back inside to Large who had continued his run just behind the South African; Ashton got back to pull Large down in a tackle but the centre returned the ball to Van Vollenhoven and, now the Springbok was able to bound clear racing round behind the posts for the killer try.

The try is a treasured memory captured by television film. Rhodes kicked the goal and then added a penalty. Wigan pushed forward and, a minute from time, Griffiths landed his third penalty of the game to make it 12-6 to Saints. It came too late for Wigan to save the match and it was St Helens captain Vince Karalius who received the Cup from Lord Derby.

THE RUGBY FOOTBALL LEAGUE

FOUNDED 1895

PATRON: HER MAJESTY THE QUEEN

PRESIDENT
THE RIGHT HONOURABLE
THE EARL OF DERBY

180, CHAPELTOWN ROAD
LEEDS, 7

SECRETARY
W. FALLOWFIELD, M.A.

TELEPHONE 4-4637/8
TELEGRAMS "NORFU," LEEDS 7

WF/MB

16th May, 1961.

The Secretary,
St. Helens R.L.F.C.
Knowsley Road,
ST. HELENS.

Dear Sir,

Congratulations on winning the Cup and on your teams fine display in what turned out to be a memorable Cup Final.

The number of tickets which each competing Club sold was higher than in any other year and helped to establish a capacity crowd for the first time in ten years.

When the excitement of having the Cup has died down a little will you please let me have it back in order to repair the damage which it sustained during the previous twelve months.   The Cup has to be inspected by our Insurance Agents before being repaired.

Yours sincerely,

Secretary.

A letter to St Helens from League secretary Bill Fallowfield after their 1961 win over Wigan.

CHAPTER 48

TRINITY TALES- CONTINUED

Traditionally the Challenge Cup finals which attract the most attention are those that have competing teams from either side of the Pennine hill chain. Besides the interest it creates in the north of England with its distinct tribal differences, the rest of the country always relishes the results of a meeting between sporting bodies from the Red and White Rose counties.

Throughout the history of the competition, however, there have been notable struggles between clubs from one county who made it through to the final. As we saw earlier, the seeds of Rugby League's Challenge Cup competition were in the Yorkshire County Rugby Union Cup and, in 1962, the White Rose stranglehold on the trophy became complete; just for a year.

By the time the competition had reached the last four all the big Lancashire clubs had been eliminated. Widnes went in the first round, Oldham and St Helens in the second while Wigan were Wakefield Trinity's third-round victims.

That left Featherstone Rovers, Huddersfield, Hull and Wakefield to decide among themselves who went forward to Wembley. The Rugby League wisely decided that both ties should be played in Yorkshire and selected Bradford's massive Odsal Stadium as the venue for both matches; the two games were played on separate days because all four semi-finalists came from the same county and the League have subsequently maintained the separation.

Huddersfield went through to Wembley by virtue of a 6-0 win over Hull KR. It was the Fartown club's first appearance in the final since their 1953 triumph over St Helens and the eighth time they had reached this stage in the Cup.

This was, however, to mark the end of a long connection with the Challenge Cup final for Huddersfield, one of Rugby League's most famous clubs, because after the 1962 final they have gradually slithered down the scale of importance.

For Wakefield and Featherstone it was a repeat of 1960 when they met in the semi-finals at Bradford. The end result was the same too. Wakefield took the decision and, after a year's absence, they returned to Wembley.

One of the factors in Wakefield's rise had been the signing of Welshman Don Vines from Oldham. The tough forward, together with his former Watersheddings team mate Derek Turner, added fire and steel to the Trinity pack. He was on the verge of playing in three successive Wembleys. In 1960 he was on Wakefield's winning side and was then transferred to St Helens playing in the side that beat Wigan. The hat-trick was, however, denied to him because he failed a fitness test on an injured knee in 1962.

In Yorkshire they take their sport seriously. While Rugby League is not taken lightly, neither is their summer love, cricket. But on 12 May 1962 there was a split loyalty as Wakefield Cricket Club found out.

It was reported locally that Wakefield CC were putting on a 'brave show' against Dewsbury-based club Hanging Heaton in spite of having half their side in London to watch the Rugby League Cup final.

Huddersfield were the surprise team of the 1961-62 season. Even their local evening newspaper, the Examiner, was surprised by their progress. 'Team without a chance now in two Cup finals!' they proclaimed when announcing that the men from Fartown were in both the Challenge Cup and Championship play-off finals.

There was a heavy South African influence in the Trinity team. Centre Alan Skene earnt it a place in the Wembley team while his fellow countrymen, winger Colin Greenwood and centre Jan Prinsloo, who had joined Wakefield from St Helens, did not. Perhaps the League were influenced by Trinity's policy of finding South African players because the touring team who were due to leave for Australia and New Zealand were sched-

Widnes hooker Keith Elwell releases a pass in the drawn 1982 final at Wembley against Hull.

Delighted Hull players show the Cup to their fans after winning the 1982 replay against Widnes at Elland Road, Leeds.

A York player tries to avoid a tackle by Wigan pair
Brian Case and Colin Whitfield in their water-
logged 1984 semi-final at Elland Road, Leeds.

Wigan prop Brian Case puts the Widnes
defence under pressure in the 1984 final.

Steve Evans of Hull tries to outpace the Wigan cover in the classic 1985 final.

Australian forward Steve Muggleton, who played for Hull, is tackled by winger Henderson Gill in the 1985 final.

Castleford coach Malcolm Reilly acknowledges the fans after his side's win over Hull KR in the 1986 final.

Left: *Referee John Holdsworth watches Warrington's Paul Bishop set up a pass to winger Des Drummond in the 1990 final against Wigan.*

Below left: *Castleford's John Joyner holds the Cup up in 1986 after their Wembley win over Hull KR.*

Below: *Oldham defenders close in on a Castleford attack in their 1986 semi-final meeting at Central Park, Wigan.*

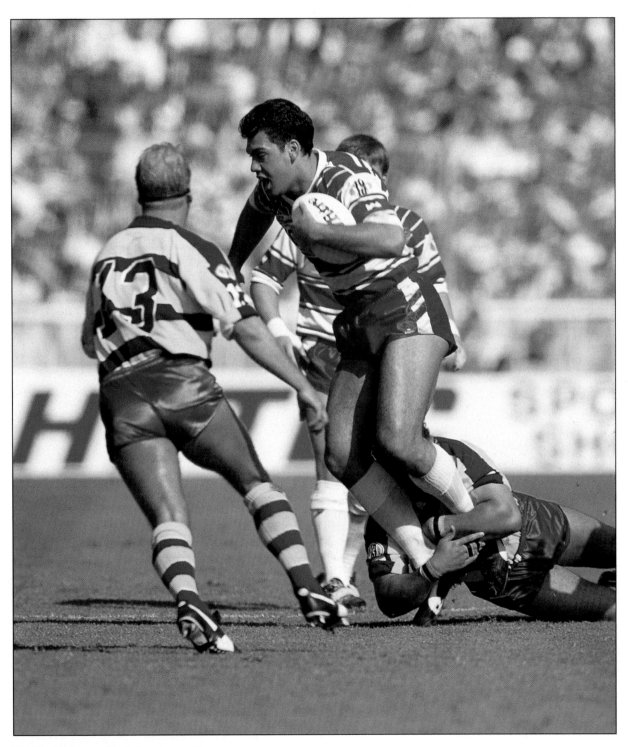

*New Zealand centre Kevin Iro tries to pull
out of a Warrington tackle as Wire loose
forward Mike Gregory moves in during the
1990 final.*

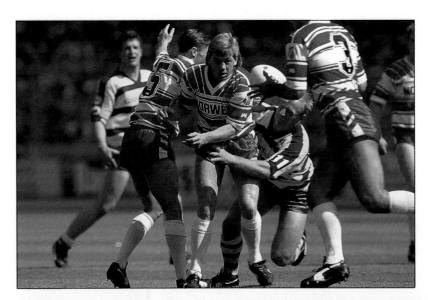

It's all action as Wigan's Steve Hampson passes to Kevin Iro during the 1990 final.

Below: St Helens forward Roy Haggerty unships the ball during the 1989 final.

Wigan captain Ellery Hanley and coach John Monie bask in the glory with the Cup after beating Warrington in 1990.

Hanley urges restraint on full-back Steve Hampson during the 1990 final.

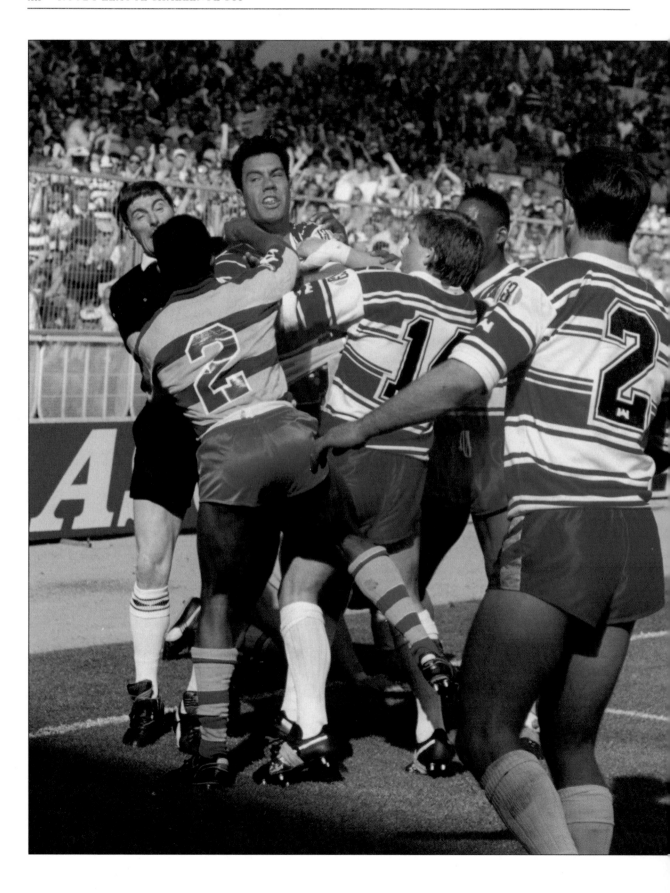

Referee John Holdsworth has his hands full after a flare up on the Warrington try-line during the 1990 final against Wigan.

Janette Smith, the first woman physiotherapist to be employed in a Rugby League Challenge Cup final, attends to centre Paul Loughlin during the 1991 Wembley clash with Wigan.

St Helens forward Bernard Dwyer is helped off after seriously cutting his ear in the 1991 final.

St Helens' Welsh halfback Jonathan Griffiths tunes in to a personal stereo to aid his concentration before the start of the 1991 final against Wigan.

A young Wigan fan reaches out to touch a player's winners' medal. Maybe a star in the making.

The man in a white suit. Cabaret artist Vince Miller leads the fans in community singing before the start of the 1991 final between St Helens and Wigan.

The changing face of the Challenge Cup

uled to play in the land of the Springbok on their way home.

It was yet another attempt by Rugby League to break out of the narrow four-nation international straightjacket in which it was contained by Rugby Union and other problems.

Huddersfield had just two survivors from their 1953 team in the 1962 final team line-up; veteran Wigan-based prop Ted Slevin and stand-off half Peter Ramsden, who as a 19-year-old captured the Lance Todd Trophy in his first Wembley appearance.

The final was not to be one of Wembley's classics but it did make its own mark in the history book because it was the first in which there was no successful place kick at goal.

In fact Neil Fox had, what the tabloid press fondly refer to as, the 'drop' on Huddersfield because he landed three drop goals during the game; they were decisive.

At that point in Rugby League history a drop goal – players drop the ball to the ground before striking it between the posts – was still valued at two points.

In modern Rugby League it is a much practised skill but in the early 1960s it was rarely employed. His hat-trick was, therefore, a notable feat and he remains the only player to have achieved such a hat-trick at Wembley. Another addition to the Fox legend.

Fox stood over this final like a colossus. Besides the three drop goals which were despatched by his left boot he also scored a 20th minute try and the quality of his display earned him the coveted Lance Todd award.

Fox's first drop goal and try against a try by Huddersfield scrum half Tommy Smales saw Trinity leading 5-3 at half-time. The second drop goal followed by a try from winger Ken Hirst, the man who had kept new signing Prinsloo out of the side, saw

Trinity build their lead up to 10-3.

Three minutes from the end Huddersfield staged their final effort when Ramsden went over the Trinity line to touch down but another arcing drop goal from Fox two minutes later ensured that Wakefield took the Cup with a 12-6 victory.

Trinity, winners of the Yorkshire Cup and League that season, were now on the verge of becoming the fourth team to win four trophies in a season; a feat not performed since Swinton in 1928.

Exactly seven days after their Wembley disappointment Huddersfield gained their revenge by beating Trinity 14-5 in the Championship final at Bradford ruining the four trophy attempt.

By the time the 1963 Challenge Cup tournament was due to start Britain was in the grip of a major freeze. The whole of the country was locked in the ice and snow.

The Rugby League encouraged their clubs to play the first round games; so Huddersfield went to the trouble of hiring a mechanical shovel to shift the snow from their Fartown pitch. But it all proved to be a waste of time as the playing surface was frozen to a depth of three inches.

Just two grounds, Castleford and Widnes, were available. The Chemics had lived up to their name by spreading de-icing chemicals all over the pitch and Castleford had relied on a 60-strong barrage of braziers to keep the frost at bay. As Widnes were drawn away in the first round at Swinton they agreed to let their Naughton Park ground be used by Liverpool City, who were drawn against Barrow-area amateur club Roose.

When the first-round weekend passed with most of the ties falling victim to the wintery conditions, the League instructed their clubs to switch the games to alternative mid-week dates. That, however, was not

greeted with complete acquiescence and Wigan led a 23-club revolt against the decision. They should have saved all that hot air because the freeze continued and the first round was put back to 2 March.

During the freeze Wigan had signed a Fijian player called Kaiava Bose and he arrived from the South Sea paradise to find workmen chipping two inches of ice off the pitch!

Huddersfield were still determined. They hired a road repair machine which succeeded in shifting the ice but no sooner had it left the Fartown pitch than the water froze again.

Life became so difficult that the League said that, if necessary, clubs who could not prepare their pitch for play by 2 March then could switch the tie to the away club. That, too, was not greeted with unanimity. Wigan and Keighley felt it was morally wrong for home clubs to lose that advantage while Dewsbury and Wakefield agreed to the move if necessary.

By the beginning of March the warmth spread into the country from the West, and the Lancashire clubs were able to play their ties. The thaw was, however, slower to reach Yorkshire and Hull KR increased the brazier record to 200.

Life had changed in Rugby League since the previous Wembley final. The professional game had split into two divisions for the first time since 1904-05. Cup holders Wakefield and Wigan were both in the first division and reached Wembley.

One of Trinity's South African imports Alan Skene had returned home and there was a scrap among several Wakefield players for the right to play alongside the majestic Neil Fox. Just after the big freeze had cleared 19-year-old Ian Brooke staked his claim.

He missed the first two rounds, their wins over Bradford Northern and Liverpool City, but came in for the third-round tie at York. Some of the York team were former Trinity players and they forced a 9-9 draw with Wakefield claiming the replay 25-11.

They reached Wembley for the third time in four years to defend the Challenge Cup after a 15-2 semi-final struggle against Warrington at Swinton.

'I had been battling to keep that vital first team place for weeks,' said Brooke. 'Every week I kept saying to myself 'I must play well so that they pick me again next week'.

'And then I found out I was selected for the Cup final team. It was an incredible feeling.'

But Brooke revealed that Wakefield plotted their Wembley triumph on a famous Football League pitch.

'Queens Park Rangers were very helpful to us,' he said. 'We used their pitch to plan all the moves. Just for a bit of relaxation we used to play soccer and some of their players came out to watch.

'And our stand-off half Harold Poynton turned on a great performance for them and they were very impressed with his skill with the round ball.'

When Trinity had won in 1962 young Brooke had been a travelling reserve with their party and had watched the game from the special enclosure for the squad players. He said: 'To go on the pitch on the day before the final was awe-inspiring and the game itself was virtually over before it began for me.'

Playing on the wing next to Brooke was a South African, Gert Coetzer. He had just finished his three-month trial period with Wakefield and the two newcomers played a large part in Trinity's subsequent success. If the pair were anticipating what lay before them, prop Jack Wilkinson knew for certain what to expect because he made a record-breaking fifth final appearance; two with Halifax and three with Trinity.

In fact Coetzer was doubtful for the game with an injury and had to have two pain killing injections before walking out for the final.

Wigan, who extended their own record to ten Cup final and seven Wembley appearances, maintained an aura of power. Their path to the final was relatively untroubled as they beat Hull, Oldham and Leeds on their way to the semi-final where they beat Hull KR.

For the final on 11 May the 84,492 crowd saw a tense first half with Trinity going in at half-time with a 5-0 lead thanks to a try from 22-year-old prop forward Malcolm Sampsom while Wigan suffered a blow when their stand-off half Dave Bolton was badly concussed. As the players left the field at the interval, he was still receiving treatment. He failed to appear for the second half.

The second half belonged almost exclusively to Trinity. There were two tries for Coetzer, one for Poynton and one, their last, for Brooke while Fox kicked five goals, four conversions and a penalty. Wigan, a man down, could not hold rampant Trinity and they had to content themselves with tries by Frank Pitchford and Frank Carlton and two penalties from Carlton. Trinity won 25-10 to become the first Yorkshire team to retain the trophy at Wembley.

Wakefield's Ian Brooke (left) and Colin Greenwood (underneath) move in on Wigan's Frank Carlton in the 1963 final.

CHAPTER 49

DRAWING OUT THE AGONY

One of the guiding maxims for professional Rugby League players is: 'Win five matches and you've won the Cup!' The theory is based on the premise that there are three qualifying rounds, a semi-final and the final.

All that pre-supposes that your team is fortunate enough to avoid the dreaded deadlock, a draw. In 1964 Widnes players became virtual authorities on the tie and their route to the final was twice as long as normal because they had to play nine matches to win the right to face Hull KR.

In the first round at Leigh they had fought out a 2-2 draw. The replay at Naughton Park was squared at 11-11 but Widnes won the second replay outright, 14-2, at St Helens.

Their second round against Merseyside neighbours Liverpool City assumed an air of normality and Widnes moved through to the third round where they faced a Swinton team, who were in the second of successive championship years. Like Widnes in the first round Swinton had endured a replay and they moved on after beating Wigan at the second attempt.

Frank Myler, who was an essential ingredient in the Widnes team of the time recalls; 'There was no important reason why we kept drawing the Cup games.

'In sudden-death Rugby it is im-possible to plan for such situations but it kept happening to us. And yet all the time we had the feeling that we were going to go all the way to Wembley.'

Widnes needed to sustain that faith because their third round meeting with Swinton needed three attempts to produce a result. In the first match at Naughton Park they ended the game locked at 5-5 and they tried again at Station Road.

That replay failed to reveal a weakness in either team and they left the Lions' den still seeking a result after a 0-0 scoreline. The third attempt was made at Central Park, Wigan and this time Widnes were comfortable winners at 15-3.

The draw was fashionable in the 1964 Challenge Cup. In the first round there had been four replays and one second replay, while the third round produced that multi-confrontation between Widnes and Swinton.

It is fair to say that tied matches are, generally, a rare breed in Rugby League; the game, with its high physical contact element, encourages a clear result.

For the second time in the 1964 competition Widnes returned to Station Road, this time for the semi-final against Castleford. Once again they left without a result after a 7-7 draw against a Yorkshire team for whom halfbacks Alan Hardisty and Alan Hepworth were the emerging forces.

Wakefield's Belle Vue home was the venue for the replay and Widnes drew on all their replay experience to take the decision 7-5. The other semi-final was between Hull KR and Oldham. They too could not decide the issue first time and left Headingley still evenly balanced at 5-5.

Their replay at Swinton attracted such a great deal of attention that the kick off was delayed to ensure that as many people as possible could see the game. The match was played in the early evening and the decision to hold the start was to prove critical.

As the last minute of the match approached Hull KR looked to be on their way to Wembley but the 27,209 crowd were stunned when Oldham hooker Len McIntyre attempted a drop goal from near the halfway line. Amazingly the ball hit the target. It was later revealed that he had never kicked a drop goal before.

But it left the match tied at 14-14. There were no floodlights at Station Road and as the daylight ebbed the two protagonists were locked in an extra-time struggle. Oldham's hopes of a first-ever appearance at Wembley were boosted in the first period of extra-time when second row forward Geoff Robinson went in for a try. Hull KR were drained by the experience. They had been within sight of victory and had it snatched away.

Fate then conspired against Oldham. Referee Dennis Davies, who lived in Swinton, ruled that the game had to be abandoned with Oldham leading 17-14 in the 12th minute of extra time.

That brought a second replay at Huddersfield and this time it was Oldham, who were badly affected by having the Wembley experience ripped from their grasp. Hull KR waltzed through to their first Wembley appearance winning 12-2 against a totally disillusioned Oldham.

Widnes's support reflected their fans' flamboyant nature. Glenys Roberts, the 13-year-old daughter of 1937 Widnes finalist Bob Roberts, went to the match wearing her father's Wembley jersey, while the 52 employees of Commercial Vehicles Ltd. each took a black and white painted umbrella and stood together at the east end of the stadium. They bought the umbrellas from the local rag and bone merchant.

Myler worked at a local factory and the girls who also worked at the centre wanted to buy him a gift to commemorate the occasion. Modest Myler asked that the money be given to charity. Compromise was in the air and Widnes provided two tickets which were purchased for 87-year-old Walter Fox and 91-year-old Anthony Fillingham. Myler made the presentation at the plant and honour was satisfied all round.

For Myler, a favourite Widnes son, it was to be his sole appearance at Wembley as a player.

Both clubs produced controversial selections for the final on 9 May.

Hull KR hooker Peter Flanagan tries to pull out of a Widnes tackle in the 1964 final.

Widnes left out prop Edgar Bate in favour of the more mobile Arthur Hughes, he played in the second row, while former Wigan forward Frank Collier switched to prop.

Rovers had a change forced upon them. Their prop John Taylor had been suspended after being sent off against Huddersfield and Jim Drake, who had missed Hull's 1960 final through injury, was brought in. But he failed to pass a fitness test and that gave the place to 21-year-old Brian Mennell, who played at Wembley after just three first team games.

After the drama of the qualifying rounds Wembley was almost a disappointment. Widnes dictated the early exchanges with their forwards gradually gaining the upper hand. At the interval Widnes led 2-0 after a successful long-range penalty by full-back Bob Randall.

With the softening up process complete Widnes bought their backs into play. Their two centres, Alan Briers and Myler, each scored a try

and Randall kicked the conversion to the second. Rovers briefly resisted when international stand-off half Alan Burwell engineered a try which was converted by full-back Cyril Kellett to put the score at 10-5.

Two minutes from the end Widnes made completely sure of winning the Cup when the man of the match prop Frank Collier went over for an unconverted try. It gave the Chemics the Challenge Cup for the third time in five final appearances.

For many of the men who played that day Wembley still had a role to play in their lives. Arthur Hughes was to see his brother Eric make six appearances in Wembley finals for Widnes; Myler was to visit the stadium twice as a coach of Widnes as was the Widnes captain and loose forward of the day Vince Karalius; Cyril Kellett's time of success was still in front of him while Rovers scrum half Arthur Bunting crossed the city and suffered two Wembley heartbreaks as coach with Hull FC.

CHAPTER 50

THE DAY DAVID ALMOST SLEW GOLIATH

By 1965 televised sport had established itself in the nation. Rugby League had been ambivalent about its effect on match attendances and had yet to realise the full potential that the medium offered in terms of sponsorship.

Rugby League and the unmistakable Yorkshire tones of commentator Eddie Waring had become part of the Saturday afternoon experience and, whatever the rights and wrongs of the argument, the cameras were undoubtedly in the right place at the right time on 9 May 1965 when Wigan played Hunslet in the Challenge Cup final at Wembley.

British fondness for a David v Goliath situation had been satisfied by Hunslet, who returned to Wembley after a break of 31 years, while Wigan were making a new record ninth trip.

The width of the gap in class was perfectly illustrated by looking at the league table; the Rugby League had returned to the single division again at the end of 1964. Wigan finished in second place with eight defeats in 34 games while Hunslet had conceded 15 defeats in the same number of outings.

The Yorkshire club had followed their traditional method of building a team from players produced from the tough Leeds suburbs and nearby West Yorkshire coalfield towns while Wigan, who had been to Wembley

four times since 1958, had substantially rebuilt their team.

Reconstruction had reached such an extent that eight of their players were making their first appearances at Wembley just two years after the club's last appearance in the final.

Trevor Lake's career on the left wing for Wigan was surprisingly brief. The flier from Northern Rhodesia moved to Central Park in 1962. In 1963-64 season he finished second in the League try scoring chart and was a clear leader in the 1964-65 season when Wigan arrived at Wembley.

His stay did not last much longer because he left Central Park in 1966 after his second trip to Wembley; his legacy was a lasting impression on Wigan and the game. His placing on the left gave Wigan awesome fire power because the legendary Billy Boston provided the finishing potential on the opposite wing.

Hunslet were, however, not without assets of their own. Their forward strength was the foundation for the side; Bernard Prior, Geoff Gunney and Bill Ramsey were all players able to influence the outcome of a game.

It proved to be the classic Cup confrontation; the boxer against street fighter; the journeyman against master craftsman.

Nothing Wigan could do would shake off the gritty Yorkshiremen and the television audience were treated

to one of the all-time great Cup finals, a game which is still mentioned in hushed terms in spite of the gap in history.

Hunslet, because of their rating as clear underdog, were able to relax and that clearly helped their game. They were also not intimidated by Wigan's lofty position within the game.

On the way to Wembley Wigan had gained revenge for their 1961 final defeat by beating St Helens 7-2 in front of almost 40,000 fans at Central Park following their first-round cruise over Barrow. The rest of the way was easy by comparison with wins over Workington and Swinton.

Hunslet faced their moment of truth in the third round when they took on their bigger neighbour Leeds. They had beaten Oldham and Batley in the first two rounds and, after a mighty effort, they clinched a third round win over the Loiners 7-5. The impressive Wakefield team failed to breach their defence in the semi-final which they took 8-0.

The points flowed even from the kick off. Hunslet's Alan Marchant put the ball into touch on the full, without bouncing in the field of play, from the first kick and Wigan loose forward Laurie Gilfedder sent the penalty soaring between the posts from the centre spot.

An indication that Hunslet were prepared to trade punches, figuratively speaking, came after three minutes when full-back Billy Langton levelled the scores with a penalty from 40 metres out. Long range accuracy matched by long range accuracy.

The style of the game was set. After referee Joe Manley had disallowed a Hunslet 'try', Wigan registered the first try of the game through centre Keith Holden. Nine minutes later Langton, who was to finish third in the League's goalkicking charts that season, eased over another penalty and Wigan's lead was reduced to 5-4.

Wigan staged a mighty effort in an attempt to create some space between them and the terrier like Yorkshiremen.

Gilfedder, a former Warrington player who played a big part in Wigan's success of the period, hit the target with a 30th minute penalty and, three minutes later, Lake's spectacular pace took him over the line for a try in the corner and Gilfedder landed a superb conversion goal.

Now the Lancastrians led 12-4 and, if League form had counted for anything, Hunslet's interest in the game would have ceased at that point. But there is no return leg to a Cup final. They were simply not prepared to concede and two minutes before half-time, they gave Wigan's confidence a jolt. Hunslet stand-off half Brian Gabbitas, who was playing the game of his life, created a hole in the Wigan defence and centre Geoff Shelton cut through to score the try which Langton improved.

At the interval Wigan led 12-9 but Hunslet were still very much in contention. It was as if the Yorkshire ter-

riers had their teeth in the seat of Wigan's pants and were not prepared to let go.

As soon as the second half of the game started Wigan set off on another major surge, determined to rid themselves of an irritant. Gilfedder raced in for a long-range try and for the moment he forwent the kicking role leaving it to his captain Eric Ashton, who safely planted the ball between the uprights.

Lake, the season's leading try-scorer, then took his place in Rugby League legend by scoring one of the best looking tries in the Challenge Cup final history. Wigan full-back Ray Ashby, an acquisition from Liver-

The classic shot: Wigan winger Trevor Lake plunges over for a try in the 1965 final against Hunslet.

pool City, came from deep inside the Lancashire club's half and sent Lake racing clear of the Hunslet cover.

He was chased by Hunslet winger John Griffiths and they were committed to history when Lake's high-level plunge for the line was captured by the press photographer corps to become one of the classic pictures in the sport's album.

Wigan led 20-9 with a little over 20 minutes left to play. Victory was within their grasp but Hunslet's reaction to that situation is one of the major reasons why the 1965 final is so highly regarded.

Winger Griffiths, who had gallantly chased Lake to the line, inspired the Hunslet counter attack when he forced his way through for a 65th

minute try which was converted by Langton. The gap closed to 20-14.

Now Hunslet were running on high octane adrenalin and they were over running the tiring Wigan players. Four minutes from the end Wigan conceded a penalty and Langton placed the ball between the posts to close the gap further to 20-16.

Wigan knew that the game was within Hunslet's reach and that they could not allow another scoring situation to develop. They steeled themselves for the remaining minutes and emerged with their record sixth win at Wembley.

There were some important newcomers at the 1965 final. They did not play but their importance was to grow. This was the first year that Rugby

Joint Lance Todd Trophy winner Brian Gabbitas rounds Wigan's Frank Parr in the 1965 Cup final.

League operated a substitute system at Wembley.

In 1964 the game had allowed them to be used to replace an injured player but only before half-time while in 1965 they were allowed for any reason up to and including half-time. Their introduction to Wembley was delayed by 12 months.

And one of the all-time best finals was also distinguished by the fact that the journalists could not split Gabbitas or Ashby for the Lance Todd Trophy. For the only time in the award's history it was shared.

CHAPTER 51

MURPHY'S LAW

Alexander James Murphy is one of the greatest players ever to grace a Rugby pitch and his constant companion on his journey through the game has been controversy.

'Murph' or 'Murphy' depending on whether he played for your team or not, possessed a range of skills that has rarely been matched in Rugby League or Union. He also possesses self confidence and a strong voice and has never been afraid to exercise one or both.

He signed for his home-town club, St Helens, on his 16th birthday in 1956. His signing-on fee was £80 which was low even by the standards of the age but never was money better spent. He had been playing for his town team since the age of ten!

Coincidentally Murphy's long relationship with the Challenge Cup started before he could influence the direction of any final.

Prior to St Helens' 1956 Wembley confrontation with Halifax, the Knowsley Road club had to fulfil a punishing schedule of three matches in five days. For the last match of that grouping the club's board of directors selected a virtual reserve team giving a first senior outing to 16-year-old Murphy.

Saints' second string came through to win 21-7 and an effervescent Murphy performed from scrum half with an air of confidence that was to become the trade-mark of his entire playing career. In 1958 he was Great Britain's youngest ever player selected for a tour to Australia and New Zealand.

The confidence of St Helens coach Jim Sullivan and Great Britain in Murphy was not misplaced. He, quite simply, could not and would not be ignored. One of his major attributes was his tactical ability and he utilised this talent to good effect by extending any particular Rugby law to its fullest extent. It brought him into conflict with authority in the shape of referees but they could not crush either his self belief or desire to exploit every opportunity to win.

That vision was to play an important part in deciding the Challenge Cup final of 1966.

St Helens had one of the finest teams ever to don their famous red and white colours; it was simply heaving with talent from full-back Frank Barrow and winger Tom Van Vollenhoven to loose forward John Mantle, the former Welsh Rugby Union international.

They made two vital signings during the season. The first did not go down well with Murphy because it was another scrum half Tommy Bishop from Barrow. Murphy was switched, reluctantly, to the centre,

and shortly before the Cup signing deadline they expended a bargain £1,000 for Wigan's veteran hooker Bill 'Sos' Sayer. The value of the latter purchase was to be evident later.

In the first two rounds Saints beat Wakefield Trinity and Swinton. The third round meeting with Hull KR saw Murphy in the thick of a major row which centred on St Helens' winning try. They looked to be on the way to a shock defeat, when four minutes into injury-time, Murphy hoisted a high kick. The ball bounced out of full-back Cyril Kellett's hands and rolled towards the dead ball line.

Murphy squeezed through the mass of struggling bodies and dropped on the ball claiming the try. Referee Eric Clay, who was known as Sergeant Major because of his demeanour, awarded the try.

All hell broke loose as the Hull KR players believed that the ball had gone out of play when Murphy had touched the ball down. Referee Clay would not listen to their protests and Len Killeen kicked the goal for St Helens to stay on the Wembley trail. Clay's decision remains a bone of contention to this day.

In the semi-final they came up against Dewsbury, one of the surprise teams of the year, at Swinton.

The last-four encounter contained a little extra spice because one of the former St Helens' stars, winger Mick Sullivan, who had returned to live in his native Yorkshire, was the mainspring, loose forward in the Crown Flatt team.

St Helens won 12-5 thanks to two tries from their Rhodesian winger Killeen, who was better known for his prodigious goal-kicking feats, but the game will always be remembered for Saints fan Mrs Minnie Cotton.

Her lodger, Welsh forward John Warlow, was roughly tackled by Dewsbury forward Dick Lowe in the closing stages of the game and Mrs Cotton took the assault personally. She rushed on to the pitch and set about the unfortunate Lowe with her umbrella. He was saved from further punishment by a possee of players and police. St Helens went through to Wembley and Mrs Cotton into national headlines.

For the second time in Wembley history a classic St Helens v Wigan final was produced.

Although St Helens were the team of the moment, Wigan were one of the few teams to beat them in the League that season. The Central Park side had overcome Halifax, Whitehaven, Bradford Northern and Leeds to reach the final which was played on 21 May in front of a capacity 98,536 crowd.

Two people dictated the eventually outcome. Wigan hooker Colin Clarke, who didn't play, and Alex Murphy, who did.

The form of Clarke persuaded Wigan to agree to Sayer's transfer to St Helens but their calculations went astray when Clarke was suspended for being sent off shortly before the final. That left Wigan without a specialist hooker and the role was handed to utility forward Tom Woosey.

This was a situation that appealed to Murphy's tactical appreciation because he realised that Sayer, who was hooking for Saints, would easily outhook Woosey at every scrummage and guarantee St Helens a command of the vital possession.

Therefore, it followed, that St Helens needed as many scrummages as possible. In those days if you were caught offside at a play the infringement cost nothing more than a kick to touch followed by a scrummage.

Murphy was too astute to miss such an opportunity and throughout the whole match he was regulary penalised for being offside. That gave the lion's share of possession to St Helens, who comfortably won the Cup 21-2.

The immaculate Killeen won the Lance Todd Trophy with five goals and a try while Murphy, Bishop and Mantle were also try scorers. Wigan's only points in a demoralising result was a Gilfedder penalty goal.

The Cup victory ended an amazing season for the Saints. They won the Lancashire League, Championship and League leadership trophy while finishing as runners-up to Castleford in the inaugural BBC 2 Floodlit Trophy; they were also the first side since Warrington in 1954 to win the League and Cup double.

The League was not pleased by Murphy's exploitation of the penalty laws and at their annual meeting they changed them so that after the kick to touch the game was restarted with a tap kick to the non-offending team. Ironically the vote was 21-2 in favour!

CHAPTER 52

THE DREAM MACHINE

When Jimmy Thompson was sixteen years old one of his best friends had a prized possession, a 125cc BSA Bantam motor bike. And all the soccer playing youngster from the West Yorkshire pit village of Knottingley wanted was a pillion ride on the British-made machine.

The deal was finally struck and young Jimmy got his wish with a ride to the next village, Featherstone. Until that moment Rugby League had played absolutely no part in young Thompson's life.

'They didn't play Rugby League at my school', he explained. 'I played soccer and was quite happy with that.'

Jimmy's pal was prepared to make young Thompson's dream come true if he would agree to wait after the outward half of the journey while he finished his training with the Featherstone Rovers' under-17 team.

It seemed a small price to pay for such a treat but once they arrived at Featherstone it also seemed such a long way to go without joining in the activity. 'I thought I may as well train as just stand there waiting,' said Jim.

The raw youngster found that he adapted well to League. Within weeks he was playing for the county under-17 team and signed as a professional with Featherstone.

'I wasn't any good at much,' professed Thompson. 'But I did enjoy knocking players down.'

After nine reserve team games at the start of the 1966-67 season, Jim had forced his way into the Rovers first team. Not that any real importance should be attached to that development as admitted by Thompson himself. 'We were hardly setting light to Rugby League in those days,' he said.

'It was just one division and Rovers were in the bottom half. In fact we were so bad that Doncaster, who were below us in the table, beat us both home and away in the league that season.

'But when the Challenge Cup came around it was a much different matter. Then our team spirit became a real asset.

'Laurie Gant was the first-team coach and we worked well with his assistant Keith Goulding who fed us with his enthusiasm. Part of his job was to build our team spirit. And he succeeded.

'But we were not a big club and that team spirit from Gant to the reserve team was an essential ingredient.'

For such an unfashionable team the Cup draw could not have been more unkind. Each time they succeeded in breaking through to the next round they would be drawn against a club who was in the top four of the league at the time.

And yet each time the gallant Colliers, Featherstone's nickname, survived it. One by one they fought their way passed Bradford Northern, Wakefield Trinity, Castleford and Leeds to reach Wembley for the first time since 1952.

So that motor bike spin had taken Jimmy all the way to Wembley and he became the youngest ever forward to play at the famous stadium.

Rovers' opponents were the equally unfashionable Barrow. They had, however, fashioned a more than useful team with former England Rugby Union stand-off Tom Brophy, Test winger Bill Burgess on the right and professional sprinter Mike Murray on the left while Ivor Kelland, Ray Hopwood and Henry Delooze provided the backbone to their pack.

Their path to the final had seen them overcome Whitehaven, Liverpool City, Hull and then Dewsbury in the semi-final at Huddersfield.

For young Thompson, who like so many other youngsters in the north had never left the region, the week of the final was an eye-opening experience. 'We trained at Crystal Palace,' he explained. 'There we trained and concentrated on putting ourselves in the right frame of mind to play Barrow.

'I was sharing a hotel room with our winger Kenny Greatorex and after we had been to see a show on the eve of the final we all retired to bed.

His Royal Highness the Duke of Edinburgh meets the Barrow team before the 1967 final against Featherstone.

'But nobody, even Kenny, who was an old stager, got any sleep. You just couldn't put the thought of the game out of your mind.'

The day of the final, 13 May, was hot and sunny and that was believed to be a disadvantage for Rovers two giant prop forwards Malcolm Dixon and Les Tonks. The theory was that their bulk would be too much to carry around for the full 80 minutes.

Rovers also started as the underdogs because of their league position, tenth from bottom, while Barrow were safely stationed mid-table.

The lead up to the final had been hit by a near unfortunate clash of colours. Both were predominantly blue and white; Barrow had an all blue jumper with a white 'V' while Rovers played in a blue jersey with narrow white hoops. Fortunately Barrow ordered a new set of white jerseys with a blue 'V' and the problem was solved.

The shape of Rugby League had

been almost completely changed for this final. Until this point the team who had possession was allowed to retain it for as long as they could until they either dropped the ball or infringed the laws. Concerned at falling attendances, the game decided to impose some new device upon itself in order to increase the attraction for spectators. The result of their deliberations was to restrict the number of tackles the team in possession could retain the ball.

Initially they decided that four tackles would be sufficient after which the opposition automatically had a chance of gaining the ball. Clubs decided that after three tackles they would kick into their opponents half trying to establish a starting point where they could start their tackling effort.

By 13 May at Wembley Rugby League had played its first season under limited tackle laws and the players were still coming to terms with

the restriction the new legislation had placed on their tactical thinking.

Thompson said: 'I have always thought that because this final was played between two less fashionable clubs the quality of the football we produced that day has never been properly appreciated.

'It was an evenly fought match in which our greater team spirit eventually pulled us through.'

Rovers held the sway in the first half and they led 9-7 at half-time. Featherstone loose forward Tommy Smales and Barrow second rower Henry Delooze had penalty kicks which cancelled each other out before Brophy rounded Rovers full-back Brian Wrigglesworth for the first try in the 16th minute which Delooze converted.

The Colliers were back on level

Featherstone coach Laurie Gant rests on the back of young forward Jimmy Thompson to show off the Cup in 1967.

terms 13 minutes later when, after intensive pressure on the Barrow line, 18-stone second row forward Arnie Morgan went over for a Rovers' try and Smales tacked on the goal points.

The Yorkshiremen made a decisive break in the first quarter of the second period with tries from centre Vaughan Thomas and Smales, who also converted the first of the pair.

With a minute of the game remaining Barrow fashioned their second try through centre Mike Watson which was converted by full-back Eddie Tees. That brought them back to trail Rovers 17-12 but time ran out as they looked for the points to force a replay.

Her Majesty Queen Elizabeth II presented the players with their medals to put the finishing touches to Rovers' first Challenge Cup final win and an extra shine to Jimmy Thompson's motor bike ride to glory.

CHAPTER 53

A DROP IN TIME

Rugby League, like so many other sports, is littered with moments of destiny. Hidden within that cliché that has served so many journalistic pens remains the true meaning; a mere movement which can decide whether you enjoy success or suffer failure.

Bev Risman knew well the power of Wembley. His father Gus had been twice with Salford and once with Workington Town and the eldest son of the great man approached his moment with eyes wide open.

It was quite clear that Augustus Beverley Walter Risman was going to follow in his paternal parent's Rugby boots because he was a dominant force in both schoolboy and then university Rugby Union. He climbed the ladder of Union success with consummate ease, playing at stand-off half for England in 1959 and then gaining selection for the British Lions in New Zealand.

He was a giant in English Rugby Union until March 1961 when he chose to follow his father into the professional game. His choice, while understandable in one respect, left some room for puzzlement because he accepted the blandishments of Leigh much to the disappointment of more fashionable clubs like Leeds.

Bev spent five years with the Hilton Park club at both centre and stand-off half and, at the age of 28,

looked like ending his days with the Lancashire club.

Leeds, however, had never forgotten the cultured, quietly spoken former Union international. By 1966 the Headingley club had a glaring weakness at full-back and they finally persuaded Risman to join them just before the Cup deadline. It cost them £7,000 to acquire his services but he slotted comfortably into their number one jersey.

It proved to be a masterstroke for Leeds and Risman because his arrival took him to the heights of success that he had been denied at Leigh and it completed a part of the jigsaw that was to give Leeds one of the most successful spells in their history.

The year 1968 was to prove the summit of his professional playing career. He helped Leeds take the League Leadership Trophy, the Yorkshire League title and to the Challenge Cup final.

Liverpool City, Bramley and Oldham all fell before Leeds as they progressed through to the semi-finals and they ensured their seventh peace time final when they crushed Wigan 25-4 at Swinton.

While Leeds were moving towards one of the most enjoyable periods in the club's history, Wakefield Trinity were approaching the end of an eon. Previous season's beaten finalists Barrow were their first-round victims fol-

lowed by Salford and then neighbours Castleford. They needed a replay to beat Huddersfield in the semi-final to return to Wembley for their fifth post-war final. Leeds had finished as top of the league table and Wakefield second which gave the final an enormous potential as a footballing spectacle.

The build up to the game proved to be difficult for both the Yorkshire giants. Leeds centre Syd Hynes had been out for three weeks with an arm injury and had to have a fitness test which he passed, although John Langley stood by just in case.

Trinity's was the greater blow. The magnificent Neil Fox was ruled out with a groin injury which had troubled him for the latter section of the season. He had attempted to return the week before the final and broke down, forced to withdraw not just from Trinity's Cup squad but as captain of the Great Britain tour team as well.

Ken Hirst, who had played on the left wing for Trinity in the 1961 final, was brought in to replace the big man. Their former Wakefield Rugby Union forward David Jeanes provided a late scare suffering from a throat infection but, although he missed some of the last training sessions, he was passed fit for the final.

By the time he reached Wembley Stadium it is fair to speculate that Jeanes must have wished he had stayed in bed; torrential rain had fallen during the morning and the Wembley turf was completely flooded.

Rain earlier in the week had left the pitch in a sodden condition and as the minutes to kick-off time drifted away, there was another cloud burst and gallons of water cascaded down on to the pitch.

That left a dilemma: whether to play the game or not. The prospect of bringing the fans back 200 miles and more from the north of England again weighed heavily and it was agreed that the game had to go ahead.

Players disappeared in plumes of water as they plunged into tackles and defenders slid way past the players in possession if they failed to make contact.

Risman and Don Fox, elder brother of Neil who had been transferred from Featherstone and moved from half-back to prop by Trinity, landed penalties in the opening ten minutes. Risman added another two points from a 13th-minute penalty and, two minutes later, the first try was scored. Leeds winger John Atkinson skidded away from a ball he had well covered and Hirst touched down for Wakefield. Don Fox converted.

The pressure on York referee John Hebblethwaite to abandon the game resumed when the pitch was all but drowned in yet another major rain storm; but he bit the bullet allowing the final to be continued.

Leeds regained the lead when Atkinson was obstructed on his way to the Wakefield line and referee Hebblethwaite gave an obstruction try to which Risman added the goal points.

Two minutes from time Leeds were awarded a penalty just inside the Trinity half and Risman takes up the story. He said: 'Mick Clark our captain asked me what I wanted to do. 'Either kick at goal or put it in touch, Bev, but make sure it goes out of play!' he told me.

'We thought that the game was over and we fully expected that whatever happened after the kick the referee would blow his whistle for the end of the match and we would have won the Cup. I decided that the goal was within my range and that I could reach.

'I set the ball up and I knew from the moment I made contact it was good. The contact was so clean. The ball sailed between the posts and the fact that the referee didn't end the game caught us by surprise.

'I suppose we were still off-guard because we were disappointed that the whistle hadn't gone. But from the

Sheets of spray mask a Wakefield tackle in the 1968 final against Leeds.

kick off Hirst got to the ball before the Leeds players and fly-kicked it forward.'

As the Leeds defenders scrambled back Hirst kicked the ball over the Leeds line dropping on it to make the score 11-10 to Leeds with the goal kick to come.

Fox was left with the kick to win the Cup for Wakefield. He was right in front of the posts and the Leeds players were flattened by the turn of events and their fears that the Cup they thought they had won was about to be snatched away.

Risman, who stood right behind the posts as Fox prepared for the conversion attempt, remembered: 'We were totally depressed. Some of boys couldn't bear to watch and turned their back. Others just stared at the ground.

'I couldn't take my eyes off Don as he stepped back from the ball ready to make his kick. When he missed it took a few seconds before we realised what had happened. And then came the final whistle.

'We had won the Cup. It was almost too incredible to think about. My memories of that day, however, are not just of that goal miss by Don but of the great rugby both sides played in the terrible conditions.

'People still talk about that game, it was a memorable occasion and in a way the fact that conditions made it

so unusual have kept the memory of the match so much more vivid in peoples' minds.'

Poor Fox, who won the Lance Todd Trophy as man of the match, was unconsolable. Tears of frustration and disappointment flowed down his face.

It transpired that just as he was about to kick the ball the foot which remained on the ground had slipped on the wet turf and caused him to make a bad contact with the ball.

The match became known as 'the Watersplash final' at least sparing Fox that notoriety.

Don Fox's agony after missing a kick from in front of the goal in the last minute which would have given Wakefield the Cup in 1968.

CHAPTER 54

BY HOOK OR BY...

When Dennis Hartley arrived at Castleford in 1966 his career could have been considered to be on the wane. He was 30-years-old and had already served two Yorkshire clubs. He had spent his initial three terms as a professional with Doncaster and then moved to Hunslet for six seasons. His time with the Leeds area club was notable for their appearance in the classic 1965 final against Wigan.

Hartley was the personification of the journeyman professional, yet his ancestry in the game was among the more unusual. Before he was called up for his national service in the army his sporting ambitions were aimed more at Association Football.

'The bloke in the next bed at barracks asked me if I would help the camp rugby team out,' explained Hartley, 'and that was how it all started.'

Hartley lived in the coal mining belt north of Doncaster and south of Wakefield. He, like so many other fellow Yorkshiremen watched Rugby League, and when he returned from his army service it was natural that he should gravitate back to the game.

Now, however, his interest was heightened because his own playing exploits in the services had given him an increased appreciation of what was happening. The professional game beckoned him but he lacked the abili-

ty to make an impact on their recruiting agents.

'I used to watch both Featherstone and Doncaster regularly,' explained Hartley, 'so I used to hang about at the back of their stands after matches hoping somebody would notice me and ask if I was interested in playing.

'Eventually somebody pointed me out to a Doncaster director and it led to the start of my career.'

After his three seasons at Tattersfield, he moved up a notch to Hunslet and he was one of the three front row forwards for the Yorkshire club in the 1965 final. The following year he was transferred to Castleford.

The Wheldon Road club's hinterland for players does not extend much further than the pit tops which could be seen from their town centre but they do make exceptions. Hartley proved to be an important acquistion.

Hartley again takes up the story. He says: 'Many folk in Castleford have told me that I was the last piece of the jigsaw in that team.

'Whether that is true or not is for other people to judge but we developed into a side who could attack with great effect, defend when we had to and, if necessary, stand up for ourselves if life turned tough.'

Hartley is convinced that the arrival of Derek Turner, the former Oldham and Wakefield loose forward, as the Castleford coach was also a

contributory factor to the club' success as the 1960s turned into the 1970s.

One of the major attractions to life in Rugby League at that time was Castleford's duel with Salford. While Castleford were a team built almost exclusively of men from their own patch of West Yorkshire, Salford had acquired a free-spending reputation.

Hotelier Brian Snape had acquired the virtually moribund inner city club and, with his cash and business acumen, transformed them into a top side. They bought players from both League and Union and succeeded in capturing national headlines when they paid a club record £14,000 to Newport Rugby Union club's Welsh British Lions stand-off half, David Watkins.

Salford carried most of the game before them and yet Castleford remained their *bête noire*. It was almost inevitable that they should meet at Wembley to pursue each other. Neither side had been to Wembley since the 1930s. Salford had gone twice in the Gus Risman era in 1938 and 1939 while Castleford's only previous outing before the twin towers had been when they beat Huddersfield in 1935.

Castleford's march to the 1969 Wembley final, ironically for Hartley, started with a first-round win at Hunslet and then they disposed of Wigan, Leeds and, with great local satisfaction, Wakefield Trinity in the semi-final.

Salford, on the other hand, did not have to stray away from their Willows home. Three home draws saw them beat off Batley, Workington Town and Widnes before beating Warrington in the last four.

Hartley returned to Wembley as Castleford's only link with the Cup final. He said: 'At least I could offer guidance and advice as to what the occasion was all about.'

For the final played on 17 May Hartley walked back into the same dressing room that Hunslet had used for the game against Wigan. The coincidence became greater when he was allocated the same peg on which to hang his clothes.

'That brought back memories,' he said. 'I remember sitting beneath the peg and recalling those dark moments for Hunslet when we came back in after losing against Wigan. People

kept telling us it had been a wonderful game but we didn't know anything about that because we had just given our all and lost.

'I kept telling myself there is no way you're going to suffer that kind of disappointment today. Losing is not a consideration.'

Because both teams were known for their more expansive brand of rugby people had been expecting a Cup final in a similar vein. Expectations, however, failed to live up to reality.

Wembley was packed with 97,939 people but the match was an anti-climax. Hartley failed to endear himself to the Lancastrians after their international winger Bill Burgess was injured by one of the big prop's tackles.

Tempers were too easily tipped out of normal position especially when the Castleford players confronted Welshman Ron Hill, who had moved from Wheldon Road to Salford earlier

that season. He did have some say in the game, however, and two penalty successes against a Keith Howe try saw Salford winning 4-3 at half-time.

The Castleford loose forward was a fiery young character called Malcolm Reilly. Like so many of their side he was born virtually within sight of the ground. He was a burgeoning talent and, as the match moved into the second half, so his influence grew.

Reilly created the vital break through for Castleford by engineering a gap which stand-off half Alan Hardisty fully exploited to score a try which second row forward Mick Redfearn converted. Castleford had hit the front in the game for the first time and they would not lose that lead again.

Castleford stand off Alan Hardisty places the ball down between the Salford posts after being chased by prop Charlie Bott in the 1969 final.

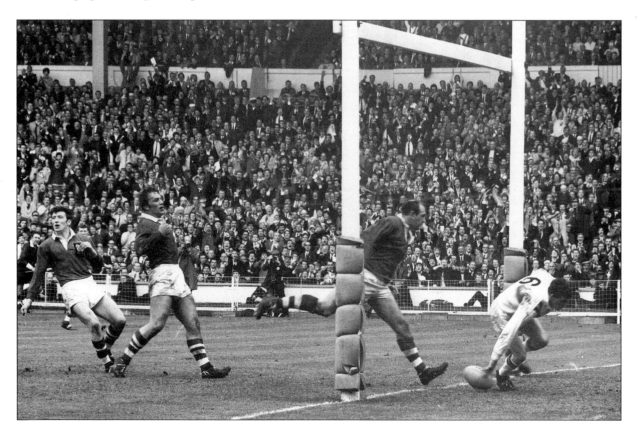

Wigan winger Kevin O'Loughlin makes a break round the Castleford cover in the 1970 final.

Hill's third penalty kept Salford in touch but two minutes from the end scrum half Keith Hepworth completed the Yorkshiremen's triumph with an unconverted try to give the final scoreline of 11-6.

Castleford's power level was maintained for the following 12 months so that they became one of the growing band of clubs who have made successive appearances at Wembley.

After they had beaten Hull and Barrow in the initial two rounds they faced old rivals from the 1969 final, Salford. Their Indian-sign over the Red Devils continued as they took the semi-final place winning 15-0 at Wheldon Road.

Their 6-3 semi-final win over St Helens at Station Road was unusual in that all the Castleford points came from drop goals by Alan Hardisty, Malcolm Reilly and second row Bill Kirkbride, who came from Halifax to replace prop Johnny Ward who, in turn, had been transferred to Salford.

On their return to Wembley they met Wigan who had been drawn away in the first three rounds, but still succeeded in beating Dewsbury, Oldham and Leigh. In the semi-final they cruised to victory by beating Hull KR.

Again Hartley takes up the story. 'There had been a couple of changes to the side but it didn't alter our capabilities,' he said.

Encouraging warm thoughts about

the game was easy for the big man because he was allocated the same changing spot in the same dressing room as the 1965 and 1969 finals.

Injuries do have an effect on the outcome of matches. Take any key player out of a side at any stage in a match and it must create problems. Full-back Colin Tyrer was enjoying a vintage season for Wigan. When he took the field at Wigan he had scored 166 goals and 17 tries. He was in incomparable form. Wigan knew that and Castleford were equally aware of his ability.

Tyrer, a former amateur international, had joined the Central Park club in 1967. He took extraordinary care with his place kicking, the time it took him first to prepare and then execute the kick infuriated the spectators and, just as often, opponents.

Nevertheless his technique, while not winning many friends, was very effective. In 1969-70 he was the league's top points scorer and he added to his tally with a first minute penalty after Welsh centre Peter

Wigan lose forward Doug Laughton searches for a break in the Castleford line in 1970.

Rowe had been obstructed by Castleford hooker Clive Dickinson.

Castleford levelled the scores five minutes later when Mick Redfearn was successful with a penalty after Wigan loose forward Doug Laughton obstructed Castleford centre Ian Shenton.

The Yorkshiremen took the lead in the 10th minute when winger Alan Lowndes touched down. The game was just 16 minutes old when Tyrer was a controversial injury victim. After a clash with Castleford scrum half Keith Hepworth, the Wigan fullback was led from the field with blood streaming from a serious facial wound. Wigan were furious and there have been many claims that the Castleford half-back should have been sent off.

Referee Fred Lindop contented himself with taking Hepworth's name.

Cliff Hill replaced Tyrer and made Wembley history because he became the first substitute to be used in a Challenge Cup final. In 1969 the Rugby League had adjusted the law to allow substitutions for any reason at any stage in the game.

The game was up for Wigan. They could not break down the dour Castleford defence, who were further encouraged when Redfearn added the only other score of the game, a penalty, in the 67th minute.

Castleford retained the Cup and as the players celebrated on the way back to the dressing room there was another pleasant surprise for Dennis Hartley. 'The League secretary Bill

Castleford show their fans the Cup after beating Wigan in the 1970 final.

Fallowfield came over to me,' explained big Dennis, 'and he told me to be prepared to leave for Australia because the players they had selected for the touring team had availability problems.'

Hartley made the trip down under and became part of a famous British team. They won the series 2-1 in Australia and, at the time of writing, no other British team has repeated their feat either in Australia or at home. And he went on to serve Castleford for another five years. What a bargain!

CHAPTER 55

MURPHY'S LAW - PROVED!

Every time Kevin Ashcroft opens his mouth the Lancashire town of Leigh falls out. The gritty hooker was born within the Lancashire town's boundaries and his variety of accent marks him down as a son of the pit borough which lies just north of the famous East Lancashire Road linking Manchester to Merseyside.

And yet he made his initial mark in the professional game in Yorkshire; he was recruited by Welshman Gwyn Davies and taken to Crown Flatt to learn the unloved art of hooking. His stay in Yorkshire was brief and he moved just across the Pennines to join Rochdale Hornets at the Athletic Grounds where he established himself as an international. Finally, in February 1967, Leigh recognised his true worth and took him to Hilton Park.

His arrival in his home town was to prove the key which opened the door to one of the most remarkable stories in Challenge Cup history. Ashcroft was a first major signing for coach Alex Murphy.

Murphy's move from St Helens proved drawn out and bitter. In October 1966 Murphy agreed to become Leigh's player-manager but St Helens simply dug their heels in refusing to sanction the transfer. Clearly they did not want one of their star players to be of any use to a neighbouring club.

In spite of being the most successful captain in St Helens' history Alex had not taken kindly to being moved out of the halfbacks to the three-quarters and declined to train or play. Australian clubs, together with some British clubs, were interested in signing him but St Helens put them all off by transfer listing him at £12,000, a staggering sum in 1966.

He was training on his own and his return to the game as Leigh's manager-coach at the age of 27 shook the League world especially as he had turned down a very lucrative offer from North Sydney.

His appointment circumnavigated the transfer fee. As he was not moving to Leigh as a player St Helens were not entitled to ask a fee and he received a five-year contract from Leigh with a weekly wage of £30.

The fight to win his playing registration took a year and eventually cost Leigh £6,000. His first match as manager was against St Helens and Leigh won. Coincidentally his first game as a Leigh player was also against Saints but this time they got their own back winning 22-0.

Murphy started to build the Leigh team and Ashcroft's arrival was an important part of the process.

'More signings came after me,' said publican Ashcroft, 'and once the men became touched by our increasing team spirit the ball just started to roll along. We were not a particularly great footballing team but we were fully committed and played for each other.

'When the 1971 Cup season started I couldn't have predicted what was going to happen but each time we overcame a team I started to believe that we were in with a chance of going all the way to Wembley.'

One by one the Leigh saw off their opponents, Bradford Northern, Widnes and Hull. Each was eliminated as Murphy's men went on to a semi-final meeting with Huddersfield which they won 10-4.

'The excitement in the town was amazing,' recalled Ashcroft, 'we were heroes in the true sense of the word.

'The excitement seemed to be never-ending and the players revelled in it all. When we were fitted for our team suits, flared trousers were very fashionable and everybody wanted their own modifications.

'In the end the tailor was so exasperated that he turned round and said to us 'You'll have what you're given!'

'But for us the final was settled at Wembley on the traditional walk about the stadium on the eve of the big game.

'Leigh arrived at Wembley wearing our official suits. We felt and looked a million dollars. Then Leeds arrived wearing leather jackets and jeans. They hardly looked like a professional sports team.

'Our winger Joe Walsh and I were

at the top of the Royal Box steps rehearsing taking the Cup, yes we were that confident, when Murphy came up to join us.

'He took one look at the Leeds players who were strolling around in their casual gear and said: 'We've got those lads beaten now'.

'Even though I'd played with some of the Leeds players at the World Cup the previous year they just couldn't bring themselves to speak to us and you could see the tension written all over their faces. Murph was spot on with his judgement.

'We went back to the hotel and the relaxed air went with us. Of course we were nervous but not frightened. Murph was sharing a room with a player who was not playing Tommy Canning. They were great friends.

'It was difficult to sleep and Alex had just dropped off at about 3.30 am when Tommy woke him up to tell

him that he had put a bet on Leigh to win the Cup. It was just that kind of team.'

When the serious business started the following day, 15 May 1971, Leigh were easily motivated to play. Ashcroft explained: 'The press had written us off. It was as if we needn't have bothered getting the coach to go to the match because Leeds were going to murder us.

'And you couldn't get away from the feeling that people were saying what right have those lads from that little pit town being here with a club like Leeds. Alex didn't have to fire us up, the press did the job for him. He just showed us the cuttings from the newspapers.

'We would have beaten anybody in the world that day. It is just the way it was. Everything we tried came off.'

Ashcroft's four-year-old son Gary was the team's mascot. At first he was

refused permission to walk out with the team but a last-minute appeal to the Wembley management saved the day.

While Leigh were playing at Wembley for the first time – their only previous Challenge Cup final was in 1921 before the game was played in the capital – Leeds were arriving for the sixth time. They had dumped Oldham, St Helens, Bramley and Castleford, winners of the Cup for the two previous years.

They were red hot favourites and Leigh were the longest odds outsiders for years.

Both teams had been disrupted before the final. Leigh scrum half Canning was injured which saw Murphy

Hail the conquering heroes! The townsfolk of Leigh welcome their team home after their surprise 1971 win over Leeds.

take over at number seven while prop Dave Chisnall missed the big day because he was suspended for four games.

Leeds lost their crucial play maker, loose forward Ray Batten and winger Alan Smith, but the pundits still favoured the Yorkshire team.

Leigh had the match in the bag by half-time when they led 13-0. They had blitzed Leeds with opportunist scoring and fierce tackling. The Headingley team were taken completely off their balance.

Prop Jim Fiddler gave Leigh the ideal start with a fifth minute drop goal and the points just kept coming, Welshman Stuart Ferguson landed two penalties and a conversion to Walsh's try while Murphy chipped in with a drop goal.

Leeds looked for encouragement and found it when full-back John Holmes kicked a penalty but that was cancelled out almost immediately by a second Murphy drop goal. Another Ferguson penalty made the score 17-2 and the Cup was clearly destined for Lancashire.

The flash point came in the 65th minute when Murphy dropped to the floor after a confrontation with Leeds' captain for the day and centre Syd Hynes.

Murphy was stretchered off and referee Billy Thompson ensured that Hynes suffered the indignity of becoming the first player to be sent off in a Challenge Cup final at Wembley. It remains a controversial incident. Hynes maintained that he did not butt Murphy and the Leigh player-

coach recovered sufficiently to resume playing six minutes later.

While the rest of the League wondered about the facts of the incident Mr Thompson had no doubts and did not hesitate in his decision.

Dave Eckersley ensured that Murphy's absence was well covered by landing a Wembley record fourth Challenge Cup final drop goal and, just before the team boss returned to the field, Ashcroft laid on a try for Eckersley with a neat reverse pass. Ferguson added the goal points.

Seconds before the final whistle Leeds 19-year-old stand-off Tony Wainwright broke through and kicked for the line. His path was blocked by Ferguson and referee Thompson awarded him an obstruction try which was converted by Holmes.

Murphy had been the inspiration to Leigh's 24-7 victory and he won the Lance Todd Trophy. He has, as far as Leeds fans are concerned, never

shaken off his part in the Hynes' dismissal with charges that he was play acting.

Ashcroft added: 'People always point to the Syd Hynes incident but Leeds were a beaten side before that happened.

'But we had won the Cup and nobody could take it away from us. We went to a wonderful reception that night but every one of the players was in bed by 12.30. We were all totally drained.

'We certainly made up for it when we got home to Leigh. I've never seen so many people who turned out to greet us. The pubs didn't close for two days and everybody wanted to buy us a drink or shake our hands.

'I don't believe as many people would have turned out even if royalty had come to Leigh.

'The amazing thing was that we were just an ordinary bunch of working lads and we had won one of the biggest prizes in sport.'

Hairstyles and fashions change but not the happiness. Alex Murphy and his wife Alice share a special moment after Leigh's 1971 Wembley triumph.

CHAPTER 56

KEL THE BOOT

The acquistion of Welsh Rugby Union players, while traditional for professional Rugby League clubs, has always been fraught with economic danger because the transition between both codes of the game is not easy, therefore, the risk of failure is consequently very high.

Although St Helens must have been reasonably confident they had made the right decision when they persuaded Welsh international full-back Kel Coslett to leave Aberavon and become a professional in July 1962, it must have been reassuring when he went on to play in all their 1962-63 games, landing an amazing 156 goals to top the league goal-kicking list and finishing as the league's top points scorer with 324.

The following season he was the season's most successful goalkicker with 138, and by the time he had been paid for playing for ten years, Coslett had moved into the pack to take over at loose forward. From the base of the scrummage he proved that, not only did he have the talent to kick a ball accurately, but he was a natural leader of men and a shrewd footballer to boot.

Kel explains the reasoning behind his move. He said: 'I broke my leg in 1965 and, when I returned to playing, I found that the injury had affected my game; I had lost some of my confidence.

'It was decided to involve me more in the game by switching me to loose forward. And it worked. I found that it actually suited me.'

At the turn of the decade he was in rare form. He led the goal-kicking charts yet again in 1970-71 and retained the same vein of form as St Helens enjoyed a purple patch in 1971-72. They won the BBC2 Floodlit Trophy and were beaten finalists in both the Lancashire Cup and John Player Trophy.

With Coslett's kicking boot as the main artillery piece St Helens set off on the Wembley mission in 1972 with a first-round win at Oldham and followed that with a home win over Huddersfield and an away victory at York. In both matches they won by a margin of 32-5 and that gave them a semi-final placing against their former stormy petrel Alex Murphy, who had left them under a cloud to join Leigh as coach in 1967 and then joined Warrington as player-coach directly after the 1971 final.

His desire to beat St Helens had proved a headache to the Knowsley Road club and it appeared that he still had that ability when they drew 10-10, but they laid that particular ghost to rest by beating the Wire 10-6 in the semi-final replay at Central Park.

Leeds, beaten so comprehensively by Leigh in 1971, were clearly in the mood to make amends to their fans, who had suffered so grievously after the humiliation of the Leigh defeat.

Perfidious fate had decreed that Leeds were given a freak chance to put Leigh in their place in the first round and, on that occasion, they did not make a mistake, winning 18-8. The difference was that this time the men from Hilton Park did not have Murphy.

A narrow 13-11 win at Castleford was followed by a third round tie at home to Wigan and Leeds took the semi-final place by winning at Central Park, 12-5, in the replay. Halifax failed to provide many problems and, a year after the nightmare ended, Leeds returned to the Challenge Cup final at Wembley.

Leeds had topped the league table and the bookmakers were still prepared to trust them, establishing them as 2-1 favourites to beat the Saints.

It appeared that those revered gentlemen who quote the odds on any sporting confrontation knew something that the rest of the world did not because throughout the week leading up to the final St Helens were savaged by a series of injury blows to their team.

Hooker Tony Karalius and forward Eric Prescott were both hit by injuries in the previous week's championship semi-final win over Bradford Northern and were ruled out of coach Jim Challinor's projections.

Welsh forward John Mantle gave the St Helens management another heart stopping moment when he was involved in a road traffic accident just before the team was due to head south to start their final preparations for the Wembley encounter.

School teacher Mantle was, however, built of much sterner stuff and, although the doctors wanted to insert 13 stitches in a nasty head laceration, he insisted on just 12 and declared himself fit to play. As a concession to safety he was to play in the game with a protective scrum cap.

Niggling minor injuries also troubled Leeds. Syd Hynes, sent off the previous season at Wembley, had missed much of the season through injury but he was passed fit to play and they were also worried about full-back John Holmes who was troubled with

an ankle injury even though he played.

Coslett recalled the moment that Saints went out. He said: 'We were a good team but we were undoubtedly disturbed by the loss of Karalius and Prescott.

'It was a drizzly day and it matched our mood.

'Speaking for myself, I was confident. I was 30-years-old and felt that I had reached my pomp. While people thought at my age I ought to be be on the way down I could honestly say that I had never felt fitter or happier playing the game.'

Two separate incidents settled the game. The first came in the first minute when, after the third tackle –

the four tackle restriction still remained in force – Tony Fisher the Leeds hooker swung the ball back for the expected clearing kick but it rolled loose.

Veteran Welsh forward Graham Rees, who had joined Saints from Swinton, raced through on to the loose ball and plunged over the line for a try in 35 seconds, the quickest in Wembley history.

Coslett converted and that early lead was the foundation on which St Helens carefully built their game. By

1972 Lance Todd winner Kel Coslett and St Helens winger Les Jones give a champagne toast after the Wembley win over Leeds.

half-time Saints led 12-6. St Helens winger Les Jones had added a second try in the 16th minute while Coslett knocked over two penalties and Leeds prop Terry Clawson had replied in kind with three successful penalty kicks.

At half-time St Helens coach Challinor had reminded his troops that they had to be on their guard in the first ten minutes of the second half. A Leeds try was the last thing he wanted but, in the first minute after the interval, Leeds second rower Phil Cookson surged over near the posts for a touch down. Amazingly, Clawson missed the conversion. Shades of Don Fox in 1968.

Although the St Helens lead had been reduced to 12-9 Leeds were badly hit by the goal miss. Coslett said: 'You could see their heads going down after that. We knew that all we had to do to win the Cup was to cut out all mistakes and tackle well!'

Coslett pushed the score along with a drop goal and penalty to complete his five goal haul and then the unlucky Clawson, who missed four goal chances including three in front of the posts, set up the big finish by landing two penalties to complete his five-goal collection and cut Saints' lead to 16-13.

St Helens were in no mood to present Leeds with a winning opportunity and when the final whistle went the Lancashire team still had their noses in front.

Kel Coslett and the Challenge Cup in 1972.

Lance Todd Trophy winner Coslett, who missed the 1966 final because he was still recovering from his broken leg and learning the loose forward trade, was ecstatic. A winner's medal at his first attempt but there was a surprise waiting for him when he finally left the arena.

'Don't ask me how he managed it', said Kel. 'Even though Wembley had provided their usual efficient security system my dad was in the dressing room waiting for me when I got back. What an emotional moment for us both.'

CHAPTER 57

FOX - MARK THREE

When Peter Fox talks about Rugby League it pays to listen. He is a man of strong conviction and persuasive view. He is also fiercely proud of his roots in Yorkshire, the coalfield area in particular.

Although as a player he had not reached the heights achieved by his two younger brothers, Don and Neil, he was, and still is, a leading coach within the professional game. In 1971 he took over at Post Office Road as coach to Featherstone Rovers and created what he firmly believes to be the finest team that ever emerged from that collection of houses, shops and pubs around a crossroads between Wakefield and Pontefract.

He used the best material that was available to him at the time, the young men of the village. In the two years that he had been with Rovers he succeeded in assembling the cream of the amateur Rugby League teams that followed their sport in the physically demanding local leagues.

Only once did he step outside the confines of the locality and that was to sign Keith Toohey from Batley. Considering the size of the community, they do well to maintain professional Rugby.

The club had won the Challenge Cup for the first time in 1967 and had enjoyed the experience. The incentive to do it over again was imbued in the players and their league form indi-cated that they were good enough to reach Wembley; they finished second in the final table behind Alex Murphy's Warrington.

Fox had blended the team to perfection. Although the veteran full-back Cyril Kellett had been signed from Hull KR before Fox's arrival, the Featherstone-based player still had a rock-like role to play in the team.

He brought veteran prop Les Tonks back from loan at Hull KR, converted Vince Farrar from a loose forward or hooker into a footballing prop forward and persuaded Charlie Stone to return to professional football. He had signed for Rovers and then become disillusioned with the professional game, returning his sign-ing-on cheque to the club.

Fox also drafted in good young players. Scrum half Steve Nash who was destined to be a Great Britain international for many years, stand-off half Mel Mason, wingers Paul Coven-try and Ken Kellett with the energy of centre Mick Smith, complimented the silky skills of partner John Newlove.

In the first two rounds they beat Salford and Rochdale Hornets at home while, in the third round, they came up against Warrington, gaining great satisfaction from their 18-14 win at Wilderspool.

There is no bigger incentive for any team from Featherstone than fac-ing neighbours Castleford at any level of Rugby League and a win in the semi-final of the Challenge Cup as-sumes even greater magnitudes than normal. The 1972 Rovers swept Castleford to one side 17-3 at Headin-gley for the right to face Bradford Northern at Wembley.

Rugby League had changed its for-mat slightly. Instead of the four tackle limit they had increased the number to six giving greater scope for players to create attacking positions and re-ducing panic kicking early in each play.

Bradford Northern were hardly high level opposition; their league form had been little short of disas-trous. In the last season before the Rugby League split back into a two-division format they were crashing around in the lower reaches.

In fact Bradford finished 23rd in the League table, just beating Hali-fax's unenviable record as being the lowest placed club ever to reach a Wembley final.

They had, however, pulled their form together for the Challenge Cup. All the teams they faced were in the top sixteen of the League which would guarantee them a place in the first division when the League was split in to two-divisions at the end of the term.

Whitehaven, Hull KR and Wigan were the stepping stones as Northern reached the semi-final where they faced eventual League Champions Dewsbury who were playing in their first semi-final appearance for 23 years! The consensus of opinion was that the heavy woollen district side, Dewsbury, were going to reach their first Challenge Cup final for 30 years.

In the event Northern, inspired by their stand-off half David Treasure, swept Dewsbury aside 23-7 giving them a place in the final for the first time since their three successive Wembley appearances in 1947, 1948 and 1949.

League form reasserted itself at Wembley. After 20 minutes everybody knew that Featherstone had won the Cup because they were leading 17-0, an unassailable lead in Cup final terms.

The veteran Kellett tormented Bradford. He initiated their agony with a third-minute penalty and then added conversions to two tries by Newlove and one from Farrar.

Eddie Tees, Bradford's full-back recruit from Barrow, spent the last eleven minutes of the first half giving Northern some respectability when he landed three penalties. But they were mere pin pricks, nuisance value, to a Rovers team who were in full command of the game.

Northern coach Ian Brooke, the former Wakefield Trinity centre who had played at Wembley in 1963 and 1968, qualified as the youngest coach to lead a Wembley team. He had substituted prop Kel Earl for the veteran Arnie Long midway through the first

half and, while it put a brake on the Rovers riot, it was never going to be the kind of move to inspire a complete change around in fortune.

Kellett started the second half in the same fashion as the first with a penalty but this time the answer was a try from Bradford winger David Redfearn.

Saturday afternoon television viewers for years after were reminded of Featherstone's 62nd minute try by centre Mick Smith. He jinked and weaved through the Bradford cover to plant the ball down near the posts for a try.

The television people were so taken by the sheer beauty of the strike that they included it as part of the introduction montage to their famous Saturday afternoon sports magazine programme 'Grandstand'. Kellett kicked the goal.

Although the game was over as a competitive situation, the points continued to flow. Bradford hit back in the 68th minute with a try from loose forward Stan Fearnley, son of the former Bradford stalwart forward and coach Albert Fearnley, and that was converted by Tees.

Featherstone substitute David Hartley scored a try five minutes from time. Kellett kicked the goal and then made his way into the Challenge Cup record books by kicking a penalty in the last minute.

By landing his eighth goal in Featherstone's 33-14 victory he had broken the Cup final goal-kicking record, which had been established by his coach Peter Fox's brother Neil in 1960.

The game might have been a one-sided affair but it too had a place in the record book. The aggregate number of points scored was the biggest in Challenge Cup final history at Wembley and the fans paid a world record £125,826.40 receipts.

Peter Fox on the shoulders of his victorious Featherstone Rovers team after beating Bradford Northern in the 1973 final.

CHAPTER 58

IT'S THAT MAN AGAIN!

Warrington and Rugby League are virtually the same thing. The Cheshire town – it was extracted from Lancashire in the 1974 local government re-organisation – which sits on the middle reaches of the River Mersey played a contributory role in the development of the 13-a-side game.

But by the end of the 1960s the Wire were in trouble; financially they were shambolic and extinction was a real possibility. The club's tradition and contribution to the town's persona remained valuable, however, and Ossie Davies, the driving force behind one of the country's leading construction companies, led a rescue party to save the Wilderspool club for future generations.

Development of the stadium and club on a professional basis was his intention and he had as his example what had been achieved at Salford by Brian Snape. The introduction of a restaurant, variety club and other sporting facilities like squash courts had brought the club wealth and fame. Wilderspool was transformed.

While reconstruction of the stadium was safe in the hands of somebody who understood the business of bricks and mortar, Davies knew that on the pitch he needed somebody who knew about rebuilding shattered teams and in the midst of Leigh's post 1971 Wembley celebrations, Davies temp-ted Murphy into becoming the new Warrington player-coach.

The Leigh public and club were stunned. Murphy, however, after leaving his initial professional club St Helens has always believed in following destiny; the challenge of constructing a team and club virtually from the foundations appealed to him.

It did not take long for the effects of his leadership to come to the surface. In the 1971-72 season they finished midway up the final one-division league and reached the Challenge Cup semi-final, where they took Murphy's former club St Helens to a replay which they eventually lost while Saints went on to win at Wembley.

Their stature continued to grow in the game as Murphy brought in new players. Two years later they were a major power in the game. They finished fifth in the first division table having taken the last old fashioned league leadership trophy the previous season, were winners of the sponsored John Player Trophy as well as taking two ill-fated competitions, the club championship, an amalgam of all merit marks from all the professional game's competitions and the Captain Morgan Trophy, another sponsored tournament.

A Cup final appearance at Wembley was, therefore, a natural extension to their highly successful season.

They used Huddersfield, Huyton, the successors to Liverpool City, and Wigan as rungs in the ladder to the semi-final, where they overcame Dewsbury to assure themselves of a first Wembley final since they drew with Halifax before the Twin Towers in 1954.

Yet another Murphy miracle was achieved. Two clubs as player-coach and two Wembley finals. He had now trodden on that famous turf four times and, up to 1974, had yet to experience defeat.

Featherstone Rovers had enjoyed their lifestyle as Challenge Cup holders and fought their way back to defend the trophy they won in such spectacular style the previous year.

Peter Fox still held the reins at Post Office Road although the shape of his Wembley team was different in substance from his 1973 side. They should have known what was going to happen when they were drawn away in all of the first three rounds and none of the ties proved easy. They came through 11-3 at Barrow, 12-9 at Hull KR and in a repeat of the previous year's final at Odsal they beat Bradford 5-0.

Before a disappointing 7,971 Headingley crowd they traded blows with Leigh and came through to take the Wembley place by winning 21-14.

The battle of minds between top tacticians Peter Fox and Alex Murphy appealed almost as much as the game itself on 11 May.

Murphy held one advantage over Fox. He was playing and could have a direct bearing on what transpired. His influence was clear throughout the whole of what turned out to be a very bad tempered game by Wembley standards.

The respective goal-kickers Derek Whitehead of Warrington and Harold Box of Rovers were the leading performers in the opening acts. In the first half-hour Whitehead had chalked up four successful shots on goal while Box had two to his credit. Oldham referee Sam Shepherd had been busy giving rulings as the two teams' discipline slipped away.

A rib injury forced Murphy to leave the field ten minutes before the end of the first half and, without his on-field guidance, Warrington saw Rovers force their way back into the game. Just before half-time Warrington's 8-4 lead was lost as Featherstone captain and stand-off John Newlove went over for a try and Box added the conversion to take Rovers in leading 9-8.

In the Warrington dressing room there was feverish activity. Murphy's presence was essential if they were to win the Cup in front of 25,000 Wire fans who had made the pilgrimage to Wembley. He underwent five painkilling injections and went out to play the second half.

Within four minutes his inspirational leadership rescued the lead for Warrington as he sent hooker Kevin

Ashcroft, who had followed him from Leigh, in for a try which Whitehead converted.

Whitehead's accurate goalkicking brought two more penalties and Murphy continued to introduce some space between Rovers and the lead with two drop goals. Warrington's triumph was completed when former Aberavon forward Mike Nicholas shot past four defenders for a try, but Whitehead's conversion miss robbed him of the chance to join Featherstone's Cyril Kellett as Wembley record holder with eight goals although he had the consolation of being voted as the Lance Todd Trophy winner.

Murphy, as ever, held centre stage, with accusations that he had employed gamesmanship to gain a hold on the match. His clash with Rovers centre David Hartley in the third

Warrington's Derek Whitehead (left) and Welshman Bobby Wanbon (right) show the Cup off after beating Featherstone in 1974.

minute had been pinpointed as the starting place of the ill temper.

Fox, never a man to mince his words, was reported by a Yorkshire newspaper as saying: 'I think the referee was totally irresponsible. The first incident of the match was a stiff arm tackle by Murphy on Hartley and this caused all the trouble later. We were suffering through penalties and this upset the lads.'

Warrington had, however, won the game 24-9 and returned home to a 100,000 crowd for a victory parade. The old League saying: 'Winners can laugh, the rest can please themselves' once again held water.

CHAPTER 59

BULL IN A CHINA SHOP

Vince Karalius went to Wembley four times as a player, three times as an unbeaten Cup finalist and once as a winning Test player. He associated the place with success. But when he took over as Widnes coach he put Cup final glory to the back of his mind.

'The place was a shambles,' said Karalius, who had well earned his nickname, 'the Wild Bull of Pampas' from the dazed Australians, who had tried to block his progress to the try line.

The former St Helens, Widnes and Great Britain loose forward was the forerunner of the modern Rugby League professional and the term: 'fitness fanatic' might have been invented for this man who pioneered the use of intensive weight training and fitness programmes in the sport. He was a lone voice in the mid-1970s but his theories have been widely adopted, although they have been re-imported from Australia where they were employed on a very effective scale.

'When I walked into Naughton Park as the coach for the first time they were on their uppers,' he explained. 'My first priority was simply to get them fit enough to play Rugby League.'

The tale in Widnes was that at his first training session with the Widnes players Vince, a craggy, long-jawed man, walked into the dressing room

and asked what the rags in the middle of the room were.

'That's our training kit', he was told. Karalius threw the offending items out of the room and replaced it with brand new equipment the following week. Professionalism is a by-word with Karalius, who viewed his sport through serious eyes. Winning was all that mattered.

Fortunately the previous regimes, former Wigan hooker Joe Egan in particular, had been building on the club's youth policy. They had been combing the local amateur clubs for likely young men and, fortunately for Karalius and Widnes, they had chosen well.

He had willing minds in the shape of centre Eric Hughes, the younger brother of Arthur Hughes who had played for Widnes in the 1964 final, scrum half Reg Bowden, centre Mal Aspey and full-back Ray Dutton. They were to form the root of the club's major successes over the late 1970s and early 1980s.

By 1974-75 the full potential of Karalius's creation was beginning to take shape. They won the Lancashire Cup and were beaten finalists in the John Player Trophy. 'You could see what was happening,' added Karalius.

Now those thoughts about Wembley that he had stored away while he rebuilt his home-town club were brought back.

The Widnes players, however, might not have known it at the time but their Wembley preparation started even before the first ball was pulled from the velvet bag.

Karalius explained: 'Fitness is not something that you can acquire over a short period. It has to be built up slowly and it is a way of life. Every time I see Cup finalists going into special camp a few days before such a big game I have to shake my head. You can't put in what's needed for such a big game at that late stage.

'I started the fitness programme for the Cup final in January and built the players up slowly. By the time we reached Wembley all the hard work was done and my players spent the last two days effectively resting up before they played.

'The body becomes used to heavy exercise at the same time every day so if the game kicked off at 3pm I had my players training intensely at 3pm on as many days as I could bring them in.'

And when he reached Wembley Karalius adopted not just the role as fitness and tactical leader but guardian too.

'On the eve of the final I took the players to the cinema, that was always my routine at Wembley, and then we took them back for an early night at the hotel. I went round to see that every player was in his room and happy before I retired. I was like a mother hen but it was important because it was all part of my build up for the game.'

Karalius's Wembley experience paid off for his players as well. Karalius explained: 'People can say what they like about coaches but if they've played at the top level as well it helps.

'Many of my team had not been to Wembley before and I had never been licked at the place. I could prepare them for what happens the first time they walked out and, inevitably, it is a tough experience and a few words from me could help.'

Anybody who watched their Rugby exclusively at Naughton Park would have missed the Widnes Wembley mission. All three of their qualifying rounds were played away from home at Swinton, Hull where they won 13-12 and Oldham.

Rugby League was suffering one of its periodic troughs of support. The situation had, however, become more serious than in the past and a new administration was put in place. In came new secretary David Oxley, a Hull-born schoolmaster from Dover, and the game's first ever full time public relations officer David Howes.

The image rebuild had yet to start in earnest and even crowds for Cup semi-finals had yet to reach their once proud peak. For their last-four meeting with Wakefield Trinity at Odsal Widnes's 13-7 victory was seen by 9,155 people.

Suitably Widnes were to face their Cheshire neighbours Warrington, the Cup holders at Wembley. Suitably because the Wire coach was Alex Mur-

phy and his relationship with Karalius had been built up when they were both members of a very good St Helens team.

Karalius had provided Murphy with solid protection. The big six foot, 14-stone Widnesian was not a man to be trifled with and, if the opposition tried to take their frustrations out on the mercurial Murphy, it was not long before they had to reckon with Karalius.

On 10 May 1975 the two men faced each other as opposing coaches at Wembley. They both knew that each was concentrating on one thing, victory. It was how they both played the game.

In the best traditions of a western style duel in the sun one of the two men was going to lose something valuable. Neither had finished on the losing side in a Cup final at Wembley before and one of them had to lose that record. Their pride was on the line.

Karalius had been twice with St Helens in 1956 and 1961 and with Widnes in 1964 while Murphy had seen victories with St Helens in 1961 and 1966, Leigh in 1971 and Warrington the previous year.

Warrington were well established as a prominent member of the Rugby League community. Although they had not succeeded in repeating their wonderful form of the previous season,they had reached Wembley by eliminating Halifax, a much-weakened Wigan and New Hunslet, the phoenix-like recreation from the ashes of the old Hunslet club. In the semi-final they overcame Leeds ensuring

that they could go back to Wembley to defend the Challenge Cup.

For the opening spell it looked as though Murphy was going to come out on top. In the fifth minute John Bevan, the Welsh winger from the triumphant 1971 Rugby Union British Lions who won a series in New Zealand, went over for a try which Derek Whitehead converted.

Widnes, however, had their own version of a siege gun in full-back Ray Dutton and his immaculate boot brought them back in contention. He sent two penalties soaring between the posts, converted a try by giant Welsh prop Jim Mills in the 33rd minute and, on the stroke of half-time, ensured that Widnes led 11-5 by kicking a third penalty.

Whitehead lifted Warrington briefly at the start of the second half when Bowden was penalised for dissent but Widnes were not to be deflected.

A Dutton drop goal, the first at Wembley since the League reduced its value from two points to one in 1974, and then a further penalty brought Widnes victory and the Cup at 14-7. His polished kicking display also brought Dutton the vote as the Lance Todd Trophy winner.

Karalius left Wembley with his record at the London stadium still intact and then shook the whole of Rugby League by leaving the game to concentrate on his growing and thriving scrap metal business. Murphy remained to face Wembley again.

CHAPTER 60

DAD'S ARMY

The delicate balance between experience and youth has always been a formula that Rugby League clubs have sought to achieve. More often than not it has been a chance decision which has achieved that kind of symmetry in every case.

For St Helens the 1960s and early 1970s were a period of almost continuous success. Three Wembley victories, eight Lancashire Cup wins in ten finals, a Floodlit Trophy success, two League Leadership wins and three Championship final returns from six final appearances. Add into that equation numbers of international selections for their players together with a never ending arrival of new players and Knowsley Road was one of the places to be in Rugby League.

The age balance in the side reached a critical point in 1975-76. A substantial number of the team had already seen their 30th birthday. Their two Welsh forwards, John Mantle and Kel Coslett, were 34-years-old, scrum half Jeff Heaton 32, stand-off Billy Benyon and hooker Tony Karalius were both 31 and Test second row forward George Nicholls 30.

There were younger players emerging but the heart beat of the team was still their ageing stars. Their potency as Rugby players was demonstrated in 1974-75 when they took the first division title and they remained a force to be reckoned with in 1975-76. They

collected the BBC2 Floodlit Trophy while their League form remained consistently successful.

Time might have been running out on the careers of some St Helens players but they were still inspired by the prospect of a Challenge Cup campaign.

They had the ability to resist a challenge by Hull with a first round 5-3 win at the Boulevard and they followed that impressive result with another important away win at Salford, who were in massive form in the League, and then a home third round win over Oldham. Their semi-final challenge came from an unexpected quarter and was to prove almost a stumbling block.

Keighley, with just one Wembley appearance to their credit in 1937, had battled their way through to the last-four for the first time since that pre-war push through to the final. Their progress had been efficient, without being spectacular, disposing of Halifax, Workington and Leigh before facing St Helens.

The little West Yorkshire club were all but written off against St Helens and yet they had constructed the kind of workmanlike side often favoured in Yorkshire. Hardly spectacular and yet accomplished in the basic professional arts that made them so difficult to beat.

Huddersfield's Fartown ground,

which had been dropped as a venue for Rugby League's bigger games with the declining fortunes of the club, provided the stage for this uncompromising encounter.

With solid professionals like goal-kicking full-back Brian Jefferson, a long-time servant with the club, together with the guile of former Castleford forward Charlie Birdsall and the force of ex-Leeds prop John Burke, Keighley neither asked for or received any quarter and it took a saving try by Heaton to give the Lancashire club passage to Wembley as they nosed home 5-4.

St Helens, who count Wigan as their most deadly of rivals, are also very close to a number of other clubs and it takes little more than 15 minutes to drive a car from the centre of St Helens to Widnes's civic centre sprawl.

The two communities are totally different, however, although they share a similar industrial base. When it comes to Rugby League, the rivalry is fierce although players from either town can be found in both clubs at any one given time.

Rugby League enjoys its own specialist press and they were aware of the number of years piling up on the heads of the St Helens team and they were naturally christened 'Dad's Army', a label inspired by the popular television comedy programme based on the antics of a south coast Home Guard unit from the second World War.

For the third successive year the Challenge Cup holders returned to defend their trophy. Widnes, winners over Warrington in 1975, had booked their place for the final by removing Batley, Wigan, and Warrington before overcoming a 9-0 half-time deficit to beat Featherstone Rovers 15-9 in the semi-final at Station Road.

The age gap was, in sporting terms, enormous. By the time both sides had taken the field at Wembley on 8 May the St Helens front row had a combined age of 99 years while the two Widnes props Nick Nelson and John Wood were just 23 and 19-years-old respectively.

Fate, it seemed, was conspiring against St Helens. The Cup final day was hardly conducive for body contact sport as temperatures in the stadium topped 100 degrees fahrenheit. The prognosis was that the ageing Saints stars would not be able to last the pace in the heat.

It reinforced the pre-match predictions which had made Widnes clear favourites although former St Helens star Alex Murphy had faith in his old club. Enough to say in print that if Saints lost he would jump off the Runcorn bridge over the River Mersey and Murphy, although a gambler by nature, did not take that kind of silly risk. It is a long drop.

Eric Ashton, the St Helens coach, who was making his eighth visit to Wembley, had briefed his troops well and their battle plan was to frustrate the younger Widnes team, counter attacking when the opportunity presented itself.

Widnes, by now coached by Frank Myler who had taken over from Vince Karalius, set off quickly in an attempt to wear down St Helens but they found Ashton's tactics kept them in check.

In the 12th minute centre Eddie Cunningham scored a try under the posts which full-back Geoff Pimblett converted. It gave Saints the lead at 5-0 and they never lost that advantage at any stage throughout the game.

The two goalkickers dominated the scoring in the rest of the first half. Dutton, the man of the match in 1975, drove home two penalties while Pimblett, the quietly spoken Saint, dropped a goal.

Widnes closed the score gap to one point with a drop goal from hooker Keith Elwell and, while Widnes were threatening to take over the match, Pimblett took another point with his second drop goal of the game.

The Chemics knew that the decisive point in the final was approaching and they were looking for St Helens' age to start telling against them as the intensity of the game and heat of the stadium remained turned up.

In fact it was Widnes who found the heat in the kitchen too much, and 12 minutes from the end Heaton turned some creative play by Tony Karalius, brother of Vincent, into a try which Pimblett converted. The score brought new life into Saints' tiring limbs and with that touch of irony produced so often in sport they finished Widnes off with two tries from a 20-year-old Widnes-born player.

Peter Glynn had been brought on as substitute for the injured Benyon just before half-time and he struck twice, once in the 74th minute and then again four minutes later. Pimblett, the man of the match, added the conversion to the first of the pair and that completed Saints' 20-5 victory. Experience had triumphed over youth. The after-match quotes told the story.

Veteran Mantle said: 'We were like marathon runners. We may be the wrong side of 30 but we just kept going'. While Heaton, scorer of that vital try, said: 'All of us old'uns realised this could be our last major final and we were prepared to give it everything.'

Coslett, who had received the Cup from Mrs Margaret Thatcher, who was then leader of the opposition, collapsed through exhaustion in the dressing room and it took both salt tablets and cold baths to revive him.

CHAPTER 61

CUP BIRTHRIGHT

Kevin Dick was born and grew up a healthy drop kick away from Leeds Rugby League Club's Headingley home. The connection went deeper. His father Alec had played in the famous blue and amber during the 1950s and the family connection with the club was part of Kevin's birthright.

His whole adolesence and family life was centred on the club and, after a spell emerging through schools football, he joined the Leeds Colts team.

Although he is not a big man, Kevin has never been short of belief in his own ability. He is also naturally strong both in body and mind. And competitive spirit ensured that he was never intimidated even by the largest forward.

His procession through the ranks at Leeds confirmed his potential as a player. After he had assumed his professional status with the club, he was considered strong enough to go straight into the Leeds reserve team.

Second-team Rugby League has always been a curious mixture. On the one hand there is the group of young bloods who are just starting out on their professional careers and anxious to prove themselves both able and courageous enough to rate a first-team opportunity.

While, on the other hand, there are the 'old men' whose careers are usually on the wane. They know all there is to know about survival in the

professional game and it develops into a battle of the strongest.

Somewhere between these two groups come the established first-team players who are returning from injury, recovering form or stepping out after collisions with the disciplinary committee.

It remains the best possible grounding for young players and Dick's quality as a player took him through that learning experience in double quick time. After seven reserve team appearances, he was drafted into the first team.

In that era the scrum half's number seven jersey at Headingley was being contested by Peter Banner, a Welsh Rugby League international who had been signed from Salford, and another up and coming youngster Chris Sanderson.

For the 1976-77 Challenge Cup campaign Banner had possession while coach Syd Hynes used Sanderson in their League matches. Leeds and Banner made progress through the Cup rounds; Batley, Barrow, Workington and the semi-final against holders St Helens.

Then the Leeds scrum half position changed dramatically. Banner decided to quit British Rugby League and live abroad while, tragically, Sanderson died of injuries sustained in a match at Salford. For the last three matches in the approach to Wembley

in Her Majesty the Queen's Silver Jubilee year, it was Kevin Dick who filled the scrum half's jersey.

Widnes had by this time acquired the tag 'Cup Kings' because it was their third successive visit to the stadium, the first West of Pennine club to achieve the feat.

Their victims in the 1977 campaign all came from Yorkshire: Wakefield Trinity, Featherstone Rovers, York and Hull KR in the semi-final and they already had the Lancashire Cup to show for their efforts.

Following the shock of Sanderson's death Leeds made a dramatic bid for the Challenge Cup.

John Holmes, who had moved from full-back where he played for Leeds in their last Wembley final, was one of the most creative outside halves of his generation and he said: 'It was as if what happened to Chris pushed us all together again and we started to play well.'

When Hynes named his team for Wembley he had enough faith in the ability of Kevin Dick to give him the crucial scrum-half role and he joined a rare breed of player who made his debut in the competition in the final.

The youngster was involved in the game from the outset. There was little or no trace of any tension and he put Yorkshire Cup-winners Leeds in the lead in the third minute when he landed a 40 metre penalty after he was involved in an incident with Widnes's former Leeds forward Bill Ramsey.

Widnes, however, were not easily nudged off their course. They surged back, passed Leeds into a five point lead with a Ray Dutton penalty and a try by centre Mal Aspey which, his then painting and decorating business partner, Dutton converted.

Leeds staged a damage limitation exercise when Test winger John Atkinson seized on an error by his opposite number Stuart Wright to score a try, but it was too far out for Dick's conversion attempt.

The Yorkshiremen snatched the initiative back after 13 minutes of the second half when, after a controversial scrum decision by Manchester referee Vincent Moss, the precocious Dick sent centre Les Dyl through for a try with a well worked reverse pass.

Kevin Dick, the undisputed hero of the 1977 final, passing.

Dick demonstrated that he was fallible by missing the goal kick but the effect to Widnes's confidence was enormous. Leeds prop Steve Pitchford, who had worked hard running the ball at the Widnes defence, became a lethal force breaking the Chemics line virtually at will.

It was from one of his powerful surges which set up the start of an amazing 20 minutes for young Dick. After the roly-poly forward had played the ball quickly, Kevin fooled not only Widnes but most of the Wembley audience with a dummy pass and then nipped over near the posts for a try which he also converted.

Three minutes from time he added a drop goal and, with 60 seconds of normal time remaining, he added a penalty. In Leeds' 16-7 victory Dick had contributed ten points with a try, two penalty goals, a conversion and a drop goal. It was not enough to win the man of the match award and the Lance Todd Trophy went instead to Pitchford who, to be fair, had shown

such good form in the game that he was selected for the Great Britain team to tour Australia and New Zealand on the strength of it.

It was a fine tribute to the fallen Sanderson by his Leeds team-mates and they dedicated their win to his memory.

Widnes were left with their second defeat in three Wembley visits but for one of their players, hooker Keith Elwell, it was the start of something really big. He started a world record 239 successive first team matches for the Chemics at Wembley.

The next time Kevin Dick played in a Challenge Cup tie, however, was at Wembley.

Ten matches after the start of the 1977-78 season, Dick had to undergo surgery for a knee cartilage problem and that put him out of the game and first team reckoning. While he was out of action Leeds signed the long-serving Halifax scrum half Sammy Sanderson.

Recognised as a creative half-back

Sanderson, a milkman, was holding the number seven jersey as Leeds entered the 1978 Challenge Cup sequence. Halifax, Wakefield, Bradford Northern and Featherstone Rovers were all swept aside as the men from Headingley returned to Wembley for their fourth visit of the 1970s.

Dick had recovered from his surgery and forced his way back into the Leeds first team squad and for the final against St Helens at Wembley; he was one of the two substitutes.

Saints coach Eric Ashton walked through the Wembley tunnel for a record ninth time. He had six appearances as a player or player-coach and three as a coach. St Helens were playing in their tenth final and their record at Wembley in post-war finals was impressive with wins in 1956, 1961, 1966, 1972 and 1976 against one defeat in 1953. To qualify for Wembley in 1977 meant overcoming Huyton, Oldham, Huddersfield and Warrington.

It was a classic mix for a Rugby League Challenge Cup final, the Red Rose against the White Rose.

Rarely, however, do games which are built up as classic confrontations live up to that prediction and, yet, this was a match that was to stand comparison with the very best.

St Helens laid down a ten point barrage. A horrendous error between Leeds full-back Henry Oulton and winger John Atkinson saw the ball go to ground in the in-goal area and St Helens hooker Graham Liptrot dropped on the ball for a fourth-minute try. Full-back Geoff Pimblett converted.

This was followed by a swivel-hipped try from stand-off Bill Francis and Pimblett again tacked on the goal points. Atkinson atoned for his part in the opening try by marking his 400th appearance for the Leeds club with a 22nd minute try which Oulton converted to rub out his contribution to the same blunder.

Six minutes before half-time Pimblett steadied the St Helens boat with a penalty. Leeds coach Syd Hynes switched his tactics at half-time. Instead of playing to the normal Leeds pattern of expansive football, he in-

structed his forwards to use their extra weight and concentrate on attacking the centre of the St Helens line.

His new approach worked. Leeds took control of the game. A David Ward drop goal, followed by tries from winger David Smith and forward Phil Cookson levelled the scores at 12-12. Then two drop goal strikes, first by John Holmes and then by Ward, saw Leeds retain the Cup with a 14-12 scoreline.

Dick had played his part in the triumph because he had replaced Sanderson as a substitute.

His recollection of the 1977 affair was clouded by the emotion and elation of the day. He explained: 'I really couldn't remember much about it and I had to buy a video copy off the BBC who had televised the game.

'It was in the very early days of video. It cost me £200 for the copy on one of the first VHS style machines. Mind you all the lads who played eventually gave me £10 each to help with the cost so that they could relive the game too.'

CHAPTER 62

HELLO LUV!

The eve of the Challenge Cup final at Wembley can destroy even the most hardened of professional players. The pressure, the fear of failure, can all be magnified in your brain during the sleepless, dark hours.

Every Rugby League coach has his antidote to that pressure. Some like to take their players off to the cinema in an attempt to lose them in a fantasy world while others would resort to quiz and parlour games.

Most of the team leaders would, however, want to keep his players' minds fixed on the team effort and their relationship with their team mates.

Doug Laughton was different. He arrived at Widnes from Wigan aged 30 and with, allegedly, the best part of his career behind him.

Vince Karalius, the doyen of the coaches, recognised that Laughton was not only a player of considerable talent with many games left under his belt but that he was also a leader of men.

That assessment proved to be correct and it was his influence over a young, developing Widnes team that saw them become one of the most successful club sides the world of Rugby League has ever seen. Certainly, in modern terms, he helped found a dynasty that looks like being at the top end of the League game for the same length of time as Liverpool in Association Football.

Karalius, the founding father of the modern Widnes club, finished as coach after the 1975 Cup triumph and his successor Frank Myler continued until May 1978. The club did not have to look very far to find his successor because he was one of their players, Laughton.

Former Great Britain captain Laughton's impact was almost instantaneous. They collected both the Lancashire Cup and the John Player Trophy as the season progressed and, although they had missed out on the first division championship, they still had ambitions as far as Wembley and the Premiership, the end of season knockout for the top eight clubs in the League which had replaced the old championship play-off in 1975.

Workington, Wigan, Huddersfield and Bradford Northern failed to provide a barrier in the Challenge Cup and Widnes made sure of their fourth Wembley final in five years where they were to face a revived Wakefield Trinity.

As the final hours before the kick off on 5 May ticked away, Laughton chose to break with the traditional approach and he invited the players' wives and girlfriends to join them for the eve-of-final dinner at the team hotel.

Eric Hughes, who was playing in his fourth Wembley final, recalled: 'You could expend so much mental energy if you allowed yourself to think too much about the match. That was one of the problems a coach had to consider and they all have their own methods and most of the team had been brought up in the Karalius discipline; you don't drink for months as part of the preparation for the game.

'Frank Myler was different and this invitation to the wives was Doug's way. It was a quiet evening in with your lady. We were always a well disciplined team and we didn't drink even then. The girls were allowed a glass or two of wine and generally it was like being at home.

'My wife Jackie and I just talked and then, at the end of the evening, the girls all went back to their own hotel and we went to bed.

'We were like most other men. Sleeping in a strange bed and thinking about what the kids are doing or what the problems may be at home; just as bad as big match nerves. By having the girls there it helped restore an air of calm and normality.

'And the proof of any method or theory is in the eating and I don't think that anybody could argue with this method.'

The pressure was on Widnes and Hughes admitted that there was great tension in the Widnes camp following their two previous Cup final defeats.

And the 1979 final was a Wembley first for your author. Although I had covered many sporting events at Wembley, I had never enjoyed the privilege of walking on the sacred turf.

I had mentioned this in passing conversation with Mr Trevor Woodward, the then football chairman of Wakefield Trinity, and he arranged that I should make the traditional Friday walk-about at the stadium with the Trinity players.

Our journey to London started from a hotel at Egham, Surrey. We passed Heathrow Airport where Concorde was taxiing for take off. And I saw the moment Wakefield were beaten.

That was when somebody said: 'Look, there are the twin towers'. Trinity were out of the reckoning. Their players appeared to be almost completely crushed by that realisation that they had got to play the game.

Even the old stagers like former Wigan forward Bill Ashurst, who was making a comeback after a knee operation and expected to take a leading role for the Yorkshire side, was unusually subdued.

The day of the match dawned and for a change in a Wembley Challenge Cup final there was no score in the first half. Hughes explained the situation: 'I know that people didn't rate this final because it was low scoring but what they have to take into account is that both sides were defensively well equipped.

'While we were always confident of winning, Trinity certainly did not make it easy for us.'

Hughes is right. Once Widnes started to find the gaps they never looked like being beaten and Wakefield were always back pedalling.

Winger Mick Burke set the trend

with a penalty and that was followed ten minutes later by a try from winger Stuart Wright and a conversion by Burke.

Hooker Keith Elwell, by now well into his mammoth sequence of consecutive appearances for the Merseyside club, chipped in with a drop goal before Trinity right winger Andrew Fletcher registered his side's only points of the game with a try in the 65th minute.

Full-back Dave Eckersley marked the start of the last ten minutes with a drop goal, while five minutes from time Eric Hughes scored their second try after bamboozling the Trinity defence by first shaping to kick a drop goal and then racing 25 metres to the line for a try.

Widnes left with the Cup after their 12-3 win while Trinity's long-serving stand-off half David Topliss joined the growing list of players who had won the Lance Todd Trophy in a losing team. Coincidentally the previous time Trinity had reached the final, the Watersplash final, in 1968, Don Fox tasted the sweet and sour of the same situation.

Widnes collected their fourth trophy when they beat Bradford Northern in the Premiership final. Four Cups but it failed to match the Huddersfield, Hunslet and Swinton record because they did not win all the trophies available to them.

The League championship got away. But there was consolation because they picked up a £12,555 cheque as the first winners of the sponsored Challenge Cup competition.

The full set. Bradford Northern and Widnes players display their club's haul from the 1978–79 season. Northern won the Yorkshire Cup while Widnes in the lighter tops took the John Player Trophy, the Lancashire Cup, the BBC Floodlit Trophy and, of course, the Challenge Cup as well as other competitions.

CHAPTER 63

DODGER'S LAST STAND

At 5 feet 4 inches tall Roger Mill-ward looks almost too small to have been a Rugby player. He was, however, a giant among the men of League. His astute football brain and sheer speed off the mark made him one of the greatest half-backs produced by Britain since the War and some would argue that he ranks among the best ever.

Shy and retiring by nature, Millward shot to fame at a very early age. He played his amateur rugby in his home town of Castleford and, for a short time in the early 1960s, ITV took to televising schoolboy Rugby League matches and Roger, with his jinking runs and darts for the line, became known as 'Roger the Dodger'.

His fame spread with the popularity of the broadcasts and that, quite naturally, attracted the harbingers of the professional career, the talent scouts.

There was, however, little danger of him leaving the district. As a Castleford lad he was determined to turn professional with his home-town club. He achieved that ambition in September 1964. His progress was swift and he made his first-team debut in October that year.

His route to a regular senior team place was, however, blocked by a superb double act, Alan Hardisty and Alan Hepworth. They dominated the Castleford half-back positions com-

pletely and young Millward was, more often than not, trapped in the second team.

There was little other option but for him to leave Wheldon Road and that eventually came to pass in August 1966 when Hull KR paid Castleford £6,000 for his services.

In the end the move suited both parties. Millward got his wish for regular first-team placings while Castleford got £6,000, and their Hardisty-Hepworth partnership remained intact for the next four years.

Roger's career blossomed on Humberside where he soon became the darling of the Craven Park followers. His career was littered with glories both for Rovers as well as Great Britain.

He made 400 appearances for Hull KR scoring a club record 207 tries, he beat Gilbert Austin's record by almost 50, and broke a whole host of scoring records which made him a feared and marked man.

He became captain of the side in November 1969 and their player-coach in March 1977. He played in five Yorkshire Cup finals on the winning side four times, two BBC 2 Floodlit Cup winning sides, a championship winning team and a championship runners-up side.

In 1970 he was instrumental in Great Britain winning the Ashes in Australia, the last side to beat the

Kangaroos Down Under to date, on his way to 29 caps for his country.

In 1980, at the age of 32, the only thing missing from Millward's illustrious career was an appearance in a Cup Final at Wembley and a winner's medal. By this late stage it was beginning to look as though he would be one of the great players who would never grace the Wembley turf. Rovers, however, had other ideas. After beating Wigan in the first round Millward had the satisfaction of putting Castleford out in the second round.

They rode rough shod over Warrington in the third round winning 23-11 and beat Halifax 20-7 in the semi-final at Leeds.

Just to make the occasion complete the other half of the Humberside professional Rugby League scene, Hull, also invited themselves to the party.

The amateurs of Millom put up a brave fight before losing 33-10 in the first round and then Hull disposed of York, Bradford Northern and Widnes to ensure that Wembley had its first all-Humberside Challenge Cup final.

Hull, who had been promoted from the second division at the start of the previous season, had spent liberally and acquired a squad of the game's better players of the time: Steve Norton, Clive Pickerill, Charlie Birdsall and Sammy Lloyd from

Castleford; Vince Farrar, John Newlove and Charlie Stone from Featherstone and Welshman Paul Woods.

Rovers, on the other hand, relied much more on Humberside produced players with a handful of imports: Millward, Allan Agar and Brian Lockwood from the Castleford area and Welshman Clive Sullivan.

The whole of Humberside moved to London for the weekend and they were at least assured of improving their Wembley record by 100 per cent.

Since the start of the Challenge Cup competition one or other of the two professional clubs had reached the final on eleven occasions with just one success, Hull who beat Wakefield

in 1914. They could not lose in this respect in 1980.

Millward had long been one of League's favourite sons and the fact that Wembley had appeared so late in his career engendered massive sympathy from the rest of the game who were left on the fringes of this private argument. They wanted to see the little man emerge with that ambition fulfilled and poor Hull really could not win whether they took the Cup or not.

Tension was always going to be the order of the day with local pride and not just the Cup at stake. It came to the surface in the eighth minute when in the act of scoring a try Rovers winger Steve Hubbard was fouled by Woods. Although Hubbard missed

with his conversion attempt, he did score with the penalty referee Fred Lindop allowed for the foul.

Then Millward, who had already broken his jaw twice, was sent crashing to the floor by a late tackle from Hull hooker Ronnie Wileman. The Rovers player-coach had been exerting considerable influence on the game and he was a closely marked man. The extent of his injury clearly left him in great pain but it was not realised at that point that he had suffered a third fracture.

Hubbard landed the penalty and Millward courageously rejoined the

Hull KR's Test forward Phil Lowe runs into a tackle by Widnes's Eric Hughes during the 1981 final.

Steve Hubbard of Hull KR holds the trophy aloft after their 1980 Wembley win over Hull FC.

game determined not to be robbed of his full Wembley experience after such a long wait. Hull were rattled and their discipline was slipping; Stone swung a punch at Rovers prop Roy Holdstock and Hubbard inflicted another penalty success on the black and white of Hull.

Hull established a toe hold in the game when centre Tim Wilby went over for a 28th minute try but just before half-time Millward restored the Rovers momentum with a drop goal.

Rovers had the Cup in their hands from this point. There was a penalty each for Hubbard and Sammy Lloyd in the second half but Rovers, and to a lesser extent Rugby League, had got their wish a Cup winner's medal for Roger Millward with their 10-5 victory.

He smiled through pain and gritted his teeth as he held the Cup aloft

at Wembley. Had he but known it at the time he had just a few minutes left as a player. In his come-back against Batley reserves he suffered his fourth broken jaw in ten months following another off-the-ball incident. Enough was enough and he retired as a player to concentrate on his coaching career.

Millward said: 'As soon as I took the tackle at Wembley I knew the jaw was broken. The bone was out of place but fortunately I took a tackle a few seconds later which put it back.

'It was swollen and sore but it

didn't affect my game. If it had I would have gone off the pitch. But I achieved my ambition of playing at Wembley and touring with Great Britain.

'At one stage I thought after 16 attempts at reaching Wembley it wasn't going to happen for me and the relief of actually making it was tremendous.'

Roger Millward's pained moment of triumph. He lifts the Cup for Hull KR after 16 years of trying but it was later revealed he had broken his jaw.

CHAPTER 64

A RECIPE FOR SUCCESS

Nineteen was to prove a significant number for apprentice chef Andrew Gregory in 1981. A gifted, petulant footballer Gregory had become accustomed to being in the spotlight. At the start of the 1980-81 season several major clubs were competing for the signature of the Wigan St Patrick's amateur club half-back.

His performances in the junior game had demanded the attention of many professional club scouts and he was, what tabloid newspapers like to describe as, 'hot property'.

Salford were the early leaders for his signature. They even persuaded him to play a first team game when one of their regular stars was injured and he succeeded in winning their man-of-the-match award.

His financial terms required further discussion by the Salford board of directors and, while they were still deliberating, Widnes coach Doug Laughton, no slouch once he decides to sign a player, slipped in to acquire the precocious talent. How Salford have come to rue their indecision as Gregory has become one of the outstanding players in the world, never mind Britain.

Widnes were in the process of rebuilding their team. Several of the old guard: scrum half Reg Bowden, centre Mal Aspey, forward David Hull and full-back Dave Eckersley had left

Naughton Park to help establish a professional club in London, Fulham.

Besides Gregory they had pulled in forward Brian Lockwood, who played for Hull KR at Wembley the previous season, Workington Town forward Les Gorley, another forward Eric Prescott from Salford and centre Eddie Cunningham from Leeds.

The Chemics took the first round at a canter slamming luckless second division side Doncaster 50-0 but their second-round encounter with Castleford was a much more even-handed affair. The teams were locked 5-5 and a replay the likely outcome when full-back John Myler landed a decisive penalty.

Gregory's influence on the side was growing and he played an important role in their 21-5 third round win over Featherstone Rovers which gave them a semi-final placing against the favourites Warrington. The Wire had won 13 successive games but Widnes came from behind to win 17-9. It gave the Chemics their tenth Wembley appearance and the fifth since 1975.

Even though Roger Millward had retired as a player Hull KR reflected the golden era of Humberside Rugby League by reaching Wembley to defend the silverware they won against Hull the previous season.

They did not have to leave their Craven Park home in the first three rounds and the journey proved too

much for Barrow, York and Salford, while they left Humberside for the first time to cast St Helens to one side 22-5 in the semi-final at Headingley.

The importance of Gregory to Widnes was now established. He had stepped more than adequately into the boots of Bowden, now player-coach at Fulham, and his debut at Wembley was to be his 19th professional game.

Unfortunately his peaceful sleep on the eve of the final was to be severely disrupted by a toothache attack.

Gregory recalled: 'For two weeks before the final I had been suffering with the tooth. But it wasn't that bad. Even as we trained in the Wembley week it was sore but tolerable.

'But by midnight on the night before the game it became unbearable. Our team doctor had to telephone a London hospital and make arrangements with a dentist to meet us.

'We arrived at the hospital in a car and I had the tooth out. It was quite funny really because I was dressed in my Widnes track suit and several Hull KR fans were also at the hospital.

'I hadn't played that many games for Widnes and they kept looking at me wondering whether it was really me. Eventually they came across and said 'Are you Andy Gregory and if you are will you be playing tomorrow?'

'I said hopefully. They took the

tooth out and stitched up the wound. We went back to the hotel and I got a couple of hours peaceful sleep.

'But all that doctors neat sewing didn't last long. Just after I had scored a try I got a belt from Hull KR loose forward Len Casey and that burst all the stitches open. Mind you I didn't mind because we won the Cup.

'I don't remember much about the game and even today when I see a tape of the game it jogs my memory and I see something that I had forgotten.'

Rovers too had had their share of worries. Winger Peter Muscroft passed a fitness test on an ankle injury while prop Steve Crooks escaped suspension after the disciplinary committee looked leniently on his two cautions that season.

Hull KR's grip on the trophy was slipping from the first whistle. Mick Burke, Widnes's recruit from Waterloo Rugby Union club who played in

their 1979 Wembley final on the wing was, by this time, safely established as a full-back and he came through from the rearguard to score a crucial third-minute try, although he missed the conversion.

Steve Hubbard ensured that Rovers at least had a say in the proceedings when he kicked a penalty in the seventh minute but that was cancelled out by Burke in the 22nd minute.

Widnes centre Mick George scored a second try for Widnes which was converted by Burke to give the Chemics a 10-2 cushion, Rovers marksman Hubbard punished a Widnes indiscretion with a penalty and, on the stroke of half-time, Widnes captain Mick Adams chipped over a drop goal.

Two minutes into the second half Gregory, who had had been subdued in the first half, darted in for a try which Burke improved taking the

score to 16-4. The game was won for Widnes at that point although there was more scoring. Burke kicked another penalty and Chris Burton, a bargain purchase from Huddersfield, scored Hull KR's only try of the game in the 55th minute to which Hubbard added the goal points.

Widnes won 18-9 and Burke was voted the man of the match for his kicking and general contribution to the game. Gregory, however, was also in contention and his first appearance at Wembley was to mark the start of an amazing love affair with Britain's leading stadium for the young man.

Brian Lockwood equalled Alex Murphy's record of four Wembley appearances with three different clubs while Widnes drew level with Wigan's record of six Cup Final victories.

Widnes celebrate their 1981 win over Hull KR.

CHAPTER 65

TO HULL AND BACK

Reaching Wembley is the ultimate goal of the professional Rugby League players. To appear in a Challenge Cup final is the expression of achievement. At first the sheer act of making the final round at Wembley is enough until they walk out when the desire to win takes over.

Hull were no strangers to the Challenge Cup final. They had played in nine with just one win, in 1914, from those appearances. Of that total three had been played at Wembley which meant that, unlike their biggest rivals Hull KR, they had yet to taste the sweetness of victory at Britain's most famous sports stadium.

In 1981-82 the power points of British Rugby League nestled on the east coast in Hull, where Hull and Hull KR were leading the way, and on the River Mersey at Widnes. The rest picked up the scraps.

Hull FC, in particular, were the glamour team of the age with a liberal sprinkling of internationals and overseas players. They attracted massive crowds and wherever they played their famous irregular black and white hoops were to be seen flying high.

Their desire to win at Wembley even reached through to their most recent recruits. David Topliss, who had joined them after 12 years with Wakefield Trinity, explained: 'It was something the fans wanted to experience so badly, we wanted to give it to

them and that, of course brought its own set of pressures.'

There was a peculiar start to the Boulevard club's Cup campaign. They signed a player who had already played in a Cup match that season for another club.

Each season there is a deadline imposed after which players who are transferred cannot play for this new club in the Challenge Cup. But in 1981-82 Carlisle and the ill-fated Cardiff Blue Dragons joined the League taking the total number of professional clubs up to 33.

There were no amateur clubs permitted to play in the competition at that point and to reach the base level of 32 clubs necessary for the first round, a preliminary round was arranged.

Featherstone Rovers and the 1981 beaten finalists Hull KR were drawn out of the velvet bag to play the tie. Rovers protested that as they had reached Wembley they should be exempted from playing in a preliminary match. Their pleas fell on deaf ears but they qualified for the first round after beating a determined Featherstone Rovers.

After the elimination from the Cup, Rovers decided to sell their promising stand-off half Steve Evans and Hull stumped up the necessary cash to make him a Boulevard player. All this took place before the Cup

signing deadline and nothing could prevent Hull putting him in their Cup squad. Subsequently the laws were changed to prevent this happening again.

After beating Salford in the first round, Hull had the unusual experience of playing a pre-Wembley Cup tie in London. They beat Fulham and returned to Humberside to overcome Halifax in the third round.

Hull returned to Wembley after a two-year gap and their fans responded by purchasing 30,000 tickets, unprecedented even in modern times. By contrast defending holders Widnes sold 13,500.

The Merseysiders attained the semi-final stage. The luck of the draw had seen them drawn away in the three qualifying rounds and they had to withstand a spirited attempt by League newcomers Cardiff in the first round, forced a 9-7 second-round win at Wigan and required a replay to beat Bradford Northern in the third round.

They looked to be on the way out in the semi-final against Leeds at Station Road, Swinton when their captain and loose forward Mick Adams hoisted a speculative high kick. The ball bounced back into play off the crossbar and centre Kieron O'Loughlin fielded the rebound to shoot past the wrong-footed Leeds defenders to score the try which gave Widnes an

11-8 win and a ticket for Wembley.

Widnes had equalled Wigan's record of 11 Cup finals and their run of six visits to Wembley from eight finals bettered Wigan six from nine.

Hull, winners of the John Player Trophy, were the outstanding team of the season and yet their return looked like being less than expected. They had finished second behind Leigh in the championship and had been eliminated in the first round of the York-shire Cup.

Added Topliss: 'We knew people expected a great deal of us and that the Challenge Cup was going to pro-vide us with chance to show not only our own followers but the rest of the game that we were winners.

'We had won both home and away in the League against Widnes includ-ing the last game of the season so we approached the game as favourites and in a confident frame of mind.'

Widnes coach Doug Laughton had gambled on playing centre Eddie Cunningham. The former St Helens and Leeds player had been told earlier in the season that his career was in danger following a serious neck injury and he had hardly played since re-ceiving the bad news.

Laughton also had an anxious wait to see if one of his most experienced players, stand-off Eric Hughes, could avoid suspension. He had faced a meeting with the disciplinary com-mittee in Leeds on the Thursday be-fore the game, after being sent off. He and Widnes were relieved when the committee ruled in his favour and he rejoined the squad after a helicopter flight from the north of England.

Wembley Stadium on 1 May was bathed in bright sunshine and Laughton's brave selection of Cun-ningham appeared to pay off. Hooker Keith Elwell, known to all at Widnes

as 'Chiefy', gave them a good start with a fifth-minute drop goal and then Cunningham, always a powerful performer, forced his way across the Hull line for a try which Mick Burke converted.

Their 6-0 lead was, however, dissi-pated by some poor self discipline and Sammy Lloyd, Hull's former Castle-ford second row forward and goal-kicker who had been out of favour earlier in the season, brought the Humbersiders level with three suc-cessful penalties.

The amazing Cunningham broke through again to restore Widnes's ad-vantage with his and Widnes's second try in the 51st minute. Burke was in-jured and he handed the goal-kicking role to scrum-half Andy Gregory and

Widnes centre Eddie Cunningham goes over for a try in the drawn 1982 final against Hull.

he was successful with the conversion.

Steve Evans, the man who had started the Wembley trail with Featherstone and completed it with Hull, suffered the agony of seeing one of his passes intercepted by winger Stuart Wright who raced away to score in the corner. Gregory's goal kick failed.

The mood of the game changed at this point. With a Widnes victory in sight Hull started to take control. They trailed 14-6 and, with 13 minutes of the game remaining, Hull loose forward Steve Norton broke through to score a try which Lloyd converted.

With nine minutes to go Hull's New Zealand Test winger Dane O'Hara forced his way through the tiring Widnes defence for a try that tied the scores at 14-14.

Lloyd, who had a 100 per cent success rate with his four previous attempts at goal, was left with the responsibility of putting Hull in a match-winning situation but, unfortunately for him and Hull, O'Hara's try had been scored out on the wing and his goal kick drifted wide.

At the end of the 80 minutes they were still locked at 14-14. There was no provision for extra time and, for the second time at Wembley, a replay was needed. The previous time had been Warrington v Halifax in 1954.

Wembley was not available for the second attempt, the visit of Pope John Paul II ruled out any sporting events for weeks ahead.

And so the Challenge Cup Final returned north for the third time since 1929 this time to Elland Road, the home of Leeds United soccer club. Topliss recalled: 'It was a pecu-liar feeling in each dressing room. The final had been played and we both had a chance to win. But the draw left us all frustrated.'

As soon as Hull returned north, their coach Arthur Bunting started planning for the replay on 19 May.

'We had not played well at Wembley,' said Topliss, ' and yet we had been given another chance. Arthur decided to change the side for the replay. He decided to go for players with mobility.'

That brought two veterans into the plot. Bunting swapped hooker Wileman for 37-year-old Tony Duke, a loyal Hull FC servant, and brought 38-year-old Welshman Clive Sullivan, the second team coach, in for the injured O'Hara. He also introduced several other new faces.

Hull's desire for Cup success was increased when they had to settle for yet another second place in the week before the replay. They were beaten 23-8 by Widnes in the Premiership final.

Topliss said: 'We went into camp several days before the replay at a hotel in Harrogate. Arthur did that so that we would be away from the well-wishers and fans concentrating solely on the game. You could tell from the mood of determination that we were going to win this time and we went to the game supremely confident of victory.'

By now Topliss was 32, after years of striving he had been to two Cup Finals after his 30th birthday.

Both sides were determined to stamp their will on the game and Widnes looked as though they had regained the upper hand when Mick Burke landed an 18th minute penalty. That proved to be deceptive because Hull went in at half-time having taken complete control with tries by New Zealand full-back Gary Kemble and Topliss, the first of which was converted by Crooks.

Hull's lead looked distinctly shaky in the early minutes of the second half. Burke landed a 57th minute penalty and, a minute later, Stuart Wright scored a try. But Widnes were still behind at 8-7.

Topliss rallied the Humbersiders in the 62nd minute with a try that Crooks converted but Widnes remained within striking distance when Burke kicked his third penalty of the evening.

The 41,171 people who had packed the stadium were enraptured by this struggle of giants although thousands of people from Hull had missed some of the game because they were late and trying to get into the already tightly packed ground.

The decisive moment was supplied by 18-year-old Lee Crooks. The young second row forward, a painter and decorator who worked for Bunting's company, proved to be the man for the job. He had been a substitute at Wembley and showed great maturity playing from the start in the replay.

With nine minutes of the game still to play, he breached the Widnes defence for a try which he also converted to put Hull in an almost unassailable lead of 18-9.

This time Hull retained control of the game and won the Cup for the first time since 1914. They had, however, failed once again to win it for their fans at Wembley and still the legend continued to grow.

CHAPTER 66

WILD ROVERS

Allan Agar was a product of Rugby League in Featherstone. Like most of the boys from the pit village, he had developed through the junior system and joined Rovers as a professional in 1967.

His initial stay at Post Office Road was brief and he moved across Yorkshire to Dewsbury two years later. His stay at Crown Flatt was fruitful as he was part of their famous 1973 championship team and then, after a short stay with the reconstituted New Hunslet club, he moved to Humberside to join Hull KR.

With the Humberside club he won most of the honours the professional game had to offer; a championship winner's medal, two Floodlit Trophy medals and Challenge Cup winner's medal in 1980.

His coaching potential was recognised by Wakefield Trinity who bought him from Humberside to captain their side and, in May 1981, he moved into management taking over as coach to the newly-formed Carlisle. He took the Cumbrian club to promotion from the second division at the first attempt, and, amazingly, he left the club he had helped establish in June 1982.

For a while there seemed no role in the game for Agar and then, in December 1982, he was invited to return to Post Office Road 15 years after he had left to seek his fortune. He re-

placed Vince Farrar, another favoured son of the club, as coach and his first task was to inspire the team's move away from the relegation zone.

Agar knew his priorities. 'League points occupied us completely,' he said. 'But by the time the Cup ties came round I knew what the side could and could not do.

'The team contained players with the talent to play at the highest level but their mental attitude was a problem. Convincing them they could be effective was difficult.

'In each round of the Cup I felt we would win but I could not say with any honesty that I thought that we would win the Cup.'

In spite of their almost constant proximity to the bottom four in the first division, four clubs were relegated at that point in history, Rovers maintained consistent form in the Cup.

Agar added: 'You could sense the difference when we were preparing for a Cup tie. The level of anticipation among the players was much higher.'

Batley and Salford failed to prevent Rovers' progress in the first two rounds but it required a massive step up in form to beat St Helens 11-10 at Knowsley Road in the third round.

That result established Featherstone as a serious threat in the semifinals and, in the last four, they faced a Bradford Northern team coached by their former coach Peter Fox. North-

ern led 6-3 at half-time but Featherstone's second half performance ensured they returned to Wembley for the first time in nine years with an 11-6 win. Agar had been in charge at the club for four months.

The weight on Agar's shoulders had been immense throughout the campaign. Not only had he had the concerns of the League and Cup campaign on his mind but his wife Liz was also undergoing treatment for cervical cancer. It was only in the final stages of the Cup sequence that she was finally told that she was cleared of the disease.

Liz was convinced that her good luck was holding and that Rovers would win the Cup.

Hull, the Cup holders, were the high rollers of the year. They won the Yorkshire Cup and had taken the first division championship. Still within their grasp were both the Challenge Cup and Premiership. Such was their status in the game that they were the biggest favourites for many years. The odds were four to one in Humbersiders' favour with the prospect of their first win at Wembley looming larger.

Rovers, who had just beaten relegation and finished in 12th place, were considered by many outside Featherstone to be at Wembley simply to make up the numbers. It did not stop the village despatching their men to Wembley with the traditional send off. Schools broke from lessons, factories and pits took time out and gathered round the team coach. This was not Rovers going to take on the might of Hull; it was the whole village of Featherstone.

Hull's followers had seen them dispose of Blackpool Borough, Wakefield Trinity and Warrington. The prospect of another Wembley brought them in such increasing numbers that the attendance for their semi-final with Castleford (it was an all Yorkshire last four) 26,031, was the biggest for a semi-final for 11 years.

In the final on 7 May Hull set the pace, although in the 16th minute scrum half Kevin Harkin was

Featherstone forward Peter Smith is stopped in a double tackle by Hull's Steve Norton (left) and Paul Prendiville (right).

stretchered off with concussion after a collision with his opposite number Terry Hudson's boot in a loose-ball situation after a scrum.

Five minutes before half-time Widnes referee Robin Whitfield made history when he sent Hull forward Paul Rose to the sin bin for ten minutes after a high tackle left Featherstone's John Gilbert concussed. It was the first time such a punishment had been meted out since the introduction of the temporary dismissal on 1st January 1983.

Featherstone had taken an early lead through a try by second row forward David Hobbs and a Steve Quinn penalty. Rovers defended that situation until the the 42nd minute when Lee Crooks was obstructed going for a try and Mr Whitfield awarded a penalty try, to which Crooks added the goal points.

The game began to follow the pre-

dicted pattern in the 54th minute when Hull's New Zealand Test centre James Leuluai went over for a try that Crooks converted, giving Hull the lead for the first time.

Agar's memory slipped back into gear. He said: 'I remembered being asked if Rovers lost the final to name the club's man of the match.

'I turned to my assistant Keith Goulding and said 'It's our choice and I think it should be hooker Ray Handscombe'. It's funny how you see things at the time but Ray was doing a great job giving us the possession when we were behind.'

That assessment was to prove prophetic. Although Hull were leading 12-5 they were being starved of the ball and when Hobbs dived over for his second try of the game and Quinn added two more goals the scores were level at 12-12.

Hobbs believed that he had given Rovers the advantage when he dropped a goal but his celebrations were cut short when Whitfield ruled a Hull player had touched the ball before it went between the posts.

It was only postponing the inevitable, because with three minutes of the game remaining, Hull's former Featherstone player Charlie Stone was penalised for butting Rovers loose forward Peter Smith and Hobbs sent a penalty soaring between the posts to give Rovers the Cup at 14-12.

Hobbs took the Lance Todd Trophy as man of the match while Rovers, who had been 33-1 outsiders at the start of the Cup, returned to Post Office Road with the Cup. Hull's Wembley jinx lived on.

CHAPTER 67

END OF THE BEGINNING

In the Rugby League Challenge Cup the accent is on winning. Sudden death competition recognises only the winners but there are occasions when even the losers walk out of Wembley with something other than a heavy heart. Such was the case in 1984.

The last time Wigan had appeared in a Challenge Cup final was in 1970 when they were beaten by Castleford and as the 1970s progressed, so the Central Park club's fortunes declined.

They were a club living on past glories and traditions unable to come to terms with the passage of time and the changing face of professional sport. As they looked towards the 1980s Wigan suffered the ultimate humiliation, relegation to the second division.

It was, however, to prove their redemption. So many people in the town were so disturbed by the state of affairs developing at Central Park that agitation for change grew. During 1982-83 Wigan switched direction.

The first change came in the board room where the old regime were bought out by a four-man board which contained a former player Jack Hilton who became club chairman and a man destined to influence the marketing of the most famous name in Rugby League, Maurice Lindsay.

With a much more aggressive marketing policy and Alex Murphy as coach Wigan embarked on a new era of success. The first indications that

the giant, which lived on the bank of the River Douglas, had awoken from his deep sleep came in 1982-83 when they won the John Player Trophy.

The following season Wigan's Cup ambitions were almost over before they started. They were drawn away from home to second division Bramley in the first round and were lucky to escape with a 10-10 draw, with the Yorkshiremen earning a second chance with a full-back Shaun Kilner drop goal; his first of the season. Three days later Wigan trampled all over the little Leeds area club who had been reformed after a financial crisis just eight games earlier.

In their second round match they slammed six tries against Oldham to win with ease while they had to come from behind to snatch victory from the jaws of defeat against St Helens in the third round.

York reached the semi-finals for the first time since 1931 when they beat Castleford 14-12 in the third round but they failed to repeat that kind of giant-killing performance with Wembley as the next stop as Wigan won 14-8.

Widnes, now back under the control of Vince Karalius, came through to reach the final by one of the longer routes. They were drawn to play in one of the two preliminary round ties and started the Wembley trail with a win in Cumbria at Carlisle.

A home win over Dewsbury and

Widnes were on their travels again to Fulham in the second round. Victory secure, they disposed of Hull KR and Leeds to face Wigan at Wembley on May 5.

A measure of Wigan's decline was walking out alongside them that day at Wembley because two of the Widnes team were players born and raised in Wigan.

Besides scrum half Andy Gregory, who had already established himself at Wembley there was Joe Lydon, the 20-year-old centre who had been a prized signing for Widnes.

He had already been to Wembley when he signed for the Naughton Park club because he was a member of the Wigan under-11 schools team who played against Widnes in the inaugural schoolboy curtain raiser game in 1975. He had the choice of a career in either Rugby League or Rugby Union and chose to become a professional, but away from Wigan.

The expense of that failure to secure the top class talent from within their own area haunted Wigan in the 1984 final.

There was a heavy Australasian influence on the Wigan side. Besides Australian signings Mark Cannon and Wayne Elvin they also had giant New Zealand forwards Graham West and Howie Tamati. During the season they had used a temporary import Australian prop Kerry Hemsley from Sydney club Balmain.

and League schoolboy international, they had signed that season and he became the youngest player to appear in a Challenge Cup final at 17 years, six months, 19 days beating Keighley's Reg Lloyd, who was 17 years, seven months in 1937.

This was the first Challenge Cup final to be played following a major overhaul of the Laws of the Game. In November 1982 the International Board handed down seven changes or amendments, the chief of which was that the value of the try was to be increased from three points to four and that if a team still retained possession of the ball on the sixth tackle that they should hand the ball over to their opponents. They resulted in radical changes to the appearance of the game. It speeded up play and, generally, created a more attractive spectacle.

Considering the opportunities afforded by the change in the law the final was generally disappointing. Widnes led 12-2 at half-time and the outstanding feature of the half had been a long distance try by Lydon.

In the second half Lydon produced yet another long-range effort which is generally considered to be one of the best solo efforts ever seen in the Challenge Cup Final while Hemsley repaid at least some of his air fare from down under with Wigan's only try of the game.

Then vice-chairman, now chairman, Maurice Lindsay admits to being bitterly disappointed by Wigan's 19-6 defeat. He says: 'Looking back it wasn't a particulary distinguished Wigan team and we made so many mistakes.

'After I had been in the dressing room to commiserate with the players I had to come out into the tunnel which led to the pitch to control my emotions. Just as I was fighting to gain control again Widnes's Eric Hughes came across to speak to me.

'I shall never forget his words. He said: 'I know you're upset but don't worry, your star is on the way up and Wigan will be back. But next time keep one thing in mind, leave your emotion until after the game.

Jim Farrell and his poster fighting for recognition in the Wembley crowd watching the 1984 final against Wigan.

Widnes postman Jim Farrell outside Wembley passing on the gospel.

Hemsley, a huge prop whose trade mark was a long flowing hairstyle, had impressed Wigan during his short stay with them and they persuaded Balmain to allow him to fly back especially for the big game just as Widnes had done for Chris Anderson in the 1975 final.

They came up against a Widnes side which, apart from the two Wigan born players, New Zealander Kevin Tamati, the cousin of the Wigan recruit, and Cumbrian Les Gorley, were all products of their district network.

For the final the League had handed the honour of refereeing the game to Huddersfield's Billy Thompson who was retiring at the end of the season because he had reached the age of 50.

Still on the subject of age Wigan gave a place in their team at full-back to Shaun Edwards, a former Union

Widnes (left) and Wigan (right) stride out to do battle in the 1984 final.

Widnes's Joe Lydon looks for a way round Wigan's Dennis Ramsdale.

'Wigan came to enjoy the final but Widnes came to win a match.'

'What he said made me think. I recalled the meal at the hotel the day before the final when Kerry Hemsley, the man we had flown all the way back from Australia, had ordered a bottle of claret with his meal and realised that we had to become much more professional.

'While everybody looks at the 1984 Cup final and says that's where the great Wigan recovery began I can't agree. We were just lucky to get there that year because the real magic started when we knew what had to be done as we walked out of the gates at Wembley that night.'

Widnes had shown Wigan the way. The Chemics had won the Cup for a record seventh time in 12 Wembley finals which equalled Wigan's own record.

Widnes captain Eric Hughes, forward Mick Adams and hooker Keith Elwell each collected a record fourth winner's medal in a record seven visits as players.

CHAPTER 68

ANNIVERSARY PRESENT

From the moment British Rugby League saw the 1982 Australian touring team in action in their first game at Hull KR they realised two salient points. First, and most immediate, they were in deep trouble because of the quality of Frank Stanton's Kangaroo team and, second, that something special was happening in front of their eyes.

In 1978 the British had been defeated 2-1 in a home Test series and there were signs of trouble which the discerning could see, if they wanted. The Australians had worked hard on their fitness and professional approach to the game. The British game by comparison was stagnant. Players were content to allow semi-professional attitudes and fitness standards rule their game.

By 1982 the Australians had realised and put into practice athleticism and, in that opening game at Craven Park, they hammered the Robins 30-10.

When the Kangaroos had arrived in the UK everybody believed that Canterbury-Bankstown scrum half Steve Mortimer was the first choice in his position but, for the match against Rovers, coach Stanton brought in a comparatively unknown Peter Sterling from Parramatta. Mortimer was never again to figure as Australia's number one scrum half. Once in the driving seat Sterling took over the direction of their game.

That day at old Craven Park, they moved to a new stadium at the start of 1989-90, Sterling played in a half-back partnership that was to send the Lions crashing to a 3-0 Test defeat and the Australians return unbeaten on a European tour for the first time. He linked up with his Parramatta team-mate Brett Kenny.

The 1982 Kangaroos were held in awe by more than the British and French Rugby League audiences. The publicity they generated brought Rugby Union people to see and admire their athleticism, skill, fitness and dedication.

After their return down under the members of the squad were eagerly sought by success-hungry British clubs. In 1983 St Helens started a trend when they persuaded centre Mal Meninga to join them on a short term contract and, whatever St Helens do, Wigan always believe in matching or beating if they can.

For the 1984-85 season they arranged for Kenny to join them, while across the other side of the country Peter Sterling was settling into his second spell with the Airlie Birds, Hull's nickname based on a street name near their Boulevard ground. Both players attracted huge audiences and success to their respective clubs.

That success was primarily reflected in the Challenge Cup. Wigan, under the influence of Kenny

who had arrived at Central Park in December 1984, sunk second division Batley without trace at Burnden Park, Bolton because Central Park was ice-bound, won through at Warrington, battled through the third round with an 8-7 win over Bradford Northern, thanks to a winning try by former Northern player Henderson Gill, and ensured a quick return to Wembley by beating Hull KR in the semi-final.

Hull, on the other hand, had progressed with a handsome first round win over Carlisle, a comfortable second round victory at Halifax, a re-played third round against holders Widnes and then a classic semi-final against Castleford.

In the last-four match at Headingley Sterling's Hull side were held to a 10-10 draw at the first attempt. In the replay there were six tries, a brawl and controversy, but Hull eventually made it through to Wembley after winning 22-16.

It was already destined to be a special Cup final. It was the 50th time the Rugby League Challenge Cup, by now sponsored by Silk Cut, had been staged at the famous old stadium since 1929. A parade of players who had played in each of the years provided the highlight of the preamble.

When the two teams came out into the sunlight Kenny seemed totally disinterested in the whole affair. He sullenly thrust his hands into his track suit top pockets and brushed aside the

Wigan celebrate their classic 1985 final win over Hull.

Wigan skipper Graeme West lifts the Cup aloft in triumph after the 1985 final.

traditional pre-game greetings and presentation.

But in the anniversary final the two Australians created a masterpiece for the British game and television audience. It ranks alongside the best that British sport has ever produced.

From the moment Widnes referee Ronnie Campbell sounded the first whistle the game was played at break neck speed with devastating individual performances as well as exceptional team skills.

Wigan's was almost too much to believe especially in the first half. They built up a 28-12 lead thanks to two tries by Australian winger John Ferguson, who had been flown back after being forced to return to Australia after his short-term contract at Central Park expired earlier in the season, a classic long distance try by winger Henderson Gill, an artistic touch down from Kenny and a try just after half-time by full-back Shaun Edwards. Centre David Stephenson had kicked one goal and Gill three more.

Wigan's Shaun Edwards signals his delight at scoring a try in the 1985 final against Hull.

It looked as though Kenny and Wigan were to take the Cup. Whether Wigan's early pace reached them, or they subconsciously relaxed, believing they had won, will never be explained but they lost their grip on the game.

Although Kenny had been the dominating factor throughout for Wigan with his evasive running and timely passing skills, from this point forward it was Sterling who ran the show.

New Zealand centre James Leuluai playing his first match after a three-week absence with a shoulder injury went in for a try, prompted by Sterling who appeared in an approach move twice. Substitute Gary Divorty forced his way over for a 74th minute try and Leuluai sprinted virtually unopposed for 70 metres for a try which made the scores 28-24.

Unfortunately for Hull, Lee Crooks could not convert any of the three tries and that left Wigan with just four minutes to hang on to their precious four-point advantage.

Just once Hull looked likely to break-away when Steve Evans threatened up the Hull left flank but Wigan survived to win 28-24 in the greatest Wembley final of them all.

It was the first time in 20 years that Wigan had won the Cup, their previous victory being another memorable final against Hunslet in 1965. Brett Kenny became the first Australian to win the coveted Lance Todd Trophy and they lifted the Cup for a record-equalling seventh time at Wembley.

Hull were still left waiting for their first win at Wembley knowing that they had scored more points than any other losing side at Wembley, only four winning sides have ever scored more in a final, and after six visits they still had to savour the taste of victory on the day.

The game had produced a record ten tries and 52 points and included a record ten overseas players added to which Wigan's New Zealand captain Graeme West became the first overseas captain to lift the Cup for 28 years denying Lee Crooks the pleasure of becoming the youngest ever winning captain.

The wonder of television took the match to an audience of millions and did more to enhance Rugby League's cause as a serious sport than almost anything it had achieved in its history up to that point.

Wigan scrum half Mike Ford and skipper Graeme West confer about tactics in the 1985 final.

CHAPTER 69

FLUSHED AND CONFIDENT

Malcolm Reilly is a man who knows what he wants from Rugby League. All through his life he has dedicated himself to fitness and pursuit of victory.

There are those who would say that his zeal in both respects have often gone over the proverbial top but the development of the modern game, both in Australia and now Britain, has proved that his kind of single-minded dedication does bring positive results. He has been vindicated.

In 1969 and 1970 he played an important part in taking the Challenge Cup to his home-town club of Castleford. For the first of the two appearances at Wembley against Salford he was named man of the match, the winner of the Lance Todd Trophy, and after their win over Wigan the following year together with his contribution to the Lions Test series win in Australia, he moved down under to join Sydney club Manly Warringah.

The £15,000, a record for the time, they paid Castleford was a bargain. The power he injected into their pack brought them the Sydney Premiership in 1972 and 1973. Reilly, however, remained a Yorkshireman, happiest in and around his beloved Castleford. He returned to Wheldon Road as player-coach in 1975 and, even hampered by a long-standing knee injury, he continued to be a player of major

significance on the British club scene.

In 1986 Reilly had retired as a player and was concentrating on the coaching role with Castleford. His team were sound, rounded footballers who maintained a high degree of good results without achieving the level of success that their open, expressive type of football often deserved.

Up to 1986 Castleford had played in three Wembley finals and had never been beaten. They had remained tantalising close to a fourth appearance in three of the four previous years when their attempts to reach the final ended at the semi-final stage.

The luck of the draw did not give Classy Cas, as they are known throughout the world of Rugby League, an even break. In each of the first three rounds they were drawn away from Wheldon Road.

The first round was easy as they cleaned Hunslet out 60-6, the second round was a little more difficult as they won 30-6 at Barrow while the third round proved the most difficult as they beat holders Wigan 10-2.

Castleford's league form had been typically erratic but, as Reilly points out, he was competing on a low budget against some of the biggest spending clubs in the British game: 'We had built a team with players from the junior game and other sources. I don't think that in all the time I was at the

club I spent more than £30,000 and that imposed certain limitations on the side.'

Castleford returned to Central Park for their semi-final against Oldham who were still seeking their first trip to Wembley. Reilly's charges punished some mistakes and went through to the final after winning 18-7.

Hull KR started their Cup campaign with a derby win over Hull and followed up with comfortable victories over York and Leigh. Their semi-final against Leeds was a high-scoring 24-24 draw which has been labelled as the best Cup tie to be played away from Wembley.

In the replay, the score at half-time was still 0-0 but Rovers survived the experience in better shape and won 17-0 after a great second-half display of fire-power.

Rovers started as favourites, they had won the Yorkshire Cup and were the beaten finalists in the John Player Trophy, but that did not deter Reilly. He remained completely confident in his charges to such an extent that he even indulged himself by writing his victory speech for the celebration dinner on the night before the game.

'To have confidence is to put yourself in with a good chance of winning the game' he says. 'Our preparation both mental and physical was good and I could see no way for Hull KR to win the final.

'I knew the Hull KR players. We had analysed their game completely and my players knew exactly what they had to do.'

Reilly's connections in Australia meant that Castleford were one of the pioneers in bringing antipodean players into the game.

One such recruit was a little Aborigine half-back called Jamie Sandy. Reilly explained: 'He was recommended to me by a friend in Australia and I watched several video tapes of him in action. I liked what I saw and brought him across. He was a useful player but for the final I had to play him on the wing.'

In fact the Aborigine almost missed out on the chance to play with Castleford because a fear of hijacking and terrorism in Europe played on his

Hull KR forward Des Harrison is stretchered off after being concussed in a tackle against Castleford in 1986.

mind. He was, however, persuaded to come and was to figure largely in the 1986 final.

Hull KR had also invested heavily in overseas talent, they had two Australian forwards Peter Johnson and Gavin Miller, an Australian stand-off half John Dorahy and New Zealand Test centre Gary Prohm.

Miller was the key man of the four. His play-making from the loose forward berth created so much room for the rest of the players to utilise their skills. There was, however, a crucial hamstring injury to the man from Cronulla-Sutherland in training on the eve of the final. It was a closely guarded secret until after the kick off when the whole world could see that he was struggling way below his usual form.

Castleford held a 7-6 advantage at half-time after a Tony Marchant try which was converted by Martin Ketteridge and a Bob Beardmore drop goal against a converted try by Prohm a minute before the interval.

Castleford's John Joyner holds the Cup aloft after their win over Hull KR in 1986.

Scrum half Bob Beardmore made it 11-6 to Castleford three minutes into the second half and Castleford looked

to have the whole affair in their pocket as Sandy raced over for their third try in the 62th minute.

Rovers, who had lost second row forward Des Harrison, stretchered off concussed in the 56th minute, fought their way back into the game through Prohm, who redeemed his error with a 67th minute try.

In the last minute of normal time Rovers' substitute John Lydiat forced his way over in the corner for a try which made the score line 15-14 to Castleford.

If Dorahy could land the goal Rovers would be in front for the first time in the game. But 'Joe Cool', as Dorahy was known in Britain, who had been in wonderful goal-kicking form all season, missed the target.

Although there were four minutes of injury time to endure, Castleford held on to win the Cup for the fourth time in their history.

Reilly's victory speech did not have to be ripped up. He remained ebullient. 'The fact that Rovers came so close to us in the end was a disap-

pointment for me,' he admitted. 'But my players held up well under that intense pressure, especially in the last moments of injury time.

'I just knew we were going to win. Our preparation had been immaculate'.

Castleford players celebrate their 1986 Wembley win over Hull KR. Try-scoring hero Jamie Sandy is on the right hand side of the Cup.

CHAPTER 70

THE FAX OF LIFE

When Mick Scott left his home-town club Halifax in 1981 to join Wigan he was determined to acquire a share of the glory which was associated with the Central Park club. He had learned his Rugby the hard way after being signed from the junior club five years earlier.

He was recruited for Central Park by former Thrum Hall coach Maurice Bamford who had taken over as Wigan coach and moved to Lancashire as part of a £50,000 joint deal with goal-kicking full-back Jimmy Birts.

While the demanding Wigan public virtually hounded poor Birts out of the club and town after he failed to find the form that made him such an important player at Halifax, Mick Scott settled in well to football life west of the Pennines.

He succeeded in becoming an important part of the Wigan team at a time when they were going through a major rebuilding process both on and off the pitch. In 1981-82 and 1982-83 Scott was such an integral part of the side that he was virtually an ever-present in the team. But, after Alex Murphy took over as manager-coach, his first-team appearances became less and less frequent.

As for every other professional player, the prospect of playing in a Challenge Cup final at Wembley was of paramount importance and he

achieved that ambition in the Wigan team beaten by Widnes in 1984. But it was still a blow when he was told there was no place for him in the 1985 Wembley squad. Mick decided that it was more than he could bear and retired from the game.

While he had been away Halifax's fortunes had bottomed out. Financial troubles had weighed them down and yet they had forced their way out of the second division as champions in 1983-84 under the coaching stewardship of Colin Dixon, their former international second row forward.

In the summer of 1984 the club persuaded David Brook, the dynamic Halifax-born head of a building supplies company based in Harrogate, North Yorkshire, to join the board of directors. His drive and enthusiasm rubbed off all round Thrum Hall and he recruited heavily from the Australian game to bolster the club's playing strength. His policy was severely criticised by the rest of the League world but it was one of the major reasons why Halifax survived in their initial season back in the first division.

During that first season back in the first division, the antipodean policy had introduced pressures in the dressing room and Dixon found his position untenable. He left the club and was replaced by Australian Chris Anderson, who was transferred from Hull KR where he had just started a con-

tract after leaving Sydney club Canterbury-Bankstown.

Halifax finished tenth in the first division and having survived both their promotion season and the dressing room upheaval, Anderson set about restoring harmony for the 1985-86 season. An overseas player quota of five per club had been introduced and the Thrum Hall club used all their available placings.

They needed more players with first division experience to ensure that they did not lose the place they fought so hard to maintain. Scott provided that kind of knowledge and, for a small fee to Wigan, was returned to the Halifax playing register.

The rate at which Halifax was being rebuilt by the building supplies man was phenomenal. They took the British game by storm and, against all expectations, they ended the 1985-86 season as first division champions. Predictions that the Thrum Hall bubble would burst quickly were thrown back in the faces of their critics.

As League champions they found life more difficult in the league during 1986-87 but the fairy-tale quality of the Halifax revival continued with the Challenge Cup.

In fact they started their Cup campaign where it normally ended, in London. The first round draw took them to Fulham but the capital's only professional club were swept aside

38-10. They followed that with wins over Hunslet, Anderson's former club Hull KR and a semi-final win over a powerful Widnes side at Headingley. Victory gave them their first appearance at Wembley since the drawn final with Warrington in 1954.

St Helens had been nine years without a Wembley appearance since losing in that dramatic final against Leeds. Their team was now under the control of Alex Murphy and the desire to earn a return to the game's elite was uppermost at Knowsley Road.

Drawn away in the first two rounds, they dismissed Dewsbury and Oldham, and returned to Knowsley Road to trounce poor Whitehaven. Their path to Wembley was blocked by Leigh but, in spite of a spirited performance in the semi-final at Wigan, the Hilton Park team could not deflect Murphy's Saints.

The incentive for St Helens to win was given a lift when their non-league soccer neighbours St Helens Town shifted some of the glare of publicity normally reserved for the town's illustrious Rugby League club by taking the FA Vase by beating Warrington Town at Wembley.

Saints had flown stand-off half Brett Clark back from Sydney especially to play at Wembley, he had flown back to play for his Australian club, Western Suburbs, after completing a short-term contract with St Helens earlier in the season.

Most respected forecasters predicted that St Helens' much younger, more mobile team would win the Cup and they approached Wembley in a confident, relaxed frame of mind.

Halifax, however, had more Wembley experience than it was generally appreciated; player-coach Chris Anderson had played for the 1975 winning Widnes team when he too was flown back specially for the game, while scrum half Gary Stephens, Welsh utility back Brian Juliff, full-

back Colin Whitfield and loose forward John Pendlebury had all featured in the beaten 1984 Wigan team.

Halifax caused consternation at Twickenham by using Saracens Rugby Union club ground for training purposes, a facility arranged by their hotel management, but a donation to the club funds ensured that the London club did not suffer retribution without recompense.

On the day of the final the fanatical Halifax supporters ensured that both of their local amateur cricket leagues suspended operations for the day while any shopkeeper who sold

Halifax scrum half Gary Stephens holds the Cup up to the fans supported by forward Mick Scott.

beers, wines and spirits had enjoyed a bumper week of trading.

St Helens appeared to freeze in the tension of the game and Halifax took full advantage of the situation. They took the lead with a try by winger Wilf George, their first try at Wembley since 1939 in their fifth visit to the stadium, and Whitfield added the conversion points.

Although centre Paul Loughlin pulled two points back with a 19th minute penalty on his Cup final debut, Saints were still struggling to find the right gear. Halifax, meanwhile, were revelling in the atmosphere and they gave themselves a healthy half-time lead of 12-2 when Irish-born hooker Seamus McCallion scored their second try which Whitfield again improved.

One of the theories expressed before the final was that Halifax's veteran full-back Graham Eadie, who they had tempted back to playing three years after he had retired in Australia, would be vulnerable to speedy attacks down the flanks but he countered that belief by making some determined tackles in the first half. But 'Wombat', as Eadie is known, was beaten by a rangy run from St Helens New Zealand centre Mark Elia for a try early in the second half which Loughlin converted.

Eadie balanced the books when he scored a converted try which was just as well for the Yorkshiremen as Loughlin was a try and goal scorer for St Helens shortly after. In an attempt to stem the rising St Helens tide Pendlebury landed a drop goal on the hour but it did not deter Saints for whom substitute forward Paul Round scored a try which Loughlin converted.

There were 14 minutes to play and Halifax were still hanging grimly on to a 19-18 lead.

Elia, the earlier try-scorer for Saints, proved to be the man on whom Halifax's fate hung. Twice he crossed the Yorkshire team's line and each time referee John Holdsworth refused to allow a try. In one lunge it appeared he had lost the ball over the line but television replays later revealed Pendlebury had, during a flying tackle, dislodged it before the Kiwi could make the Wembley turf.

St Helens seemed fixated with the desire for a try and ignored chances to level the scores with a drop goal which would have taken them into a replay at Manchester United's Old Trafford home. Halifax's torment continued as their defence held stubbornly against the increasing desperate red and white jerseys.

The release of tension at the final hooter was enormous. Halifax had won the Cup for the first time for 49 years, veteran Eadie marked the late autumn of his career by being named as man of the match and Scott, one of just three Halifax-born players in the side, did see Wembley as a player again.

Happiness is winning the Challenge Cup. Halifax at Wembley in 1987.

CHAPTER 71

THE LOWE DOWN

Graham Lowe arrived at Central Park in August 1986. He was never under any illusions about what he had taken on because he was already a coach of some repute when he was persuaded to leave the southern hemisphere.

Wigan, by his own admission, was different. The previous season Wigan had won the Lancashire Cup and the John Player Special Trophy, as well as the annual Charity Shield, but that was not good enough for the ambitious Central Park board of directors. It had not been, by any stretch of the imagination, a poor season; many other clubs would have counted that return of two major trophies as a triumph, but Wigan wanted more.

They controversially parted company with their joint coaches Alan McInnes and Colin Clarke and then brought Lowe in to take over the side. He had successfully coached club sides in both Australia and New Zealand before taking charge of the New Zealand international side which challenged the might of Australia and tied the 1985 series against Great Britain.

Lowe is a man who speaks his mind and that bluntness, together with a series defeat by Australia, saw him leave the international coaching scene and become available for hire. Wigan moved in to take him out of the job market and it was to be the

start of an amazing era in British Rugby League, never mind Wigan's history.

In his first season with the club success arrived virtually daily. They took the first division championship, the John Player Special trophy, the Lancashire Cup and Premiership. The major omission from that list was, of course, the Challenge Cup.

Their interest in the competition had ended dramatically on 4 February 1987 when they were beaten 10-8 by Oldham in a result that left the game stunned because it defied the grain of their results for the season.

It was to remain a result of great significance, not just for Rugby League who soon consigned it to the history files, but to the Wigan players and coaching staff. They stored away the shock and pain and each season they brought it out, dusted it down and used it to kill off any complacency.

At the end of the season Wigan checked out their trophy haul but more than one at Central Park said that they would have swapped them all for a return to Wembley indicating the power of the competition over the professional game.

It is always hard to play Wigan at Central Park. Their following is almost as formidable as their players and for the 1987-88 Challenge Cup, Lady Luck smiled benevolently on the

cherry and white hordes because they were drawn at home in each of the three qualifying rounds.

They battled to a 2-0 victory over Bradford Northern in the first-round mud, sunk Leeds easily in the second round and then, in a controversial tie, beat Widnes 10-1. The Chemics had two touch downs which referee Jim Smith turned down as tries.

Because Wigan had been drawn against Salford in the semi-finals they needed a convenient neutral venue and they joined a growing number of big Rugby League matches to be played at the Burnden Park, ground of nearby Football League club Bolton Wanderers.

Wanderers won few friends by playing a soccer match on a wet pitch the night before the Rugby game but Wigan made light work of the mud trampling Salford 34-4, which was just one point short of Huddersfield's peace-time semi-final record score.

Cup holders Halifax were starting to find life a little more arduous in the first division but, under Chris Anderson's guidance, they remained a tough middle-of-the-table side and they were, however, determined to hang on to the Challenge Cup. It was Anderson's last season with the club; he was to return to Australia at the end of the season to extend his coaching career in his native land.

The Thrum Hallers hammered

St Helens prop Tony Burke tests the Halifax defence at Wembley in 1987.

York amateurs Heworth 60-6 in the first round and then they put Rochdale Hornets and Hull KR out of the competition to make sure of a semi-final date with Hull.

Two weeks before the last-four match Hull coach Len Casey quit his post and caretaker-coaches Tony Dean and Keith Hepworth took them to Headingley to face Halifax. Defences ruled the game and neither side could bring a decision about even though Hull had four drop goal attempts and Halifax three.

Hull led the replay 3-0 after 63 minutes but Halifax's Australian prop Keith Neller sent his countryman and centre team mate Tony Anderson over for an unconverted touchdown to snatch a 4-3 win and a place at Wembley.

A capacity 94,273 crowd (Wembley believe that Rugby fans were physically bigger than their soccer counterparts and reduced the upper crowd limit for Rugby League finals) paid a new world record £1,102,247.00 for the privilege of watching the game.

There was, however, not to be a second fairy tale. The professional standards required by Lowe of his player ensured that Halifax were ground down completely. Although they prevented Wigan from scoring for 27 minutes Halifax collapsed to concede the Cup and the final in the next 11 minutes.

Two tries from New Zealand centre Kevin Iro and one each by Henderson Gill and Joe Lydon saw Wigan lead 16-0 at half-time. If they had been able to add the conversion points Halifax would have been in much deeper trouble.

The creative genius of Wigan scrum half Andy Gregory was simply ripping the Halifax defence to shreds. He dropped back into that role as the second half started and sent winger Tony Iro, brother of Kevin, in after 45 minutes for a yet another unconverted try.

There was no respite for poor Halifax. Wigan hit them again from the kick off. Lydon cut them to the quick with a gliding run through their defence and he sent skipper Ellery Hanley on a curving arc to the line.

Gregory landed the first goal of the match for Wigan who now led 26-0.

With a record defeat staring them in the face Halifax burst into life and full-back Ian Wilkinson, who had been called up for the Great Britain tour squad just two days earlier, opened up a gap in the Wigan defence long enough for Australian Tony Anderson to go in for their opening try. Colin Whitfield kicked the goal.

Wigan cancelled that out immediately with a try from New Zealand centre Dean Bell which was converted by Lydon, but Halifax at least reached double figures when prop Neil James touched down for a try which Whitfield converted.

The 32-12 scoreline had seen the 30 point barrier beaten for only the fifth time in Challenge Cup final history and Wigan had achieved the feat for the second time.

Gregory deservedly took the man of the match award in his record fourth unbeaten appearance at Wembley while, for Wakefield referee Fred Lindop it marked the end of his senior career because he reached the compulsory retirement age.

The victory also completed Graham Lowe's remarkable second season in the British game; he had now won everything it had to offer.

New Zealander Lowe was not alone as an antipodean at Wembley that day. Halifax had fielded five Australians, they had one extra place above the quota of four allowed because of their long-term contractual situation, while Wigan had four New Zealanders, including prop Adrian Shelford who had escaped a disciplinary ban two days before the final because an official caution had not been recorded.

CHAPTER 72

SWEET REVENGE

The air at Wembley on 27 April 1989 smelled particulary sweet to 27-year-old Wigan full-back Steve Hampson. It was not because the fair-haired drayman had not been to the stadium before or because he had not seen a Rugby League Challenge Cup final before, because he had. The fact of the matter was that he was walking out with Wigan.

The former Vulcan Rugby Union club full-back was like every other professional player. He wanted to play for his club in the Challenge Cup final at Wembley but he, in particular, looked as though he had offended the particular spirits who made it their business to look after the competition.

Three times before he had assisted Wigan through to Challenge Cup finals only to be robbed of the honour of playing in the big game itself by a succession of broken bones.

He missed the previous final against Halifax because of a broken arm sustained in a late league match against Salford and that had been a double blow. Not only did it rule him out of the final but also out of the Great Britain party to tour Australia and New Zealand. A broken leg had ruled him out of the 1984 final and a broken arm out of the 1985 final.

As soon as Wigan had qualified for Wembley from their semi-final in 1989 the first person the press corps wanted to speak to was Hampson.

'Would he,' they asked, 'be playing again between then and the final?'

Hampson's attitude as it had been in the previous years was positive.

'I will not be wrapping myself up in cotton wool,' he said. 'My main ambition is to play at Wembley. But I want to maintain my form so that I merit selection in the side for the final.'

Wigan already had the Lancashire Cup and the John Player Trophy safely locked up in the Central Park trophy cabinet when they set out to defend their Challenge Cup in 1989.

Lady Luck certainly made it as difficult as she could for a team which looked capable of an historic clean sweep. All they needed for that to happen was the Challenge Cup, Championship and Premiership. A tall order, but it looked well within Wigan's compass. Their first three Cup rounds were all away from home at Doncaster, Bradford Northern and sweet revenge over Oldham at Water-sheddings, the scene of their previous Challenge Cup exit two years earlier.

Soccer giants Manchester City loaned their Maine Road stadium to Rugby League for the semi-final between Wigan and Warrington. The biggest semi-final crowd for 20 years of 26,529 spectators saw Wigan go through after a titanic struggle inspired by a massive drop goal by Joe Lydon.

Widnes looked to be on a collision course with Wigan. Sporting their major signing from Welsh Rugby Union, Jonathan Davies, they were being freely tipped to reach Wembley for the first time since 1984 but St Helens took them by surprise in the semi-final at Central Park winning with a last gasp try from winger Les Quirk.

It also happened to be his 100th try in senior Rugby and also a club record as he had scored a try in his tenth successive game. Widnes had not been helped when second row forward Richie Eyres was sent off for tripping.

To reach the semi-final stage Saints had overcome Swinton, Barrow and Featherstone Rovers.

It created the third Wembley derby between two of Rugby League's bitterest rivals and the the 1961 and 1966 defeats by St Helens still rankled with the Wigan followers.

They lived with the defeats so badly that the Wigan coach Graham Lowe recalled with clarity the first thing that happened to him when he got out of his car to start work on his first day at Central Park.

He remembered: 'I was just crossing the car park when a Wigan fan came up to me. He looked me straight in the eye and said 'I don't care what else you do with this club just make sure you beat St Helens every time!'

'Then I knew that any game

against Saints was never going to be another game. It meant too much to the people in Wigan and, no doubt, St Helens.'

Already the reports about Lowe's future were filtering through and before too long he made it clear that he would be leaving Wigan at the end of the season for the next stop in his search for a coaching challenge, Sydney, Australia.

St Helens and Wigan had already met three times in the season and, ironically, their last meeting was six days before the Wembley match. Although Wigan had beaten Saints both at Central Park and Knowsley Road in the League, they came unstuck at home in the Premiership first round; the end of their clean sweep hopes.

St Helens, who had shaken Widnes in the semi-final with a team devoid of Australian stars forward Paul Vautin and wing Michael O'Connor who had played expensive short-term contracts for them earlier in the season, elected to bring them

back from down under for Wembley. It was a move not appreciated by many of the players who felt that the men who had put them in the final should be allowed to finish the job.

The final became little else but a record book exercise for Wigan. They crushed St Helens 27-0 with a display of clinical, professional Rugby League providing ample revenge for the two defeats in the 1960s.

They became the ninth side in Challenge Cup history to retain the Cup and the second to achieve that feat twice. St Helens were the first side not to score in a Challenge Cup final since 1950 when Wigan beat Willie Horne's Barrow 10-0 while the scoreline was the widest margin of defeat for 29 years.

It was Wigan's 19th appearance in a Challenge Cup final. It was their tenth win, nine of which had taken place at Wembley and they had made 14 visits to the twin towers.

Wigan held a 12-0 half-time lead and their points came from tries by Kevin Iro (2), Andy Gregory, man-of-

The 1989 winners Wigan celebrate their win over St Helens.

Moment of magic. Ellery Hanley receives the Cup in 1989.

the-match Ellery Hanley and, deliciously, their last try four minutes from time went to Steve Hampson, the man who had to wait so long for his chance to play at Wembley. Joe Lydon kicked three goals and Gregory a drop goal.

Gregory's Wembley record was also extended to five undefeated visits, four wins with Wigan and a draw with Widnes while Wigan's second row forward Denis Betts was the sixth player who had appeared in the under-11 curtain raiser to progress through to the final.

It was the first final played under the new all seater restriction and the 78,000 crowd saw the most one-sided game in the final's history.

The fact that the statistics mattered more than the match reflected on the poor quality of the St Helens

Southern Counties amateur league players and players from the former Soviet Union after their curtain raiser game before the 1990 final.

performance. How their coach Alex Murphy must have regretted sending a telegram to Central Park after the 1961 final saying: 'Roses are red, violets are blue, St Helens 21, Wigan 2'. It came home to roost in the end.

CHAPTER 73

THE CENTRAL REASON

Wigan started the 1990 Challenge Cup competition unbeaten in a record 15 consecutive ties and they are without doubt the Kings of the Challenge Cup whose throne is at Wembley.

Although Bradford Northern appeared in three successive finals in 1947, 1948 and 1949 they were not all winning appearances as they lost to Wigan in 1948; the prospect of that record-breaking achievement was the target for Wigan.

New Zealand coach Graham Lowe had moved out of Central Park at the end of the 1988-89 season and, in spite of all the success he achieved with two Challenge Cups, one league championship, four Lancashire Cups, three Regal Trophies and one charity shield, it was difficult not to agree with his decision that time was up for him with both Wigan and British Rugby League. He joined Sydney club Manly-Warringah and, coming from Australia to replace him, was the quiet, thoughtful coach John Monie from Parramatta.

It did not disturb the thoroughly professional way in which Wigan attacked their job and Monie added a defensive provision that made them almost impossible to score against and an attention to game planning rarely equalled even in his native Australia.

The question for him was whether he could maintain the level of success achieved by Lowe and expected by the townsfolk of Wigan. After six years of virtually uninterrupted success they had come to expect it once again.

The cherry and whites set off in fine style. The Regal Trophy, the successor to the John Player Trophy, was already back in the pavilion and the League championship was to follow.

Hull KR had pushed them all the way in the first round before Wigan won 6-4 and then they ensured that neither Dewsbury or Wakefield Trinity had any further interest in the 1990 competition.

Standing between Wigan and a third successive final stood, almost inevitably, St Helens who were now working under new coach Mike McClennan following Alex Murphy's mid-season departure from the Knowsley Road.

The last-four tie positively bristled with interest especially in view of Saints' humiliation at Wembley the previous year.

Wigan had lost one of their major driving forces in captain Ellery Hanley for a large proportion of the season after he had suffered a major pelvic injury while playing for Sydney club Western Suburbs the previous summer. He had returned to action midway through the season and was beginning to run into something like the kind of form that had seen him labelled as the best player in the world.

There was no hint of a walk-over for Wigan this time. St Helens proved doughty opponents. In fact the first half of a compulsive semi-final belonged to them with tries by scrum half Sean Davine and winger Les Quirk each goaled by Paul Loughlin, against one by Wigan by Steve Hampson converted by Joe Lydon.

Two Lydon penalties cut St Helens' lead to 12-10 but Loughlin gave them two points to cushion their load with a further penalty. The atmosphere was stiff with tension and Wigan responded with a try from their utility player Ged Byrne; Wigan led 14-12.

Still St Helens were within range of Wigan and a return to Wembley. They drew level with a Loughlin penalty but, two minutes from the end, Hanley burst through the St Helens defence, drew in the remnants of the rearguard, and slipped the ball to forward Andy Goodway, who scored a killer try which was converted by Lydon.

Wigan were through to their 16th Wembley Cup final with a 20-14 scoreline from one of the most memorable semi-finals in the history of the tournament.

The Central Park side had won 14 successive Cup ties having scored 297 points and conceded just 89. No wonder they were 7-4 on favourites to complete their hat-trick of Challenge Cup Final wins.

Warrington went back to Wembley for the first time in 15 years. Under Australian coach Brian Johnson, who had spent some time as a player on the Wilderspool playing staff before his retirement, they had become a respected, if not particularly successful, side. They had won the Lancashire Cup to show that they were developing along the right lines but, after that county cup victory, their form became erratic and they were hit by a crop of injuries.

Nevertheless they put together a sustained burst for the Challenge Cup. Featherstone and Trafford Borough, the long-term successors to the former Blackpool club which had stayed briefly in the outskirts of Wigan and then Chorley before moving in with the south Manchester area

non-league soccer outfit Altrincham, were early victims.

They came through a tough third-round battle at Bradford Northern who were also entertaining serious Challenge Cup hopes to reach the semi-final where they faced Oldham.

It was a match Oldham coach Tony Barrow relished because Warrington had sacked him before his move to Watersheddings. The second division club were also chasing promotion to the first division but there was not a person in the town who would not have forfeited that privilege for a Cup final place at Wembley. The club have yet to taste that particular pleasure and they are one of the most senior clubs left without that honour on their club roll of honour.

They had earned the right to play Warrington with a shock win over Jonathan Davies's Widnes and, for a while, they had Warrington on the

rack. But the pressure exerted by the first division team proved too much to bear and, in the last 20 minutes, they allowed Warrington into the game. Substitute forward Mark Thomas set up match-saving tries for Martin Crompton, who had gone to the match as a spectator but had to play after Paul Bishop had suffered a badly cut hand in a domestic accident on the day of the match, and winger Mark Forster.

After the tension, entertainment and drama of the semi-finals the final on 28 April proved to be a disappointment.

Again Wigan's power ensured that it was a one-sided affair. Warrington stayed in touch for the first half but

Wigan's Shaun Edwards showing the effects of his serious facial injury backs up his captain Ellery Hanley in the 1990 final against Warrington.

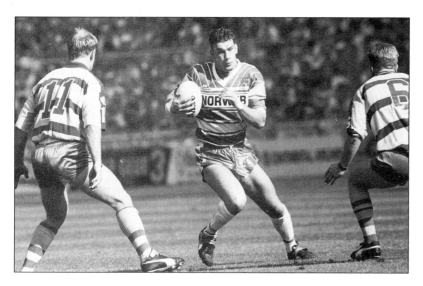

Wigan forward Ian Gildart challenges Warrington's Bob Jackson (number 11) and Martin Crompton (number six).

they folded badly in the second. Their points in that first 40-minute spell came from a 39th minute try by their loose forward and captain Mike Gregory and two goals by Bishop.

No match between Warrington and Wigan is ever likely to be a genteel affair and Wigan stand-off Shaun Edwards showed immense courage when, after a jarring tenth-minute facial injury, he refused to leave the field for treatment and it was later revealed he had played with a badly depressed fracture of the cheekbone near the eye socket.

Tries by forward Denis Betts and winger Mark Preston together with four goals by Joe Lydon against a Bishop penalty gave Wigan a 16-2 lead but Warrington gave themselves some hope when a minute before the interval skipper Mike Gregory, who was labouring with an achilles tendon injury, scored a try that was converted by Bishop.

Bishop, the son of former St Helens star scrum half Tommy Bishop, was beginning to have some say in the game early in the second half but a crushing tackle from Lydon left him

concussed. With his senses went Warrington's last chance of staying in the final.

It was one-way traffic in winning with tries from Preston, skipper Ellery Hanley and Kevin Iro. They led 32-8 with 15 minutes remaining and Wakefield's 1960 record score of 38 looked under serious threat.

But Warrington's pride brought them a 70th minute try by David Lyon and a goal by replacement goalkicker Paul Darbyshire.

With their flow of thought interrupted Wigan could manage just one more try through Iro leaving them two points short of Trinity's best against Hull at 36-14.

Again Wigan had rewritten a large portion of the record book in one match. Gregory had played through his sixth unbeaten appearance at Wembley to become only the second player to win the Lance Todd Trophy twice, following Warrington's Gerry Helme in 1950 and 1954.

He also created a new record for picking up his fifth winners medal although he deserved another because he was playing under the handicap of a major groin injury which was to rule him out of Great Britain's summer tour to New Zealand and Papua New Guinea.

Wigan had won the Cup for a record third time in succession, their hat-trick saw them score 95 points and concede just 26, their third major trophy of the season. Now the cherry and whites had proved their right to the Cup King title by winning 11 times in 20 Cup Final appearances, both new records, as well as appearing at Wembley for the 16th time, again creating a new best performance. New Zealander centre Kevin Iro picked up two tries for the second year in succession taking his total for Challenge Cup finals to six which is twice as many as any other player. He had one try disallowed and that could have made him the first player to score a hat-trick at Wembley.

Fuelled by the concentrated atmosphere of the country's top professional club, Denis Betts' quality of performance accelerated at such an impressive rate that he made appearances on the first-team sheet: twice he was named as a subisitute in 1986-87.

In August 1986 Wigan had recruited former New Zealand national team coach Graham Lowe. Schooled in the ways of the Australian game after a spell coaching in Brisbane and honed by control of the Kiwi Test team, Lowe moved to Central Park following an acrimonioussplit with the New Zealand League authorities.

Lowe recognised Betts' true potential not just as a journeyman League professional but as a player who could perform at the highest levels of Test Rugby. In the following season 1987-88 Betts appeared twice more on the Central Park team senior sheet; this time the pair included his debut in the starting line-up and another substitute's placing.

During all the time Betts was forcing his way into contention for the first team Wigan were assuming even more power in British Rugby League. Two Lancashire Cup victories, a win in the John Player Trophy, a Premiership victory, a league championship and a triumph over Halifax at Wembley. They accumulated honours at an impressive rate.

In 1988-89 Betts, whose strong-running style was being nurtured by Lowe, had arrived as a regular first-team player. It was to be an incredible season for the Central Park club; they collected another Wembley win - this time against their old rivals St Helens - with Betts appearing as a substitute for eight minutes, the league championship, the Lancashire Cup and Regal Trophy. Only the Premiership eluded the tiring Wigan team. It takes a little under 30 minutes to drive from downtown Salford to Wigan. But in Rugby League terms the journey is usually completed in the opposite direction with the conveyor belt type production line of the former mining town endlessly rolling the overflow products down to bolster the more meagre supply of the soccer-biased inner-city area.

Denis Betts is an exception and he reversed the trend. He turned his back on a greater national awareness in a soccer career with Manchester United, the soccer colossus whose Old Trafford ground casts a shadow over most of his native Salford from the banks of the Manchester Ship Canal. He wore the famous red and white shirt as a schoolboy registered player with United but the lure of soccer failed to hold him: Blackburn Rovers and Port Vale also failed to tempt him too.

The young Betts was so sportingly adept that he was able to perform with aptitude at any discipline that took his fancy. It was, therefore, natural to assume that his ease with soccer together with the proximity of Old Trafford to his Salford home, United would provide his final destiny.

Betts, however, rejected that course. His first taste of Rugby had

been on the razed pitches of Clarenden High School in deepest Salford not more than a lusty goal kick from the decaying dockland left high and dry by the onset of containerisation - and Old Trafford.

Life is never easy in an inner-city environment. Packed in between massive urban renewal programmes and the remaining 'Coronation Street' landscape, sports facilities are both rare and, usually, careworn. Once Betts turned his back on soccer he added extra height to the mountain he was expecting to scale.

Encouraged to use his increasing physical size to best effect on the Rugby field, he played for the city's schoolboy side. Betts took his first step outside the protection of his inner-city environment by joining Leigh Rangers amateur club. Considering that he was also brought up within a mile of Salford's Willows ground that was an unusual situation. Nevertheless it was to be the next point on his journey to winning the Lance Todd Trophy in the historic 1991 Challenge Cup final. He explained: 'I used to be taken to the games by Sean Devine's father. Sean, a friend who lived in Leigh, later joined St Helens but we both started from the same amateur club.'

While Leigh's professional team has flirted briefly with League's greatest honours, the town's major advantage, as far as League players are concerned is that it has several accomplished amateur clubs which regularly attract talent scouts from the surrounding professional clubs; Leigh, St Helens, Warrington, Widnes, Wigan and others.

Rangers provided what was not available in Salford: quality youth rugby. Betts' game developed under their tutorage to such an extent that Wigan succeeded where soccer failed. They tempted him into the professional ranks.

At this point Lowe's connection with Wigan was severed. Denied the oxygen of inspiration, he had inspired a golden era for a club who had started the decade in the second division, the New Zealander left Central Park to join one of Australia's top clubs, Sydney's Manly-Warringah, with the reputation as one of the world's top coaches.

From the moment he knew he was leaving Central Park Lowe tried to persuade the fast-maturing Betts to ply his trade, even on a limited summer contract basis, with the Sea Eagles. The young man from Salford, however, was sufficiently street-wise to husband his resources. He preferred to stay in Britain and concentrate on building his career, maintaining his fitness levels without risking injury or fatigue in back-to-back Australian-British seasons.

With the temptation to try Rugby League in the southern hemisphere safely pushed behind him, 19-year-old Betts found an important part of Australia had come to him in England. Replacing Lowe as Wigan coach came John Monie, who had established himself as a team organiser of some repute with Parramatta from the all-powerful Sydney competition, the Winfield Cup.

Monie, like Lowe, utilised Betts' burgeoning talent to the full and when it came to the 1989-90 Challenge Cup final against Warrington Denis was again included among the starting line-up.

This was his third visit to the Wembley pitch. Besides playing as a substitute the previous year, he trod the lush turf for Salford Schools in 1981 in the traditional pre-final under-11 match against Castleford which they lost 13-0; he was the sixth player to complete that long journey.

It was Wigan's third successive Challenge Cup final. No side had previously succeeded in winning on all three visits and the incentive for this record-breaking team was enormous. With contemptuous ease they swept Warrington aside winning 36-14 with Betts scoring the first try for the cherry and whites in the 22nd minute.

The game was hardly noteworthy as Warrington failed to provide any serious opposition to the most sophisticated machine in the British professional game, but it did succeed in adding to the tales of courage that abound from the Challenge Cup final. Wigan stand-off half Shaun Edwards was felled by a head-high tackle in the tenth minute and he refused to leave the field after treatment.

After playing his part in building an historic Wigan triumph, Shaun was cajoled into leaving the action for the last few minutes of the match and it was later revealed he had sustained a double fracture of the eye socket as well as a depressed cheekbone. It was to cost him his place in the Great Britain squad to tour Papua New Guinea and New Zealand later that year.

By the time they had arrived at Wembley to defend the Challenge Cup for a record-breaking fourth time Wigan had already made the 1991-92 season extra-special. They battled through from just after Christmas without defeat and emerged from one of the most serious end-of-season fixture pile-ups as league champions: they had played their last eight matches in 19 days including four games in the final week.

That punishing schedule was completed two weeks before the Challenge Cup final against St Helens. The physical signs of deterioration were still visible on their bodies and Featherstone Rovers eliminated them from the end-of-season Premiership competition before they reached Wembley. On the big day loose forward Ellery Hanley had nerve-blocking injections on a torn thigh muscle while the rest of their walking wounded queued for pain-killing injections from club Doctor Ansar Zaman.

Betts recalls: 'In spite of the mental and physical tiredness, I felt more comfortable at Wembley than in any of my three previous visits. It was as if I had come to terms with the place.

'The adrenalin flowed. The sheer uncertainty of who was playing introduced the necessary edge of competition for the whole squad. Joe Lydon did not pull out of the game until the eleventh hour and we trained normally all week before the game.

'We gained enormous inner strength from enduring the adversity together and, by the time the final started, we were pleased to return to simply playing Rugby. I seemed to cruise through the game and everything we did paid off.'

'In the last 20 minutes, however, the pain in my whole body grew and exhaustion found its mark. We just wanted it all to end.'

No wonder even the substantial Betts frame was beginning to creak. He had played in every one of Wigan's 39 matches before the final, plus four more with Great Britain.

The match statistics told it all. In the first half the power of Betts had savaged St Helens but in the agonising second half he had a ten-minute

More Wigan celebrations. This time it's following their record fourth successive Wembley win in 1991.

breather on the wing and touched the ball a total of four times. What he achieved in the first half had, however, found great favour with the men from the media and he comfortably won the vote for the Lance Todd Trophy as man of the match.

The pedigree of this Wigan team was established: they were all-time greats. They had won the game's two major trophies in an incredible run through the second half of the season and, at the same time, virtually rewritten the Challenge Cup final record book.

They were the first side to win four successive challenge Cup finals, it was their eleventh win in 17 appearances at Wembley, they equalled Oldham's record of four successive finals at any venue, captain Ellery Hanley became the first skipper to lift the Cup on three successive occasions and he equalled the record established by Derek Turner and Eric Ashton of captaining three winning sides; it was their 20th successive Challenge Cup victory - their previous defeat had been by Oldham in 1987 - and their second win over St Helens in three years.

They had won the Challenge Cup for the 12th time and played their 21st final, while on an individual basis Andy Gregory was yet to be beaten in seven appearances at Wembley - he had one draw and six wins to his credit.

Saints' contribution to the record-book was provided by second row forward John Harrison, who at six feet, seven inches, was the tallest man ever to play at Wembley.

Even though Wembley has reduced capacity following the stadium's all-seater conversion the 75,532 fans who saw the game paid a new record £1,610,447 for the privilege.

Martin Offiah's arrival in Rugby League was hardly greeted with a fanfare of trumpets. Compared with many other signings from Rugby Union his decision to join Widnes from Rosslyn Park Rugby Union Club for £20,000 was almost as mundane as a major signing from the amateur Rugby League game.

Offiah is, however, as far distant from ordinary rugby playing mortals as can be imagined. His frustration at failing to make progress in Rugby Union ensured that he was vulnerable to blandishments from the professional game and, once Widnes's scouting system had been attracted following his performance in a seven-a-side tournament, probably one of the greatest natural rugby talents to be produced in Britain for many years was lost to the fifteen-a-side game.

The London-born son of Nigerian parents was given the gift of speed. His fleetness of foot is remarkable not only for his acceleration but the ability to sustain speed over long distances while remaining aware of all the tactical and technical problems.

Doug Laughton has always been a determined man. As a person he has never allowed many things to stand in his way particularly once he has seen that a rugby player has talent. Offiah was persuaded by the Widnes coach's picture of the professional game and what it had to offer a player and he moved to the north of England.

Laughton has the ability to assess players' potential in Rugby League almost in an instant. He persuaded Jonathan Davies, John Devereux and Paul Moriarty to leave successful careers in Welsh Rugby Union, snatched Alan Tait from the Scottish international side and, after seeing Tongan second row forward Emosi Koloto on television playing for Wellington against a touring Welsh side, flew out to New Zealand to complete the signing.

Offiah soon justified the Widnes chief's faith. After failing to score in his professional debut against Halifax on 30th August 1987 he surged through the rest of the season to finish on top of the League try-scoring list with 42. He also impressed sufficiently to earn a cap for Great Britain.

He became one of the players around when the national side was built and did enough on the 1988 tour of Australia to earn short-term contract offers from the dollar-rich Australian clubs; there were long term offers too.

By the end of the 1991-92 season he had become the first Englishman to lead the try-scoring lists in four successive seasons: Australian Albert Rosenfeld holds the record with five for Huddersfield whilst Welshman Johnny Ring did it four times for Wigan. Offiah recorded the fastest ever century of tries, established the Widnes record for 58 tries in a season and scored a record five tries in one match for Great Britain against France.

In short the number of challenges left open to him in the British game with Widnes were reducing. Nevertheless it still came a major shock when on the day of Widnes's Premiership final against Hull at Old Trafford it was revealed that he had asked for a transfer.

He stated that he wanted a fresh stage on which to perform and then left for a summer contract with Sydney club St George. The war of nerves between the player and club continued across the world and Offiah gradually started to burn his bridges behind him. Eventually he told Widnes he no longer wished to play for them under any circumstances.

Widnes kept their council until Offiah returned from down under when he made good his threat to withhold his services. Stalemate resulted. The club held their position until Offiah made a token gesture of returning to training and then they placed him on the transfer list at

£500,000, a world record by more than the proverbial mile.

Although he trained regularly he failed to make more than one reserve team appearance, citing an injury sustained in Australiaas the reason for his absence. The months of the British season drifted by and Offiah was left outside of the game.

Despondency at the situation set in and although a number of clubs made propositions to Widnes nothing substantial ever materialised. His agent Alan McColm threatened to switch him away to the United States to play grid-iron football or back to Australia. Eventually after a bid from Hull faded when Widnes would not

drop their price, it was left to between Laughton and his new club Leeds – he had left Widnes at the end of the previous season – and Wigan.

In the opening days of 1992 the situation reached a critical point. The 6th January at noon was the last date decreed by the league on which registrations for the Challenge Cup would be accepted and, just three days earlier Wigan, who had two previous bids rejected, finally persuaded Widnes to sell this precocious talent for a new world record transfer fee of £440,000.

If Offiah was looking for a suitable stage then Wigan and Central Park certainly provided it. The successive League and Cup doubles, as well as

the World Club Challenge victory, established them as the team to beat and, fuelled by the ever present desire to reach Wembley for a fifth successive year, maintained their ambition at boiling point.

He made his debut for Wigan against Wakefield Trinity and failed to score. The old try-scoring habit soon restored itself and he scored a hat-trick against Halifax in his third appearance with cherry and white.

Wigan reached the semi-finals

Andy Gregory and Martin Offiah show off the Cup after Wigan's record-breaking fifth successive Wembley in 1992 when they beat Castleford.

against Bradford Northern after disposing of Salford, Warrington and St Helens. Then Offiah provided a corner-piece five tries out of thirteen in what was to be a remarkable 71-10 victory at Bolton Wanderers' Burden Park home to ensure a return to the Challenge Cup Final.

By the time Wigan reached Wembley on 2nd May 1992 they had known for two weeks that the League championship, and the first leg of a third successive double, was safely in the bag but the challenge presented by Castleford seemed, on paper at least, certain to prove a real test for Wigan.

The Yorkshiremen had enjoyed a reasonable spell in the run up to the end of the season although their form had returned to a more accustomed erratic pattern following their 8-4 semi-final win over Hull. They had, however, an impressive Wembley record to defend with four wins from four appearances and something was certain to give in this head-to-head confrontation.

Offiah, who had said that one of the reasons for joining Wigan was to play in a Cup Final at Wembley, used his speed early in the piece, bursting through after five minutes to pounce on a mistake by full-back Graham Steadman and score a try. The touch-line conversion by Frano Botica gave Wigan a 6-0 lead and from that point they never looked back.

In time added on at the first half, Offiah struck again. Shaun Edwards launched a forward kick from near the halfway line and it looked as though two Castleford defenders would field the ball safely. The pace of Offiah stunned the two defenders, the Wembley crowd and a vast television audience.

He burst between the Castleford pair and won the race for the ball as it crossed the line. Botica converted and Wigan led 19-0 at half-time.

No player has ever scored a hat-trick at Wembley and the stage was set for that piece of Rugby League history to fall to Offiah. His Wigan team-mates were determined to help him reach that goal, they tried to engineer chances in his favour. For a few seconds it seemed as though he had succeeded when he broke away to touch the ball down but his celebrations were cut disappointingly short when Widnes referee Robin Whitfield brought him back almost 40 yards after a touch judge revealed Offiah had knocked the ball forward.

As he admitted the disappointment was intense."It was a good try and it took me 15 minutes to recover from that blow. But by that time it was too late to recover. I'll be back to try again," he said.

While Wigan led comfortably in the first half, Castleford showed some competitive mettle in the second. They indicated that they were still a credible force with a 45 minute try by New Zealander Richard Blackmore and it looked as though a second was on its way when speedy back Ian St John Ellis broke away.

The ball was free and Ellis within reach when Offiah blistered through to push the ball behind the deadball line to safety. Wigan accelerated away and, although Castleford did score a second try through prop Keith England in the 68th minute, the game was effectively beyond them after Offiah's intervention.

Although he missed his hat-trick Offiah was given the Lance Todd Trophy as man of the match and Wigan won 28-12. "I would rather have had the hat-trick," he admitted later.

Wigan had won the cup for a record-breaking fifth successive year and gone an amazing 25 Challenge Cup ties without defeat. Watched by the newly victorious Prime Minister John Major, it was the kind of victory that indicated Wigan would still be winning the Cup even when the next general Election came round.

CHALLENGE CUP
ROLL OF HONOUR

Year	Winners		Runners-up		Venue	Attendance	Receipts
1897	Batley	10	St Helens	3	Leeds	13,492	£624.17.7
1898	Batley	7	Bradford	0	Leeds	27,941	£1,586.3.0
1899	Oldham	19	Hunslet	9	Manchester	15,763	£946.16.0
1900	Swinton	16	Salford	8	Manchester	17,864	£1,100.0.0
1901	Batley	6	Warrington	0	Leeds	29,563	£1,644.16.0
1902	Broughton R.	25	Salford	0	Rochdale	15,006	£846.11.0
1903	Halifax	7	Salford	0	Leeds	32,507	£1,834.8.6
1904	Halifax	8	Warrington	3	Salford	17,041	£936.5.6
1905	Warrington	6	Hull K R.	0	Leeds	19,638	£1,271.18.0
1906	Bradford	5	Salford	0	Leeds	15,834	£920.0.0
1907	Warrington	17	Oldham	3	Broughton	18,500	£1,010.0.0
1908	Hunslet	14	Hull	0	Huddersfield	18,000	£903.0.0
1909	Wakefield T.	17	Hull	0	Leeds	23,587	£1,490.0.0
1910	Leeds	7	Hull	7	Huddersfield	19,413	£1,102.0.0
Replay	Leeds	26	Hull	12	Huddersfield	11,608	£657.0.0
1911	Broughton R.	4	Wigan	0	Salford	8,000	£376.0.0
1912	Dewsbury	8	Oldham	5	Leeds	15,271	£853.0.0
1913	Huddersfield	9	Warrington	5	Leeds	22,754	£1,446.9.6
1914	Hull	6	Wakefield T.	0	Halifax	19,000	£1,035.5.0
1915	Huddersfield	37	St Helens	3	Oldham	8,000	£472.0.0
1920	Huddersfield	21	Wigan	10	Leeds	14,000	£1,936.0.0
1921	Leigh	13	Halifax	0	Broughton	25,000	£2,700.0.0
1922	Rochdale H.	10	Hull	9	Leeds	32,596	£2,964.0.0
1923	Leeds	28	Hull	3	Wakefield	29,335	£2,390.0.0
1924	Wigan	21	Oldham	4	Rochdale	41,831	£3,712.0.0
1925	Oldham	16	Hull K R.	3	Leeds	28,335	£2,879.0.0
1926	Swinton	9	Oldham	3	Rochdale	27,000	£2,551.0.0
1927	Oldham	26	Swinton	7	Wigan	33,448	£3,170.0.0
1928	Swinton	5	Warrington	3	Wigan	33,909	£3,158.1.11
1929	Wigan	13	Dewsbury	2	Wembley	41,500	£5,614.0.0
1930	Widnes	10	St Helens	3	Wembley	36,544	£3,102.0.0
1931	Halifax	22	York	8	Wembley	40,368	£3,908.0.0
1932	Leeds	11	Swinton	8	Wigan	29,000	£2,479.0.0
1933	Huddersfield	21	Warrington	17	Wembley	41,874	£6,465.0.0
1934	Hunslet	11	Widnes	5	Wembley	41,280	£6,686.0.0
1935	Castleford	11	Huddersfield	8	Wembley	39,000	£5,533.0.0
1936	Leeds	18	Warrington	2	Wembley	51,250	£7,070.0.0
1937	Widnes	18	Keighley	5	Wembley	47,699	£6,704.0.0
1938	Salford	7	Barrow	4	Wembley	51,243	£7,174.0.0
1939	Halifax	20	Salford	3	Wembley	55,453	£7,681.0.0
1940	*No competition*						
1941	Leeds	19	Halifax	2	Bradford	28,500	£1,703.0.0
1942	Leeds	15	Halifax	10	Bradford	15,250	£1,276.0.0

Year	Winners		Runners-up		Venue	Attendance	Receipts
1943	Dewsbury	16	Leeds	9	Dewsbury	10,470	£823.0.0
	Dewsbury	0	Leeds	6	Leeds	16,000	£1,521.0.0
	Dewsbury won on aggregate 16-15						
1944	Bradford	0	Wigan	3	Wigan	22,000	£1,640.0.0
	Bradford	8	Wigan	0	Bradford	30,000	£2,200.0.0
	Bradford won on aggregate 8-3						
1945	Huddersfield	7	Bradford N.	4	Huddersfield	9,041	£1,184.3.7
	Huddersfield	6	Bradford N.	5	Bradford	17,500	£2,050.0.0
	Huddersfield won on aggregate 13-9						
1946	Wakefield T.	13	Wigan	12	Wembley	54,730	£12,013.13.6
1947	Bradford N.	8	Leeds	4	Wembley	77,605	£17,434.5.0
1948	Wigan	8	Bradford N.	3	Wembley	91,465	£21,121.9.9
1949	Bradford N.	12	Halifax	0	Wembley	*95,050	£21,930.5.0
1950	Warrington	19	Widnes	0	Wembley	94,249	£24,782.13.0
1951	Wigan	10	Barrow	0	Wembley	94,262	£24,797.19.0
1952	Workington T.	18	Featherstone R.	10	Wembley	72,093	£22,374.2.0
1953	Huddersfield	15	St Helens	10	Wembley	89,588	£30,865.12.3
1954	Warrington	4	Halifax	4	Wembley	81,841	£29,706.7.3
Replay	Warrington	8	Halifax	4	Bradford	102,569	£18,623.7.0
1955	Barrow	21	Workington T.	12	Wembley	66,513	£27,453.16.0
1956	St Helens	13	Halifax	2	Wembley	79,341	£29,424.7.6
1957	Leeds	9	Barrow	7	Wembley	76,318	£32,671.14.3
1958	Wigan	13	Workington T	9	Wembley	66,109	£33,175.17.6
1959	Wigan	30	Hull	13	Wembley	79,811	£35,718.19.9
1960	Wakefield T.	38	Hull	5	Wembley	79,773	£35,754.16.0
1961	St Helens	12	Wigan	6	Wembley	94,672	£38,479.11.9
1962	Wakefield T.	12	Huddersfield	6	Wembley	81,263	£33,390.18
1963	Wakefield T.	25	Wigan	10	Wembley	84,492	£44,521.17.0
1964	Widnes	13	Hull K R.	5	Wembley	84,488	£44,840.19.0
1965	Wigan	20	Hunslet	16	Wembley	89,016	£48,080.4.0
1966	St. Helens	21	Wigan	2	Wembley	*98,536	£50,409.0.0
1967	Featherstone R.	17	Barrow	12	Wembley	76,290	£53,465.14.0
1968	Leeds	11	Wakefield T.	10	Wembley	87,100	£56,171.16.6
1969	Castleford	11	Salford	6	Wembley	*97,939	£58,848.1.0
1970	Castleford	7	Wigan	2	Wembley	95,255	£89,262.2.0
1971	Leigh	24	Leeds	7	Wembley	85,514	£84,452.15
1972	St Helens	16	Leeds	13	Wembley	89,495	£86,414.30
1973	Featherstone R.	33	Bradford N.	14	Wembley	72,395	£125,826.40
1974	Warrington	24	Featherstone R.	9	Wembley	77,400	£132,021.05
1975	Widnes	14	Warrington	7	Wembley	85,098	£140,684.45
1976	St Helens	20	Widnes	5	Wembley	89,982	£190,129.40
1977	Leeds	16	Widnes	7	Wembley	80,871	£241,488.00
1978	Leeds	14	St Helens	12	Wembley	*96,000	£330,575.00
1979	Widnes	12	Wakefield T.	3	Wembley	94,218	£383,157.00
1980	Hull K R.	10	Hull	5	Wembley	*95,000	£448,202.90
1981	Widnes	18	Hull K R.	9	Wembley	92,496	£591,117.00
1982	Hull	14	Widnes	14	Wembley	92,147	£684,500.00
Replay	Hull	18	Widnes	9	Leeds	41,171	£180,525.00
1983	Featherstone R.	14	Hull	12	Wembley	84,969	£655,510.00
1984	Widnes	19	Wigan	6	Wembley	80,116	£686,171.00
1985	Wigan	28	Hull	24	Wembley	*97,801	£760,322.00
1986	Castleford	15	Hull K R.	14	Wembley	82,134	£806,676.00
1987	Halifax	19	St Helens	18	Wembley	91,267	£1,009,206.00
1988	Wigan	32	Halifax	12	Wembley	*94,273	£1,102,247.00
1989	Wigan	27	St Helens	0	Wembley	*78,000	£1,121,293.00
1990	Wigan	36	Warrington	14	Wembley	*77,729	£1,360,000.00
1991	Wigan	13	St Helens	8	Wembley	75,532	£1,610,447.00
1992	Wigan	28	Castleford	12	Wembley	77,286	£1,877,564.00

* Indicates a capacity attendance, the limit being fixed annually taking into account variable factors.

INDEX

Aberavon 45, 46, 145
Aberdare 23
Abertillery 46, 89, 109
Abram, Syd 57
Ackerley, Alvin 92, 110
Adams, Len 63
Adams, Leslie 66, 71, 72, 73
Adams, Mick 165, 166, 173
Agar, Alan 162, 169, 170
Agar, Liz 169
Aldershot 71
All Blacks 74, 79, 101
All Golds 25, 66, 79
Allerton 3
Altrincham 13
Altrincham FC 189
Ammanford 55
Anderson, Chris 172, 180, 181, 183
Anderson, Tony 184
Anderson, Willie 25, 28
Anfield 74, 96
Anlezark, Alec 29
Archer, Harry 114
Arkwright, Jack 61
Ashcroft, Ernie 86
Ashcroft, Kevin 142, 143, 151
Ashby, Ray 128, 129
Ashton, Eric 113, 114, 115, 116, 120,
    121, 128, 155, 158, 193
Ashurst, Bill 160
Askin, Tommy 72
Aspatria 50, 74
Aspey, Mal 152, 157, 164
Association Football 8, 13, 17, 18, 20,
    104, 111
Astley and Tyldesley Collieries 71
Aston Villa 3
Atkinson, Arthur 72
Atkinson, John 136, 157, 158
Athletic News 54
Athletic Grounds 12, 41, 47, 50, 82
Austin, Gilbert 49, 161
Australia 25, 28, 34, 38, 46, 47, 53, 64,
    66, 76, 80, 96, 98, 101, 106, 111, 113
Australasia 48
Autey, Wilf 11
Avery, Bert 19, 30

Baker, Ambrose 49
Balmain 171, 172
Bamford, Maurice 180
Banks, Billy 101, 103
Banner, Peter 156
Barber, Ken 78
BBC 106, 107
BBC Radio 102
BBC 2 Floodlit Trophy 131, 145, 154,
    161, 169.
Barmouth 9

Barrow 14, 21, 44, 47, 51, 66, 71, 75, 81,
    84, 85, 86, 90, 91, 96, 97, 99, 101,
    106, 107, 108, 109, 127, 130, 132,
    133, 135, 140, 149, 150, 156, 164,
    177, 185, 186
Barrow, Frank 130, 134
Barry 23
Barry West End FC 80
Bartle, Ike 13
Barton, Frank 86, 91
Barton, Tom 36
Baskerville, Albert 25
Bate, Edgar 126
Bassett, Arthur 84
Bateson, Peter 116
Bath, Harry 94, 95, 104
Bath RUFC 49
Batley 3, 10, 12, 17, 19, 23, 25, 28, 29,
    32, 39, 40, 45, 65, 67, 86, 96, 99,
    101, 109, 111, 127, 139, 148, 155,
    156, 163, 169, 174
Batten, Billy 21, 33, 38, 42, 44, 85
Batten, Eric 84, 85, 89, 91, 93, 99
Batten, Ray 144
Bawden, Jeff 101, 103
Beardsmore, Bob 178
Bell, Dean 184
Belle Vue 44, 64, 68, 82, 86, 90
Belle Vue Rangers 78, 91, 102
Belle Vue Stadium, Manchester 81
Bennett, Bill 83
Bennett, Jack 42
Benyon, Billy (Oldham) 49
Benyon, Billy (St Helens) 154, 155
Bethlehem 119, 120, 121
Betts, Denis 187, 190, 191, 192
Bevan, Brian 94, 102
Bevan, Jim 83
Bevan, John 153
Beverley 23
Beverley, Harry 70, 83
Beverley Victoria 15
Blackburn Rovers FC 191
Blackpool Borough 115, 170
Blackpool Golf Club 79
Blan, Billy 86, 91, 97
Blan, Jack 86
Blaydon RUFC 93
Blewer, Henry 50
Birdsall, Charlie 154, 161
Birkenhead Wanderers 7
Birts, Jimmy 180
Bishop, Paul 189, 190
Bishop, Tommy 130, 131, 190
Board of Trade 85
Bolton, Dave 116, 124
Bolton Wanderers 54, 183
Bone, E.J. 12
Booker, Dennis 117

Boscow, Tom 59
Bose, Kaiava 123
Boston, Billy 113, 116, 120, 127
Boulevard, The 42, 115, 154
Bowden, Reg 152, 153, 164
Bowkett, Len 67, 77, 108
Box, Harold 151
Bradford 3, 7, 8, 11, 14, 15, 17, 18
Bradford Northern 7, 23, 24, 28, 39, 50,
    58, 62, 64, 82, 84, 85, 89, 90, 91, 96,
    97, 101, 105, 109, 115, 124, 131,
    132, 142, 145, 148, 149, 150, 158,
    159, 160, 161, 166, 169, 174, 183,
    185, 188, 189
Bradford Park Avenue 18, 24
Bradman, Donald 81
Braund, Cyril 39
Bramley 3, 5, 13, 23, 32, 38, 40, 49, 69,
    81, 82, 104, 135, 143, 171
Bridgend 39, 72
Bridgewater Albion 41
Briers, Alan 126
Brighouse Rangers 3, 13
Brindle, Fred 66, 67
Brisbane 28, 190
British Lions 111
British Open 76
Broadbent, Benjamin 7
Broadley, Tom 7
Brockbank, Betty 97
Brockbank, Chris 50, 51, 73, 94
Brockbank, Herbert 50
Brogden, Stanley 71
Broken time 3
Brook, David 180
Brooke, Ian 149
Brookes, Billy 21
Brookland Rovers 14, 15, 16, 37
Brooks, Ernie 19
Brophy, Tom 132, 133
Brough, Alf 47, 49, 50
Brough, Jim 74, 75, 106, 114
Broughton Moor 41
Broughton Rangers 3, 7, 9, 11, 12, 13,
    15, 16, 17, 19, 21, 28, 29, 34, 39, 40,
    47, 50, 77, 78, 84
Brown, Lou 55, 57, 62, 63
Brownlie, Cyril 74
Buck, Harold 44
Bulmer, Billy 13
Bunting, Arthur 126, 168
Burgess, Billy 132, 139
Burke, John 154
Burke Mick 160, 165, 167, 168
Burnden Park 174, 183
Burton, Chris 165
Burwell, Alan 126
Byrne, Ged 188

Campbell, Ronnie 175
Canning, Tommy 143
Cannon, Mark 171
Canterbury-Bankstown 174, 180
Captain Morgan Trophy 150
Cardiff 1, 42, 45, 46, 53, 80, 89
Cardiff Blue Dragons 166
Cardiff Scottish RUFC 79
Carlisle 74
Carlisle RLFC 166, 169, 171, 174
Carlton, Frank 109, 110
Carnforth 11
Carter, Bill 44
Casey, Len 165, 184
Castle, Frank 96, 106, 107, 109, 120, 124
Castleford 3, 6, 11, 13, 55, 65, 68, 71, 78,
    84, 85, 86, 91, 101, 109, 120, 123,
    125, 131, 132, 135, 138, 139, 140,
    141, 143, 145, 148, 154, 161, 162,
    164, 167, 170, 171, 174, 177, 178,
    179, 191
Cawoods 23
Celtic FC 80
Central Park 40, 46, 49, 50, 51, 55, 58,
    65, 79, 86, 90, 109, 113, 114, 119,
    120, 125, 127, 131, 145, 171, 174,
    175, 177, 180, 183, 185, 186, 187,
    188, 190, 191
Chadwick, John 83
Chalkley, Dennis 93
Challinor, Jim 105, 145, 147
Chambers, Reverend Frank 1
Chambers, Reverend J.H. 47, 56
Charity Shield 183
Cheltenham 27, 48
Cherrington, Norman 115
Chisnall, David 144
Chorley RLFC 189
Clarendon Park School, Salford 191
Clark, Brett, 181
Clark, Doug 32, 37, 38
Clarke, Colin 131, 183
Clarke, Mick 136
Clarkson, Tommy 40
Clawson, Terry 147
Clay, Eric 130
Cleator 37
Cliff, The 40
Clifford, Joe 32, 37
Clues, Arthur 90
Coetzer, Gert 124
Coldrick, Percy 46
Collier, Frank 113, 121, 126
Condon, Michael 92
Cook, Bert 90, 97
Cook, Harry 119
Cook, Terry 109
Cooks, G. 30
Cookson, Phil 147, 158

Cooper, Fred 7, 16
Cooper, Lionel 101, 103
Corsi, Angelo 42
Corsi, Jack 41
Corsi, Joe 41, 47, 49, 50
Corsi, Louis 41
Coslett, Kel 145, 146, 147, 154, 155
Cottingham 55
Cotton, Minnie 131
Coventry 30, 50, 67, 77
Coventry, Paul 148
Cornwall 41
Cox, Jack 83
Craven Park, Barrow 66, 97, 106
Craven Park, Hull 161, 164, 174
Craven, Peter 93
Crompton, Martin 189
Cronulla–Sutherland RLFC 178
Crooks, Charlie 61
Crooks, Lee 168, 170, 176
Crooks, Steve 165
Croston, Jim 71, 73, 86, 87
Croyden 83
Crown Flatt 62, 79, 85, 131, 142, 169
Crumlin 42
Crystal Palace 8, 53, 54, 132
Cumberland 14, 37, 52, 98
Cumbria 14
Cummersdale Hornets 2
Cunliffe, Jack 86, 115
Cunniffe, Bernard 71, 72
Cunningham, Eddie 155, 164, 167
Curran, George 85

Daly, John 99, 100
Daniels, Arthur 105
Daniels, Sam 36
Darbyshire, Paul 190
Darwell, Joe 40
Davies, Bill 44
Davies, Dai (Warrington) 52, 73, 78
Davies, Dai 15, 16
Davies, Dennis 126
Davies, Dick 63
Davies, Evan 49
Davies, Gwyn 142
Davies, Jonathan 185, 189
Davies, Ossie 150
Davies, Wattie 4, 10, 11
Davies, W.T.H. (Willie) 89, 90
Day, Ernie 95, 105
Dean, Ken 92
Dean, Tony 184
Deane, Syd 29
Dechan, James 17, 24
Delooze, Henry 132, 133
Delves, Walter 110
Dennett, Jack 61
Derby, Lord 54, 69, 75, 121
Derwent Park 106, 114, 115
Devereux, Jimmy 34
Devine, Sean 188, 190
Devon 41
Devery, Pat 101, 103
Dewsbury 12, 28, 29, 30, 32, 42, 47, 54, 55, 56, 57, 62, 66, 75, 78, 85, 91, 104, 122, 123, 130, 131, 132, 140, 149, 150, 169, 171, 181, 188

Dewsbury Celtic 106
Dick, Alec 156
Dick, Kevin 156, 157
Dickinson, Clive 140
Dickinson, Todder 110
Dinas Powis 79
Dingsdale, Bill 67
Divorty, Gary 176
Dixon, Malcolm 133
Dobson, Mr J. S. 75
Doherty, Bob 6
Doncaster 132, 138, 164, 185
Dorahy, John 178, 179
Douglas, Peter 61
Douglas, River 171
Dover 153
Drake, Bill 118
Drake, Jim 115, 126
Dreadnoughts, The 23
Dublin 71
Duckworth, George 119
Duffy, Abe 61
Duke, Tony 168
Dunbavin, J. 17
Durham 14
Dutton, Ray 152, 153, 155, 157
Dyl, Les 157

Eadie, Graham 182
Eagers, W.J. (Billy) 14
Earl, Kel 149
Eastern Suburbs 67
Eastmoor 3, 9
Eaton, Cyril 84
Ebbw Vale 23, 46
Eckersley, Dave 144, 160, 164
Eddon, Jack 63
Edgar, Brian 106, 107, 114
Edward, Prince of Wales 67
Edwards, Alan 79, 84, 85
Edwards, Shaun 172, 175, 190, 192
Egan, Joe 86, 96, 152
Egerton 17
Egham 160
Egremont 51
Elia, Mark 182
Elizabeth, Princess 101
Ellaby, Alf 32, 60, 61
Elland Road, 81, 168
Ellenborough 37
Elvin, Wayne 171
Elwell, Keith 49, 155, 157, 160, 173
Emery, Wyndham 39
England 7, 8, 17, 28, 41, 46, 50, 53, 71, 74, 75, 76, 111
Entwistle, Terry 116
Etty, John 111
Evans Bryn 49
Evans, Frank 49
Evans, Jack 49, 52
Evans, Jack Jnr 49
Evans, Ray 100
Evans, Roy 113
Evans, Steve 166, 168, 176
Everton FC 80
Examiner, Huddersfield 122
Eyres, Richie 185

F.A. Cup 47, 54, 64
Fallowfield, Bill 107, 141
Fallowfield Stadium 8, 9
Fairfax, Arthur 109
Fairfax, S.V. 49
Fairhirst, Frank 67
Farrar, Fred 21
Farrar, Reg 49
Farrar, Vince 148, 149, 162, 169
Fartown 5, 15, 20, 21, 25, 26, 28, 64, 86, 97, 122, 123, 154
Fattorini and Sons 3
Faulder, Ken 107, 108
Faulkner, Max 76
Fawcett, J. 26
Fearnley, Albert 149
Fearnley, Fred 11
Fearnley, Stan 149
Feather, Harry 18, 48
Featherstone Rovers 36, 49, 52, 62, 75, 84, 99, 106, 114, 115, 117, 122, 132, 133, 134, 136, 138, 148, 149, 150, 151, 155, 158, 155, 162, 164, 166, 168, 169, 170, 185, 189, 192
Ferguson, Joe 30
Ferguson, John 175
Ferguson, Stuart 144
Fiddes, Alex 71, 73, 101
Fiddler, Jim 144
Fillingham, Anthony 126
Finn, Tom 116
Finnan, Bill 110
Fish, Jack 11, 15, 16, 17, 19, 49
Fisher, Tony 146
Fitton, Tommy
Fitzgerald, Dai 4, 10
Fletcher, Andrew 160
Fletcher, Tom 8
Flimby 14
Flimby and Fothergill 49
Football Association 54, 64
Forster, Mark 189
Foster, Trevor 89, 90, 93
Fox, Don 117, 136, 137, 147, 148, 160
Fox, Neil 117, 118, 123, 124, 135, 148, 149
Fox, Peter 117, 148, 150, 151, 169
Fox, Walter 126
France 79, 106, 111, 117
Francis, Alf 34
Francis, Bill 158
French, Fred 81
Fulham 164, 166, 171

Gabbitas, Brian 128, 129
Galia, Jean 68
Gallant Youths 4
Gant, Laurie 132
Garforth, Clem 84
Gath, Jim 28
Gear, Albert 81
Gee, Ken 86, 96, 97
Gelder, Ron 105
George Hotel, Huddersfield 3, 86
George, Mick 165
George, Wilf 181
Gibson, Eppie 106, 108
Gilbert, Bert 34

Gilfedder, Laurie 127, 128, 131
Gill, Henderson 174, 175, 184
Glassblowers 51
Gleeson, Tommy 32
Gloucester 44, 49
Glynn, Peter 155
Gnoll, The 77
Goldthorpe, Albert 8, 20, 21, 22
Goldthorpe, James 20
Goldthorpe, John Henry 20
Goldthorpe, Walter 8, 25
Goldthorpe, William 20
Goodall, Jack (Warrington) 83
Goodall, John 6, 11
Goodfellow, Herbert 86, 88
Goodway, Andy 188
Goole 12
Gorley, Les 164, 172
Gorseinon 111
Goulding, Keith 132
Gore, Bill 119
Great War, The 31
Greatorex, Ken 132
Greenwood, Colin 122
Gregory, Andrew 164, 165, 168, 171, 184, 186, 187, 190, 193
Gregory, Mike 190
Grenoble 117
Griffin Hotel, Leeds 53
Griffiths, Fred (Punchy) 115, 120, 121
Griffiths, John 129
Griffiths, Tyssul 104, 105, 110, 116
Gronow, Ben 32, 37, 38, 101
Grundy, Jack 96, 106, 108, 109
Gullick, Don 103
Gunney, Geoff 127
Gwynn, Dai 1

HMS Indomitable 86
Hadwen, Herbert 13, 15
Halifax, 3, 13, 14, 15, 17, 19, 20, 23, 24, 25, 29, 31, 34, 40, 42, 49, 51, 62, 63, 64, 75, 77, 78, 81, 82, 83, 84, 85, 91, 92, 93, 94, 103, 104, 105, 109, 110, 112, 115, 117, 120, 124, 130, 131, 140, 145, 148, 150, 153, 154, 157, 158, 161, 166, 168, 174, 180, 181, 182, 184, 185, 190
Hall, H. 38
Hall of Fame 31
Halsall, Hector 50
Hall, Trevor 58
Hampson, Steve 185, 187, 188
Handscombe, Ray 170
Hanging Heaton 122
Hanley, Ellery 184, 187, 188, 190, 192, 193
Hardgrave, Roy 58
Hardy, Belson 67
Hardisty, Alan 125, 139, 140, 161
Harkin, Kevin 170
Harris, Billy 28
Harris, Eric 64, 65, 75
Harris, Fred 75
Harris, Tommy (Rochdale) 41
Harris, Tommy (York) 118
Harrison, Des 179
Harrison, Jack 34

Harrison, John 193
Harrogate 168, 180
Hartley, Dennis 138, 139, 141, 149, 151
Hatfield, Don 91
Hawick RUFC 17
Hay, Vic 84
Haydock 76
Headingley 6, 13, 16, 17, 24, 25, 29, 32, 35, 40, 41, 44, 49, 62, 64, 65, 74, 75, 77, 85, 86, 90, 99, 106, 111, 125, 148, 150, 156, 158, 164, 174, 181, 184
Healey, Bill 106
Healy, Ken 92
Heathrow Airport 160
Heaton, Jeff 154, 155
Hebblethwaite, George 136
Hebron, Robert 38
Heckmondwike 11
Helme, Gerry 95, 105, 190
Hemsley, Kerry 171, 172, 173
Henderson, Peter (Halifax) 110
Henderson, Peter (Huddersfield) 101
Hepworth, Alan 125, 161
Hepworth, Keith, 140, 141
Herbert, Norman 106, 107, 114
Herman, Hilton 49
Hesketh, George 38, 49
Heworth ARLFC 184
Higgins, Laurie 63
Higginshaw 78
Higson, John Willie 21
Hill, Mr A. 88
Hill, Cliff 141
Hill, Ron 139
Hilton, Jack 91, 97, 171
Hilton Park 102, 135, 142, 145, 181
Hitler, Adolf 66
Hobbs, David 170
Hockenhull, Ted 19
Hodgson, Martin 51, 52, 65
Hoey, Jimmy 61
Hogg, Andrew 12
Holbeck 9
Holden, Keith 116, 128
Holding, Billy 67, 94
Holdstock, Roy 163
Holdstock, John 182
Holland, Major 34, 38
Holliday, Tom 74
Holliday, Tosh 50
Holmes, John 144, 146, 156, 158
Horne, Willie 96, 97, 106, 108, 186
Hopwood, Ray 132
Horsfall, H. 52
Howe, Keith 139
Howes, David 153
Howley, Tommy 46
Hubbard, Steve 162, 163, 165
Huddart, Dick 120, 121
Huddersfield 1, 10, 15, 19, 28, 30, 31, 32, 34, 35, 36, 37, 38, 40, 44, 46, 47, 49, 51, 55, 62, 64, 66, 67, 68, 69, 71, 72, 73, 75, 76, 77, 81, 84, 85, 86, 89, 92, 93, 96, 101, 103, 122, 123, 126, 132, 135, 138, 142, 145, 150, 154, 158, 159, 160, 165, 183
Hudson, Barney 79, 85

Hughes, Arthur 126
Hughes, Eric 126, 159, 160, 172, 173
Hughes, Jackie 159
Hull, 3, 7, 13, 14, 17, 19, 20, 21, 24, 25, 26, 33, 34, 35, 38, 42, 46, 47, 51, 62, 64, 75, 77, 80, 84, 85, 89, 92, 104, 110, 115, 117, 118, 120, 122, 124, 126, 132, 140, 142, 153, 154, 161, 162, 163, 166, 168, 169, 170, 174, 176, 177, 184, 190
Hull, Dave 164
Hull KR 13 15, 16, 25, 29, 32, 33, 37, 42, 49, 51, 58, 62, 66, 69, 80, 94, 115, 122, 124, 125, 126, 130, 140, 148, 150, 156, 161, 162, 163, 164, 165, 166, 169, 171, 174, 177, 178, 179, 180, 181, 184, 188
Hunslet 3, 8, 12, 15, 16, 20, 21, 22, 24, 29, 32, 33, 35, 46, 47, 50, 51, 58, 68, 69, 70, 71, 77, 78, 82, 84, 86, 89, 90, 94, 104, 115, 127, 128, 129, 138, 139, 153, 160, 169, 176, 177, 181
Hunslet Carr 13
Hunter, Johnny 101
Hurcombe, Danny 46, 47
Hurst, Ken 123, 135, 136, 137
Hutt, Lou 58
Hutton, Colin 94
Huyton 150, 158
Hynes, Syd 135, 144, 146, 156, 158

Ibrox 12
Ireland 8
Iro, Anthony 184
Iro, Kevin 184, 186, 190
Irving, Hudson 91
Isherwood, D. 16
Issac, Iowerth 75
Italian 41
Ivill, Billy 107
Ivison, Billy 98, 100, 106

Jack Lane School, Leeds 13
Jacklin, Tony 76
Jackson, Phil 96, 106, 107
Jackson Tom 12
James, Carwyn 111
James, Sam 12
James, Neil 184
James, Willie 12
Jeanes, David 135
Jedforest RUFC 49
Jefferson, Brian 178
Jenkins, Bert 27
Jenkins, Dai 84
Jenkins, Emlyn 79
Jenkins, Griff 76
Jerram, Sid 38, 46
John Player Trophy 145, 150, 159, 167, 171, 177, 183, 185, 188, 190
Johnson, Abe 49
Johnson, Brian 189
Johnson, Paul 178
Jolley, Bill 38
Jolley, Stan 87
Jones, Bob 42
Jones, Dai 84
Jones, Johnny 86

Jones, Les 147
Jones, Lewis 111, 112
Jukes, Bill 21
Juliff, Brian 181

Kangaroos 22
Karalius, Tony 145, 146, 154
Karalius, Vince 110, 120, 121, 126, 153, 155, 159, 171
Keegan, Arthur 116
Keighley 16, 17, 25, 32, 36, 49, 55, 64, 77, 78, 85, 86, 104, 111, 123, 154, 172
Kelland, Ivor 132
Kellett, Cyril 126, 130, 148, 149, 151
Kellett, Ken 148
Kemble, Gary 168
Kennedy, F. 53, 54, 56
Kennedy, J.E. 42
Kenny, Brett 174, 175, 176
Kershaw, H. 34
Ketterridge, Martin 178
Kielty, Stan 91, 93, 105
Killeen, Len 130, 131
Kilner, Shaun 171
King Edward VII 11
King George V 37, 67
King George VI, 90, 101
Kinnear, Roy 57
Kirk, Billy 52
Kirkbride, Bill 140
Knapman, Ernest 47, 49
Knottingley 132
Knowleden, Bryn 95
Knowsley Road 103, 130, 145, 154, 169, 181, 186, 188

Laidlaw, Alex 18
Lake Trevor 127, 128, 129
Lancashire Cup 27, 39, 48, 49, 58, 65, 67, 79, 81, 96, 99, 101, 113, 145, 152, 154, 156, 159, 183, 185, 188, 189, 190, 191
Lancashire League 58, 62, 65, 79, 131
Lancashire Senior Competition 27
Lane End United 29
Langfield, George 102, 103
Langley, John 135
Langton, Billy 128
Large, Ken 121
Laughton, Doug 141, 159, 164, 167
Lawkholme Lane 77, 78
Lawrenson, Johnny 84, 98, 100
Leadership Trophy 135, 154
Leake, John 53
Leeds 3, 11, 14, 16, 20, 21, 25, 26, 28, 34, 35, 42, 44, 47, 49, 50, 58, 62, 64, 65, 66, 67, 69, 71, 74, 75, 81, 83, 84, 85, 90, 92, 94, 97, 104, 106, 110, 111, 115, 120, 121, 124, 127, 131, 132, 135, 136, 138, 142, 143, 144, 145, 146, 147, 153, 156, 158, 161, 164, 166, 167, 171, 177, 181
Leeds Mercury 44
Leeds Parish Church 9, 11, 20
Leeds United FC 168
Lees, Sammy 8
Leigh 3, 8, 17, 21, 24, 36, 39, 40, 49, 55,

67, 99, 101, 114, 125, 135, 140, 142, 143, 144, 145, 150, 151, 153, 154, 167, 177, 181
Leigh Rangers 191
Leuluai, James 170, 176
Lewis, George 61
Lewthwaite, Jimmy 96
Leytham, Jimmy 27
Lindop, Fred 141, 162, 184
Lindsay, Maurice 171, 172
Line-out 13
Liptrot, Graham 158
Little, Billy 13, 14, 15, 81
Liverpool FC 74, 80
Liverpool City 123, 124, 125, 128, 132, 135, 150
Liverpool Stanley 77, 80
Llandudno 53
Llanelli 45, 46, 49, 96, 111
Llewellyn, Steve 103, 109, 110
Lloyd, Reg 77, 78, 85, 172
Lloyd, Sammy 161, 163, 167, 168
Lockwood, Brian 162, 164, 165
Lockwood, Hubert 83, 85
Lomas, Jim 13, 16, 18, 33
London 53, 54, 56, 61, 62, 72, 75, 88, 110, 122, 160, 162, 166, 180
London Highfield 68, 71
London Irish RUFC 46
Long, Arnie 149
Longstaff, Fred 35, 36
Loughlin, Paul 181, 182, 188
Lowe, Dick 131
Lowe, Graham 183, 184, 185, 186, 188, 190, 191
Lowndes, Alan 141
Lydiat, John 179
Lydon, Joe 171, 172, 184, 185, 187, 188, 190, 192
Lyman, Joe 55
Lyon, David 190

Maine, George 11
Maine Road 110
Manchester 8, 78, 81, 82, 85
Manchester City FC 80, 105, 185
Manchester Guardian 54
Manchester United FC 79, 80, 191
Manley, Joe 128
Manly-Warringah 177, 188, 191
Manningham 3
Mantle, John 130, 131, 145, 146, 154, 155
Maoris 1
Marchant, Alan 127
Marchant, Tony 178
Markham, Ray 66
Marlor, Rothwell 49
Marsden, George 17, 18
Maryport 81
Mason, Len 62, 77
Mason, Mel 148
Mawson, Frank 91
McCallion, Seamus 182
McCue, Tommy 77, 78, 84
McCutcheon, Billy 1, 48
McDowell, Hugh 69
McGurrin, Bernard 114

McKeating, Vince 108
McInnes, Alan 183
McIntyre, Len 125
McLoughlin, Eddie 41
McTigue, Brian 113, 115, 116, 120, 121
Meek, Mel 84
Mennell, Brian 126
Merthyr Tydfil 23
Messenger, Dally 25
Mid-Rhondda 23
Midland Hotel, Manchester 53
Miller, Gavin 178
Miller, Joe 27
Miller, Willie, 99, 100
Millington, Harry 84
Millom 161
Mills, Ernie 55, 66, 67, 72
Mills, Jim 153
Millward, Roger 161, 162, 163, 164
Mitchell, Norman 100
Moffatt, J. 8
Monie, John 188, 191
Mooney, Walter 40
Moorhouse, Stanley 32
Moores, Jeff 64
Morecambe 3, 11, 16, 77
Morgan, Arnie 134
Morley, Johnny 13, 15
Morrell, Cyril 70
Morris, Oliver 85
Mortimer, Steve 174
Moss, Vince 157
Mount Pleasant 4, 11
Mountford, Cec 97
Mountain, Stanley 72
Mudge, Johnny 98, 100, 106
Munns, J. T. 6
Murphy, Alex 120, 130, 131, 142, 143,
    144, 145, 148, 150, 151, 153, 155,
    165, 171, 180, 181, 187
Murphy, Harry 86
Murray, Mike 132
Murrayfield 113
Muscroft, Peter 165
Myler, Frank 125, 126, 155, 159
Myler, John 164
Mysons 23

Nash, Steve 148
Naughton, Ally 94
Naughton, Danny 94
Naughton, Johnny 94
Naughton Park 58, 94, 123, 125, 152,
    153, 164, 171
Neary, J. 30
Neath 39, 46, 49, 77, 111
Neller, Keith 184
Nelson, Nick 155
New Zealand 25, 27, 43, 48, 58, 59, 62,
    63, 79, 86, 106, 111, 113
New Zealand All Black 25
Newbould, Tommy 23, 24
Newcastle 48
Newlove, John 148, 149, 151, 162
Newport RUFC 1, 4, 49, 63, 89, 104,
    138
Newton Abbot 41
Nicholas, Mike 151

Nicholls, George 154
Nordgren, Brian 86, 87, 88, 96
Normanton 24
Normanton St Johns 28, 29
North Western League 14
Northampton 83
Northampton St James 8
Northern League 13, 18, 20, 39, 96
Northern Rugby Union 3, 4, 5, 10, 13,
    14, 17, 18, 19, 20, 23, 25, 28, 29, 32,
    35, 41, 79
Norton, Steve 161, 168

Oakland, Joe 6
O'Connor, Michael 186
Odsal Stadium 83, 84, 85, 90, 94, 97,
    104, 105, 112, 114, 117, 120, 122,
    150, 153
O'Hara, Dane 168
Old Trafford 182, 191
Oldham 1, 6, 8, 9, 10, 13, 19, 20, 21, 24,
    27, 29, 30, 32, 33, 35, 38, 42, 47, 48,
    49, 50, 51, 52, 62, 69, 82, 84, 85, 90,
    92, 93, 102, 104, 112, 113, 117, 122,
    124, 125, 126, 127, 135, 138, 140,
    143, 145, 151, 153, 154, 158, 171,
    177, 181, 183, 185, 189, 193
Oldham Athletic FC 98
O'Loughlin Keiron 166
O'Neill, Paddy 40
O'Neill, Stanley 40
Oppy Wood 34
O'Reill, Tony 119
Osbaldestin, Harold 79
Osbourne F. 84
Oster, Jack 67
Other Nationalities 17, 28
Oulton, Henry 158
Oxley, David 153

Padden, Dicky 41
Palin, Harold 94, 95, 96
Pansegrouw, Jan 92
Parker, Gwyn 75
Parker, Reg 106
Parker, Tommy 46, 47
Parkin, Jonty 34
Parkinson, Billy 40
Parramatta 174, 188, 191
Parsons, George 109
Pascoe, Don 63
Paskins, Tony 98, 106, 108
Peel, Mr F. 81
Pemberton 27
Pendlebury, John 181, 182
Pepperell, Russ 101, 102
Phillips, George 103
Phillips, Tom 36
Pickerill, Clive 161
Pickles, Captain 71
Pimblett, Geoff 155, 158
Pitchford, Frank 124
Pitchford, Steve 157
Platt, Don 113
Platt, Joseph 1
Plymouth Albion RUFC 49
Pontefract 15, 148
Pontypridd RUFC 46

Pope John Paul II 168
Port Talbot 45
Port Vale FC 191
Portrush 76
Post Office Road, 99, 117, 148, 150, 169,
    170
Powell, Wickham 45, 46
Poynton, Harold 124
Premiership 159, 160, 168
Prescott, Alan 103, 110
Prescott, Eric 145, 146, 164
Prescott, Frank 42
Prescott, Robin 85
Preston, Mark 190
Pretoria 119
Price, Dai 39
Price, Gareth 92
Priestley, Mr J. 26
Prinsloo, Jan 122, 123
Prior, Bernard 127
Prohm, Gary 178, 179
Prosser, Jack 39

Queen Victoria 6
Queens Park Rangers 124
Quinn, Steve 170
Quirk, Les 185, 188

Ramsden, Peter 101, 102, 103, 109, 123,
    157
Ramsey, Bill 127
Randall, Bob 126
Randall, Jack 21
Rangers FC 80
Ratcliffe, Albert 61, 70
Ray, Stephen 67
Read, Jack 49
Red Devils 79
Redfearn, David 149
Redfearn, Mick 139, 141
Redruth 41
Rees, Billo 49, 52
Rees, Dai 63
Rees, Dai (Bradford Northern) 89
Rees, Graham 146
Regal Trophy 23, 52, 188, 191
Reid, Paddy 92
Reilly, Malcolm 139, 140, 177, 178, 179
Resolven 77
Rhodes, Alan 120, 121
Rhodes, Austin 109, 110
Rhodes, W. 30
Rhodes, William 56
Richards, Gwyn 67
Riley, Joe 15
Ring, Johnny 45, 46, 47
Risman, Bev 135, 136, 137
Risman, Gus 79, 80, 81, 84, 85, 98, 100,
    106, 135, 138
Rix, Syd 50
Roberts, Bob 126
Roberts, Glenys 126
Robinson, Geoff 126
Robinson, Roy 110
Rochdale Hornets 3, 12, 17, 19, 25, 28,
    29, 36, 41, 42, 45, 46, 47, 49, 50, 64,
    82, 90, 96, 106, 113, 142, 148, 184
Rodney Parade 89

Roffey, Fred 46, 47
Roma, Walter (Rattler) 35
Roose ARLFC 123
Roper, John (Sol) 108, 114
Rose, Paul 170
Rosenfeld, Albert 32, 38, 66, 101
Rosser, Mel 63
Roughyeds 50
Round, Paul 182
Rowe, Peter 140
Royal Navy 111
Royal Engineers 71
Royal Hibernian Military School 71
Ruddick, George, 28
Rugby Football League 43
Rugby Football Union 2, 29
Runcorn 3, 13, 14, 19, 24, 27, 155
Ryan, Martin 86
Ryder, Ron 95

Saddler, Ted 71
Salford 1, 8, 9, 11, 12, 13, 17, 18, 19, 21,
    24, 25, 29, 32, 33, 36, 38, 46, 47, 50,
    62, 66, 75, 76, 79, 80, 81, 82, 83, 84,
    89, 90, 98, 106, 108, 120, 135, 138,
    139, 140, 148, 150, 154, 156, 164,
    166, 169, 177, 183, 185, 191
Salford Ex-Players Association 85
Salterhebble 13
Sampson, Malcolm 124
Sayer, Bill 130, 131
Scala Ballroom 96
Sanders, J. 25
Sanderson, Chris 156, 157
Sanderson, Sammy 157, 158
Sandy, Jamie 178
Saracens RUFC 181
Scotland 3, 4, 8, 64, 111
Scott, Elisha 74
Scott, Mick 180, 182
Scott, R. 65
Seaton 14
Seeling, Charlie 46, 52
Service, Alex 102
Shankland Bill 67, 75, 76, 94
Shannon, Tommy 77, 78, 94
Sharlston 34, 86
Sharrock, Jimmy 28
Shelford, Adrian 184
Shelton, Geoff 128
Shenton, Ian 141
Shepherd, Sam 151
Sherburn, Joe 77, 78
Sherwood, Herbert 73
Silcock, Nat 78
Simms, Herbert (Dodger) 4
Sinton, Bill 17
Skene, Alan 122, 124
Slater, Harry 23
Slevin, Ted 101, 123
Sloman, Bob 49, 50
Smales, Tommy (Huddersfield) 123
Smales, Tommy (Featherstone Rovers)
    133, 134
Smith, Alan 144
Smith, Charlie 83, 84
Smith, David 158
Smith, Fred 21

Smith, Fred (Wakefield Trinity) 117
Smith, George 25
Smith, Jim 183
Smith, Mr J.H. 6
Smith, Len 70
Smith, Mike (Featherstone Rovers) 148, 149
Smith, Mike (Hull FC) 118
Smith, Peter 170
Snape, Brian 138, 150
Somerset 41, 42
South Africa 58, 119
Southward, Ike 106, 114, 115
Sporting Chronicle 53, 100
Springboks 111
St James' Park 27
St Helens 3, 6, 10, 14, 24, 32, 36, 41, 46, 55, 58, 59, 60, 61, 67, 68, 80, 82, 91, 94, 98, 101, 102, 103, 104, 106, 109, 113, 117, 119, 120, 121, 122, 125, 127, 130, 131, 140, 142, 143, 145, 146, 147, 150, 152, 153, 154, 155, 156, 158, 164, 167, 169, 171, 174, 181, 182, 185, 186, 187, 188, 191, 192, 193
St Helens Recs 3, 38, 58, 80, 82
St Helens Town AFC 181
Stanton, Frank 174
Station Road 51, 52, 55, 59, 67, 94, 96, 109, 125, 140, 155, 166
Stephens, Gary 181
Stephenson, David 175
Sterling, Peter 174
Stockport Rangers 3, 12
Stone, Billy 42
Stone, Charlie 148, 162, 163, 170
Stott, Billy 87, 88
Streatham and Mitcham 75
Stroud 79, 80
Sullivan, Clive 162, 168
Sullivan, James 45, 46, 47, 49, 55, 56, 57, 74, 101, 109, 110, 130
Sullivan, Mick 113, 115, 130
Sulway, Wilf 49
Swansea 1, 92
Swinton 8, 9, 15, 19, 21, 34, 36, 38, 46, 49, 51, 52, 55, 62, 63, 65, 66, 71, 73, 74, 78, 80, 86, 90, 92, 93, 94, 99, 123, 124, 125, 126, 127, 130, 135, 146, 153, 160, 166, 185
Swinton Park 34, 49

Tamati, Howie 171
Tamati, Kevin 172
Tanner, Haydn 111
Tattersfield 138
Taylor, John 126
Team of All Talents 31, 66
Tees, Eddie 134, 149
Television 102, 114
Thatcher, Margaret 155
Thomas, Emlyn 39, 40
Thomas, Gwyn 46
Thomas, Howard 63
Thomas, Johnny 39
Thomas, Malcolm 111
Thomas, Mark 189
Thomas, R.L. 8

Thomas, Rees 116
Thomas, Vaughan 134
Thompson, Billy 144, 172
Thompson, Cec 114
Thompson, Jimmy 132, 133, 134
Thompson, Joe 43, 44, 65
Thrum Hall 34, 62, 83, 84, 91, 94, 110, 112, 115, 180, 183
Todd, George 38, 83, 85
Todd, Lance 27, 79, 80
Tolson, Mark 69
Tonks, Les 133, 148
Toohey, Keith 148
Topliss, David 160, 166, 167, 168
Topping, Peter 69, 78
Toowoomba 64
Torquay Athletic RUFC 49
Tottenham Hotspur FC 80
Towill, Idris 71, 72
Townsend, Alfred 91
Trafford Arms, Wakefield 53, 54
Trafford Borough 189
Traill, Jim 69
Traill, Ken 69
Traynor, David 6
Treasure, David 149
Treen, Jack 83
Treherbert 23
Trophy, Lance Todd 88, 90, 95, 97, 100, 103, 105, 108, 116, 118, 123, 129, 131, 137, 144, 147, 151, 153, 157, 160, 170, 176, 177, 190, 191, 192
Troup, Alec 81
Turner, Derek 117, 122, 138, 193
Tyrer, Colin 140, 141
Twickenham 2, 14, 17, 29, 32, 43, 44, 45, 48, 75, 111, 181
T'Owd Tin Pot 3

Underbank Rangers 31

Valentine, Bob 9
Valentine, Dave 101, 103
Valentine, Jim 8, 9
Van Heerden, Adrian 47
Van Vollenhoven, Tom 46, 119, 121, 130
Van Rooyen, George 58, 61
Vautin, Paul 186
Vines, Don 122
Voortrekker High School 119

Wagstaff, Harold 31, 32, 37
Waide, Walter 53
Wainwright, Tony 144
Wakefield Cricket Club 122
Wakefield Trinity 3, 17, 19, 21, 23, 24, 29, 30, 32, 33, 34, 38, 43, 44, 46, 47, 49, 50, 64, 65, 71, 73, 77, 79, 82, 84, 85, 86, 87, 88, 89, 90, 91, 105, 115, 117, 118, 120, 122, 123, 124, 127, 130, 132, 135, 136, 137, 138, 139, 148, 149, 153, 158, 159, 160, 162, 166, 169, 170, 188, 190
Wales 8, 27, 43, 44, 45, 46, 49, 53, 74, 75
Walkden 6
Walkington, Jack 69
Wallace, H. 49

Walsh, Joe 143, 144
Walsh, Tom 21
Walters, Emlyn 90
War Emergency League 84
Ward, David 158
Ward, Donald 90, 91
Ward, Ernest 89, 90, 91, 93
Ward, John 140
Ward, Ted 86
Waring, Eddie 84, 127
Warlow, John 131
Warrington 3, 5, 11, 15, 16, 17, 18, 19, 25, 28, 29, 32, 39, 49, 51, 52, 58, 62, 66, 67, 75, 76, 81, 83, 85, 88, 89, 90, 94, 96, 98, 104, 105, 109, 111, 119, 124, 128, 131, 139, 145, 148, 150, 151, 153, 154, 155, 158, 161, 164, 168, 170, 174, 181, 185, 189, 190, 191, 192
Warrington Town FC 181
Wartime Challenge Cup 84
Warwick, Silas 18, 48
Waterloo RUFC 165
Waterman, Dennis 22
Watersheddings 9, 35, 48, 49, 113, 122, 185, 189
Watkins, David 138
Watson, Cliff 120
Watson, Mike 134
Weaste 28
Webster, F. 25
Webster, Fred 64
Weighill, Bob 85
Welsh Rugby Union 44, 48, 111
Wembley 47, 53, 54, 55, 57, 59, 60, 62, 63, 64, 66, 67, 68, 69, 71, 72, 73, 74, 75, 76, 78, 80, 81, 82, 83, 85, 86, 88, 90, 91, 94, 96, 97, 99, 102, 105, 106, 109, 110, 111, 113, 114, 115, 116, 117, 118, 120, 122, 123, 124, 125, 126, 127, 129, 130, 132, 133, 135, 138, 139, 140, 142, 145, 146, 148, 149, 150, 151, 152, 153, 154, 158, 159, 161, 162, 163, 164, 165, 166, 167, 168, 169, 170, 171, 173, 176, 177, 181, 184, 185, 187, 188, 190, 191
West Bromwich Albion 3
West, George Henry (Tich) 15, 16
West, Graeme 171, 176
West Ham United 54
West Lancashire Golf Club 76
West Riding 7
Wheater's Field 9, 11, 13, 19
Wheldon Road 101, 138, 140, 161, 177
Whitcombe, Frank 89, 90
White City 53
White, Len 91
Whitehaven 51, 74, 105, 112, 113, 117, 131, 132, 181
Whitehaven Recs 51
Whitehead, Derek 151, 153
Whiteley, Johnny 115
Whitfield, Colin 181, 182, 184
Whitfield, Robin 170
Widnes 3, 5, 7, 36, 40, 42, 46, 58, 60, 61, 65, 68, 69, 70, 77, 78, 86, 94, 95, 96, 99, 109, 114, 117, 123, 125, 126,

139, 142, 152, 153, 155, 156, 157, 159, 160, 161, 164, 165, 166, 167, 168, 171, 172, 173, 174, 175, 180, 181, 183, 185, 186, 191
Wigan 2, 15, 16, 24, 27, 28, 29, 30, 32, 34, 36, 38, 41, 42, 45, 46, 47, 49, 52, 54, 55, 57, 58, 59, 62, 66, 67, 71, 75, 76, 77, 79, 80, 82, 84, 85, 86, 87, 88, 90, 91, 96, 97, 99, 101, 104, 106, 110, 113, 114, 115, 116, 119, 120, 121, 122, 123, 124, 125, 126, 127, 128, 129, 130, 131, 135, 138, 139, 140, 141, 145, 148, 150, 153, 154, 155, 159, 161, 165, 167, 171, 172, 173, 174, 175, 176, 177, 180, 181, 183, 184, 185, 186, 188, 189, 190, 191, 192
Wigan Highfield 49
Wigan St Patricks 164
Wilby, Tim 163
Wilde, Hughie 42
Wilderspoon Stadium 17, 76, 94, 148, 150, 189
Wileman, Ronnie 162, 168
Wilkinson, Ian 184
Wilkinson, Jack (Halifax) 92, 110, 117, 124
Wilkinson, Jack (Hull KR) 49
Williams, Brinley 45
Williams, Dafen 46
Williams, Evan 75
Williams, Sam 8
Willows, The 15
Wilson, Harry 21
Wilson, John 53, 54, 84, 100
Wilson, Robert 11, 12, 32
Winfield Cup 191
Wood J. B. 120
Wood, John 155
Woods, Dai 42
Woods, Paul 162
Woods, Tommy 41
Woodward, Alf 49
Woodward, Trevor 160
Wookey, Bill 107
Woolsey, Tom 131
Woolwich 72
Workington Town 74, 86, 89, 97, 98, 100, 106, 108, 110, 114, 115, 127, 135, 139, 164
World Cup 111, 140
Wrigglesworth, Brian 133
Wright, Stuart 157, 160, 168
Wrigley, Edgar 32

Yeadon Airport 83
York 25, 38, 41, 44, 62, 63, 66, 68, 84, 98, 104, 117, 145, 156, 161, 164, 171, 177, 184
Yorkshire Post 24
Yorkshire County Cup 20, 32, 35, 38, 48, 71, 91, 101, 123, 156, 161, 167, 169, 177
Yorkshire County League 20, 32, 35, 38, 49
Yorkshire Senior Competition 5
Young, Fred 26